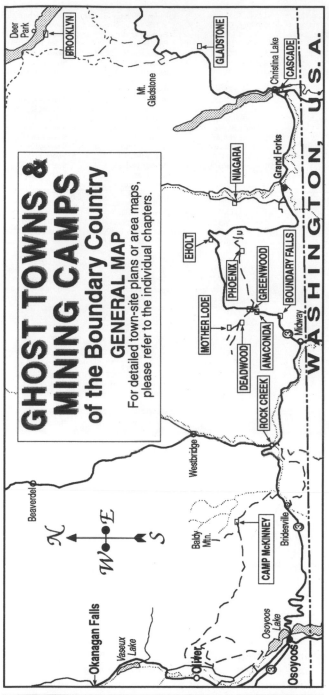

GHOST TOWNS & MINING CAMPS of the Boundary Country

GENERAL MAP

For detailed town-site plans or area maps, please refer to the individual chapters.

GHOST TOWNS & MINING CAMPS
of the Boundary Country

CANADIAN CATALOGUING IN PUBLICATION DATA

Basque, Garnet.
  Ghost towns & mining camps of the boundary country

  Includes bibliographical references and index.
  ISBN 0-919531-33-4

  1. Ghost towns—British Columbia. 2. Mines and mineral resources—British Columbia—History. 3 British Columbia—History, Local. I. Title.
  FC3820.048B38 1992   971.1'6   C92-091414-4
  F1089.B7B38 1992

SUNFIRE PUBLICATIONS LIMITED
P.O. Box 3399,
Langley, B.C. V3A 4R7

PRINTING HISTORY
First Printing — June, 1992

Financially assisted by the Province of British Columbia through the British Columbia Heritage Trust and the B.C. Lottery Fund.
Printed in Hong Kong

PHOTO CREDITS:
Public Archives of Canada: 2.
B.C. Provincial Archives: 6, 8, 12, 16, 17 (top right & bottom), 19, 21, 26, 44 (inset), 52, 53 (left), 56, 58, 61, 62 (bottom), 64, 65, 66, 70, 71, 77, 78, 82, 92 (top), 93, 94, 95, 105 (bottom), 114, 115, 116, 118, 119, 120, 123, 124, 127, 128, 132, 134, 135, 136, 138, 140, 141, 143 & 144.
Greenwood Museum: 10, 23 (top), 29, 31, 49, 59, 73, 77, 79, 80 (top right) & 113 (top).
Grand Forks Museum: 17 (top left), 84, 92 (bottom), 101 (bottom), 106 (centre & 113 (bottom).
Sunfire Archives: 23 (bottom), 33 (bottom), 42 (top & bottom left), 45 (top left & bottom), 53 right, 62 (top) & 99 (bottom).
Garnet Basque: 33 (top), 34 (bottom), 36, 37, 38, 39, 42 (bottom right), 43, 44 (main), 45 (top right), 46, 47, 48, 97, 98, 99 (top), 100, 101 (top four), 104-105 (all colour), 106 (top & bottom), 107, 110, 111 & 117.
Gary McDougall: 34 (top left & right) & 35 (top left, centre & right).
Bill Maximick: 40-41, 102-103 & 108-109.
Mildred Roylance: 54, 67, 72, 75, 80 (top left) & 81.
Wilfred Hall: 55 & 57.

Rock Creek

This is the earliest known photograph of Rock Creek, showing the town during 1860-61 when photographed by the North American Boundary Commission. This original town was established on the west side of Rock Creek.

OF all the towns that sprang into existence in the Boundary Country, Rock Creek is the only one that owes its beginning to placer mining. The history of Rock Creek also precedes all other Boundary Country communities by some 30 years. It all began in October, 1859, as a Canadian named Adam Beam was making his way from Fort Colville, Washington, to the Similkameen district. At Rock Creek, then unnamed, Beam discovered gold. Details of this first discovery are sparse, but it appears that after the initial find, Beam continued to the Similkameen, undoubtedly seeking better prospects. However, Beam apparently was not impressed by what he found in the Similkameen, for he returned to Rock Creek that December. Perhaps he tested the creek once more before returning to Fort Colville for the winter.

On May 7, 1860, Beam was back on Rock Creek, and in six weeks, according to a subsequent dispatch from Gov. James Douglas to the Secretary of State in London, he had recovered $977 worth of gold. Word of Beam's discovery soon spread, and before long there was a collection of tents and a hundred miners on the little flat beside the Kettle River.

Meanwhile, most of the gold seekers in British Columbia were preoccupied with the Fraser River diggings and had no idea a new goldfield had been discovered in another part of the colony. That all changed on July 14 when the Victoria *Colonist* published three brief accounts pertaining to the new diggings.

The first was a letter dated June 25 that James M. Thor-

pe had written by the light of a small fire while his companions slept. After providing details of their journey from Hope to Rock Creek, Thorpe related the price of supplies: "Flour is worth $25 per cwt.; beans 30 and 35 cents per lb.; quicksilver, $4 per lb.; sluiceforks, $10; shovels, $5; long-legged India-rubber boots, $16; shoes, per pair, $3; common white overalls, $2.60 per pair; over-shirt, $2.50; nails, 50 cents per lb.; rot-gut whisky, 25 cents a glass; beef, of excellent quality, 14 to 20 cents per lb."

Thorpe and a companion named William had tried their hand at prospecting for two or three days but found it difficult because of high water, and, he complained, "a purse with very little in it is of no use to a man, when he needs tools, lumber, and provisions for two or three weeks. The diggings are good, but it takes labor and a small capital, to get at anything at this stage of the water. Lumber for pumps and sluices are necessary, and for fluming, too, in many places. But if we had money we could not buy lumber. The man who buys lumber here must be a good friend and acquaintance of the man who has a whip-saw, and pays $200 per thousand for it."

Thorpe explained that there were only three whip-saws on the entire creek, and since he and his companions could neither buy nor rent one at any price, they decided to work for the man who owned one of them. For this they earned $4 per day and board, getting paid when their employer did a clean-up. "There is only one crosscut saw on the creek," Thorpe added, "and tools of every description are scarce."

In another article, E. Crockett confirmed that mining tools were not to be had at any price. Crockett also noted that the miners had recovered up to $100 a day to the hand and already four trading posts and 200 miners were active on Rock Creek. A miner named Scott, who had previously been on the Fraser River, added: "These diggings were struck in May last. They are sixty miles from Fort Colville, on the trail between that place and Hope."

Two weeks later the *Colonist* printed a notice that Ballou's Express would begin running a weekly service from Fort Hope to Rock Creek. The newspaper also published this more sombre item: "At Black Rock Bar, on Rock Creek, on the 10th instant, Frank Porter and David Barr had a difficulty about a mining claim, when Porter shot Barr through the stomach. Barr died instantly; and at last accounts the murderer has not been arrested." This was the first recorded murder in the Boundary Country.

On August 18, the *Colonist* published a letter from George Dunbar, who operated Ballou's "Pony Express" service to Rock Creek. When Dunbar left Rock Creek on August 3, there were "about 300 men at work there, making from $5 to $20 per day, and several as high as $100 per day. The miners all seem contented, and feel certain of doing well. The miners are leaving Canal River for Rock Creek. He met two trains (40 mules) coming from the Dalles with provisions for Rock Creek."

The same issue of the newspaper contained a letter from D.C. Thorne, dated July 27. Thorne, who had arrived at Rock Creek three days earlier, reported: "Plenty of gold here, and coarse at that! Ten miles of the creek is taken up. No claim has yet failed that has been worked. Several are making $20 to $30 per day and some more. Cannot buy an interest in some claims for $3,000. Provisions very scarce. Whisky (as they call it) $6 per gallon. China brandy (no other liquor here) $12 per galloon. Twelve log cabins are built and others building; two saloons, one butcher's shop, one hotel, and five stores. About five hundred men on the creek and two hundred on the river. Another town is started half-way up the creek. I would advise all my friends to come out here, plenty of diggings for all; wages are from four to five dollars per day."

The news of this new goldfield soon had its effect, for a week later the *Colonist* reported that the rush to Rock Creek had just commenced from the Fraser River. Every day boats filled with miners from between the canyons were arriving at Hope. "The occupants remain just long enough to purchase an outfit and start off for the Similkameen," said the newspaper, which, bolstered by the encouraging reports, proclaimed Rock Creek to be the "richest, and by far the most extensive of any heretofore struck in British Columbia."

The Rock Creek gold rush excitement was also spreading through Washington and Oregon as well. In a letter published in the Stilacoom *Herald*, E.C. Ferguson wrote: "We arrived at this place yesterday, all right, and find quite a lively place. Everything looks flourishing. There are about five hundred men here at present, and more on the road. . . . Judging from appearances, and the diggings in general, I think there is every prospect that there will be a rush here next spring. . . ."

The Dalles *Mountaineer*, which had reserved judgement on the Rock Creek goldfields, pending confirmation, announced at the end of August that "Old '49ers who are on the ground, say the Rock Creek mines are equal to California in its palmiest days.

"The effect of this news has been to stir up quite an excitement in our midst. Many of our oldest and best citizens have taken up the fever and are already off or preparing to start for the mines." Among the stampeders was Charles Hull, who, sensing an opportunity, took a complete sawmill plant with him. But the wave of fortune hunters descending upon Rock Creek was not only hard working miners and businessmen. They were accompanied by gamblers, ruffians and the normal riffraff that is invariably attracted by the prospect of easy riches. This latter group had no respect for British authority and, accustomed by the free-wheeling lifestyle of American mining towns, they soon turned Rock Creek into a lawless camp.

Commenting on the situation in the New Westminster *Times*, someone named "Verax" wrote: "We have got anything but a desirable population here just now, and nothing is wanted more than some protective force to teach the rowdies a lesson, and enable order-loving people to get along in some kind of peace and quietness. I could single out a dozen or two individuals who would be valuable acquisitions to your chain-gang (if you are so far advanced to possess one). A few months hard labor on bread and water would entirely cure them of their anti-British rowdyism. It is the wish of all decent inhabitants of Rock Creek — Americans as well as English — that a magistrate and constabulary should be at least once established at that place. The sooner this is done the better, in order to check the growing lawlessness in the bud. . . ."

Robert Stevenson, who would later become well known in the Cariboo, was at Rock Creek in the spring of 1860, and he later described it as being "a typical hell-roaring frontier town," with "dance halls, variety theatres, saloons and gambling dens. Money came easy. The liberality of the digger was proverbial in his indulgence in any and everything that suited his fancy. But there was one thing the miners objected to, and that was the payment of government licence fees — especially the duty on goods brought across the line. . . ."

It soon came to the attention of Gov. James Douglas that the miners at Rock Creek were causing trouble. As he had done previously in a similar incident on the Fraser River that came to be known as Ned McGowan's War, Douglas lost little time in responding to the American threat. He knew that lawlessness and rowdyism were a part of normal daily life in American mining camps, but he was determined to illustrate that that type of behaviour would simply not be tolerated on British soil. The task facing Douglas was not an enviable one, however, since the camp was comprised predominantly of Americans. This was clearly illustrated on April 14, 1861, when a census revealed that only seven of the 123 inhabitants of Rock Creek at that time were British subjects.

Nevertheless, in September, 1860, Douglas made his way to Hope. From there he commenced the long journey to Rock Creek over the Dewdney Trail. He was accompanied by the newly-appointed gold commissioner, William Cox, and secretary Arthur Bushby. Near the spot that later

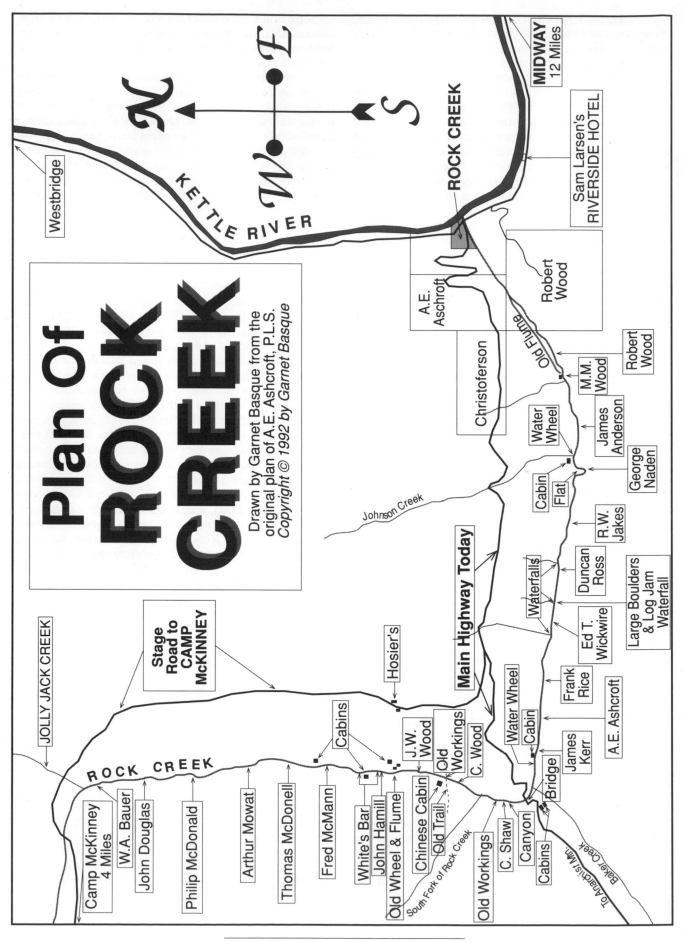

Plan Of ROCK CREEK

Drawn by Garnet Basque from the original plan of A.E. Ashcroft, P.L.S. Copyright © 1992 by Garnet Basque

KETTLE RIVER

Westbridge

N
W   E
S

ROCK CREEK

MIDWAY 12 Miles

Sam Larsen's RIVERSIDE HOTEL

A.E. Aschroft

Robert Wood

Christoferson

Old Flume

Robert Wood

M.M. Wood

James Anderson

Water Wheel

George Naden

Johnson Creek

Cabin

Flat

R.W. Jakes

Duncan Ross

Waterfalls

Ed T. Wickwire

Large Boulders & Log Jam Waterfall

Main Highway Today

Frank Rice

Water Wheel

Cabin

A.E. Ashcroft

James Kerr

Bridge

To Anarchist Mtn.

Baker Creek

Canyon

Cabins

C. Shaw

Old Workings

South Fork of Rock Creek

Old Trail

Chinese Cabin

Old Wheel & Flume

John Hamill

White's Bar

C. Wood

Old Workings

J.W. Wood

Cabins

Hosier's

Fred McMann

Thomas McDonell

Arthur Mowat

Philip McDonald

John Douglas

W.A. Bauer

Camp McKinney 4 Miles

ROCK CREEK

JOLLY JACK CREEK

Stage Road to CAMP McKINNEY

became Hosier's Ranch, the Douglas party met up with Stevenson, and Douglas asked him to go ahead and notify the miners of his arrival.

"This I did," said Stevenson, "but nearly every man jack of 'em absolutely refused to meet him. In fact, certain of the most rebellious spirits went so far as to lock up a large billiard hall where we usually held our meetings. On the governor's arrival in camp, I informed him of my ill-success in getting the boys together. He only laughed and told me that bright and early next morning to go up the creek and inform everyone that a public meeting would be held, at which he would be pleased to listen to all complaints. This I cheerfully did, begging and imploring the miners to come to camp."

Meanwhile, Douglas forced open the door to the meeting hall and made preparations for the meeting. When the hour arrived, some 300 miners packed the partially constructed saloon. As promised, Douglas listened quietly to all complaints, then rose to reply. Dressed in the full regalia of a governor's uniform, even a cocked hat, Douglas' commanding presence rivited the attention of his audience. Douglas began his speech by stating his intention to build a wagon road from Hope to Rock Creek, and by promising to look into the complaints of the miners. This was greeted by a wave of approval. After the cheering subsided, Douglas turned to the matter which had brought him to Rock Creek. He later wrote: "I did not attempt to conceal that the object of my visit. . .was to enquire into their conduct, and to suppress the disorders which were said. . .to be prevalent in that part of the country, and I assured them that I was agreeably surprised to find that those reports were unfounded. . . ."

Douglas demanded respect for British authority and promised that all miners would be treated justly and fairly. He then introduced Cox and outlined his authority and duties. Thus ended the "Rock Creek Rebellion," and in a subsequent letter to the Secretary of State in London, Douglas briefly described the settlement of Rock Creek as consisting of 15 houses with several more under construction, and "shops and buildings intended for the supply and entertainment of miners."

In November, when the final clean-up for the season was made, it was calculated that $83,000 in gold had been taken from Rock Creek by 20 individual miners and small companies of miners. In addition to this, a considerable quantity of gold was taken out by miners who left the camp without disclosing what they had made. By this time the town consisted of 23 homes and businesses of good size, some of them erected at considerable expense, besides a number of huts and cabins. The town also boasted a large billiard saloon which, Cox said, added greatly to the good appearance of the town, the inhabitants of which were anxiously waiting for the government to have the town-site surveyed.

By this time Rock Creek had settled into a peaceful mining camp. Two days after Douglas' speech, Cox had watched the creek's discovered, Adam Beam, wash out $65 in gold from a days's clean-up. That night he squandered his earnings at the gaming tables. Cox, who respected Beam, and wanted the settlement of Rock Creek to flourish, gave the professional gamblers 10 days to leave town.

Cox firmly believed that there would soon be a large increase in the population of Rock Creek, with a corresponding increase in the revenue flowing into the government coffers. Accordingly, late in 1860 he awarded a contract for construction of a government building to Leatherman & Co. The building was completed in early April, 1861 at the cost of £285. To secure government documents and receipts, Cox ordered a large iron safe, weighing about 1,200 pounds, which had to be packed in from the Dalles. In the meantime, he borrowed £240 from some cattle drovers to keep the government business running smoothly.

When next the *Colonist* reported on the activities of Rock Creek, on December 5, it came in the form of a letter dated November 6 that was reprinted from the Portland *Advertiser*.

"Cold weather — but too early — has come at last," wrote an unidentified miner, "putting an end to all further mining operations in this vicinity until about the first of March next. Miners and others who intended leaving have gone — most of them to Colville and Walla Walla. Of those remaining there are about 150 on the creek; including miners, merchants, mechanics and government officials. The miners who remain are satisfied that what they have not done this season they can do next — that is, make their 'pile.' Although a few miners and a good many discontented gamblers have gone from here and called the mines a humbug, there are a few on the creek who have done well. From the Nolan claim, the best on the creek, there has been taken out the sum of $7,000 this season. There are three men working this, and they each give it as their opinion that four times that amount will be taken out next season. From most of the other claims, sums varying from $2,000 to $5,000 have been taken out. . . .

"The British officials here are having a lively time at present, in attempting to prevent goods being smuggled into British territory. The boundary line is only three miles from here, and two trains are just outside awaiting a favorable opportunity to run their goods in and evade paying the ten per cent duty on dry goods, and $1.50 per gallon on liquors. Another dodge is to take all the goods across on the same horse, thereby saving $1.50 on each horse, that being the duty on every animal taken into British territory. Contrary to the expectations of some of our merchants, provisions are exceedingly plentiful, although the prices remain very high. Flour is selling at 20 cents per pound; Sugar, Coffee, and Dried Fruit at 40 cents; Bacon, 45; Apples, 50; Potatoes and Onions at 20. The price of lumber has fallen to $12 per hundred."

In early February, 1861, a number of pack trains loaded with supplies left the Dalles for Rock Creek. According to the Portland *Times*, Mr. Parker's 40-mule pack train was being freighted by Loebe & Co. Cyrus Smith had a train of 25 mules about to start out, as did Palmer & Jacob. Woodward & Co, with 40 mules, and Woodbury & Co., with 20 animals, were also about to get underway.

All of these supplies, and the inrushing miners, were bound for Rock Creek, then the main area of interest in southern B.C. But miners were a fickle lot, always seeking new eldorados. Some ventured further afield, and soon word filtered back to the town that gold had been discovered in Mission Creek, near the future site of Kelowna. At first the reports did not create much interest, but by the middle of February, more than one group had gone out to examine the new discoveries for themselves. One such party was headed by Adam Beam.

When Beam and his associates returned, they showed Cox some gold they had obtained from a claim where the owner, William Pion, was making $4 a day with a rocker. Beam told Cox that they had prospected nine different streams, all of which emptied into Okanagan Lake, "and found gold on each, averaging from three to ninety cents to the pan," despite the ground being frozen, which "much impeded our work. We are all quite satisfied of the richness of these streams, and shall as soon as possible, dispose of our claims on Rock Creek and leave for that section of the country where a miner can grow his potatoes and other vegetables, besides keep his cow."

The decision of Beam and the others to leave Rock Creek alarmed Cox. He feared that if too many miners abandoned their claims on Rock Creek for the new diggings, the town might be deserted. So Cox, who himself had preempted land in the area, suppressed the news. On March 1, he wrote a letter to the Colonial Secretary advising him about the new discoveries, adding: "I have not made the above statement public as it would only tend to bad results at present. The miners in this neighborhood who are heavily burdened with debt would be easily coaxed off, and the mines now in preparatory condition for being worked abandoned. Improvements going forward on buildings and farms would be checked. Townlots would be almost unsaleable, and the expected revenue seriously interfered with."

On March 28, the *Colonist* received information from "Dunbar's Express" that miners were once again at work on Rock Creek. According to Dunbar, they were doing well. "Kelly & Co. are making $17 per day to the hand; others are making from $10 to $12." Dunbar also noted that the "Oregonian pack-trains," previously mentioned, were arriving every day, "and large numbers of miners are there and on the way." Nowhere was there any mention of the new discoveries in the Okanagan.

But if the Mission Creek gold discovery was not yet general knowledge, it still continued to worry Cox. In another letter to the Colonial Secretary, dated April 27, he wrote: "Tomorrow about twelve miners leave for the Okanagan gold fields. If the mines are only of an ordinary nature, the climate and soil are of a sufficiently attractive nature to cause miners to settle there. Much money has been expended in improving buildings here and some good lumber houses have been erected, but the expected stampede to Okanagan has thrown a dismal feeling over the owners of such property."

One major cause for anxiety among the businessmen of Rock Creek, briefly alluded to in Cox's letter of March 1, was the amount of credit they had extended to the miners. In March, Cox had estimated the total debt at $16,000. This was a serious matter, and in a letter dated July 10, Cox wrote that his worst fears had come true. "Rock Creek I regret to say has not prospered as anticipated, the season is advancing and still no immigration. Miners heavily burdened with debts contracted recklessly during the late winter, escaping, flying to the Nez Perces (sic) country — the

traders disenheartened refuse credit to good men who cannot produce the cash, and without provisions cannot work their claims — in fact things have the appearance of a general bankruptcy."

Despite the problems and setbacks, Rock Creek remained a surprisingly quiet and orderly camp. In an article titled "The Rise and Fall of Rock Creek," published in 1926 in the First Annual Report of the Okanagan Historical and Natural History Society, Leonard Norris wrote: ". . . there was no drunkenness, no fighting and no brawling among the men. The American miners who came overland to Rock Creek were generally speaking, a pretty decent lot of men. Men who lived for years in a mining camp where there is no constituted authority —, no village policeman to keep order, soon learned to secure for themselves some degree of comfort and quiet by exerting themselves, each individually in discountenancing any disorder or want of decorum in the camp. It is true, drinking and gambling went on, but these in themselves are harmless amusements. Apparently during the 16 months that Cox was in charge of the camp, he reported only one crime as having been committed in Rock Creek mining camp. A man was guilty of theft and was run out of the camp, Cox declining to send him to jail on account of the expense. This crime list when the number of men — ranging from 125 to perhaps 300 or 400 occasionally — and the duration of the camp are considered, would hardly discredit a Sunday School picnic."

Norris does go on to relate that a murder was committed about six miles up Rock Creek. The victim, a Frenchman named Pierre Chebart, had invited an Indian he had just met to join him for dinner. After the meal, both men settled down for the night in a vacant cabin. During the night the Indian, who later claimed he "had a bad heart," got up, stole the knife from under Chebart's head, and stabbed him to death. The corpse was then thrown into the creek and drifted about two miles downstream, where, according to Cox, it "presented a very pitiable appearance."

For a man in Cox's position, this was a very serious sit-

A hydraulicking operation in the canyon of Rock Creek c1895. Despite all the gold mining that has taken place on Rock Creek, this stream may still hold promise for the modern prospector, for there is no record of anyone ever having reached bedrock.

uation. He could have improvised a gallows and hired a hangman, but there was no judge or jury to try the murderer. To take the man to New Westminster to await the next assizes would have been expensive. So Cox, who usually acted swiftly in such matters, procrastinated while he tried to decide what to do. Some historians believe Cox merely stalled to give American vigilantes an opportunity to resolve the problem for him. In any event, that is precisely what happened.

The Indian, who had confessed the murder to other Indians, had been turned over by the chief to the settlers at Osoyoos. He was then turned over to the American vigilantes who administered their own brand of justice. "The wretched young man was marched to a large pine tree," wrote Cox, "& there executed in the presence of his former associates & comrades."

On October 29, the *Colonist* published a brief account of the mining activities that had taken place on Rock Creek during 1861, as relayed by a miner named Richards. Rufus Henry had taken out $2,000. "Knowland, Schwartz & Co. made $2500 to the man; Bacon & Co., consisting of three men, have made $3000 each. Their claim paid about $100 to the man over expenses."

Richards told the newspaper that there were about 100 men at Rock Creek during the summer, "but at present there were not more than twenty miners. There is only one trader left."

William Cox left Rock Creek on November 15, having seen the last party of miners leave the camp for Mission Creek five days earlier. Rock Creek was now completely deserted.

The following year gold was discovered in the Cariboo, and as news of its phenomenal richness spread, miners abandoned their claims in other parts of the province like rats leaving a sinking ship. Rock Creek, Boundary Creek, and creeks in the Similkameen, Okanagan and elsewhere were virtually abandoned and forgotten.

In late August, 1862, Joseph Harrison, accompanied by two partners named Saxton and Chambers, and four others who joined them, embarked on a prospecting trip from Kamloops to Okanagan Lake, Rock Creek and the Similkameen. On October 20, the *Colonist* published details about their journey.

"At Rock Creek they found a large town of deserted buildings, many of them of a good substantial character. The Indians had played havoc amongst them, by knocking off the locks, hinges etc. and breaking the windows. Not a soul was living in the town. Above the town — one mile up — were seven Chinamen, and three white men. The Chinamen had a claim in the bed of the creek, in which they said they were doing well. Mr. Harrison estimated they were making from $5 to $6 per day. The white men were laying in a stock of provisions, and intended tunnelling during the winter. There was every appearance of good hill diggings. He found everything necessary for mining, good houses, sluice boxes, tools, and nobody to claim them. They then set to work on an old claim, erecting a dam and prepared sluice boxes, and worked for a day and a half without any satisfactory results, when the cold weather setting in and provisions getting scarce, four of the party determined to return to Hope, leaving three there undecided as to

whether they would get a supply of provisions from Colville — 75 miles distant — and winter on the creek, or not. Flour was $10 per 100 lbs., and was about the only article of `grub' on the creek, there being no bacon or beans. Harrison and two others left Rock Creek about the 2d October."

From 1862 to 1865, the rich goldfields of the Cariboo dominated the provincial mining scene, and very little news was forthcoming about Rock Creek. During 1865, despite very high water in the spring, some 50 or 60 men had made fair wages. Then in October, the *Colonist* received word from a miner named Pooly that new diggings, paying 30¢ to the pan, had been discovered on the South Fork of Rock Creek.

In early April, 1866, the New Westminster *Columbian* published a "semi-official" letter that had been received by Gold Commissioner Haynes pertaining to the new strike. "Fourteen white men and 40 Chinamen are mining on Rock Creek. Randall & Co., at the crossing, have struck very good diggings. Randall told me himself that he washed 100 buckets and got $11. There is quite a stir here about it." The letter went on to state that, owing to the excitement, men who had been hired to work on the roads had decided to leave for the diggings. "The diggings alluded to is six miles higher up the stream than the diggings hereto known, and goes far to establish the fact that Rock Creek mines are richer and far more extensive that was supposed."

But the new gold rush did not materialize, interest soon faded, and by July the *Colonist* reported that only "about ten white men are mining there, the rest being Chinamen." The paper went on to state that: "Nothing but Chinamen's wages are made in that section."

Despite sporadic placer activity, Rock Creek as a town had managed to survive, partially, of course because of mining, but also because of the increase in travellers using the Dwedney Trail which passed through the settlement. But in August, 1866, Rock Creek's fight for survival was nearly snuffed out by a disastrous fire that roared through the town.

According to the Cariboo *Sentinel*, the fire, which occurred on the night of August 7, 1866, "destroyed nearly all of the houses in the town there, and consumed a large quantity of goods. The fire originated in a dwelling house adjoining the general store of Smith & Bradford, and there being a strong breeze blowing at the time, the flames soon spread. The people had only time to get out of their houses without saving anything, when the dwellings were one sheet of flame. Everything in the store of Smith & Bradford was consumed with the exception of a small quantity of bacon and a few trifling articles, which were all injured, however, by the fire. The loss of the firm mentioned amounted to upwards of $8,000."

Although the loss was a severe blow to Smith & Bradford, they wasted little time in rebuilding. A few days after the fire Smith was making his way back from Hope "with a large train of goods," and before long the partners were conducting business as usual. A number of buildings must also have been rebuilt, for at the end of January, 1867, the *Colonist* reported that 42 white and Chinese miners had decided to spend the winter at Rock Creek. "The miners did very well during the summer season," continued the paper, "and show considerable oro as a result of their work."

For the next 20 years, mining activity at Rock Creek remained sporadic, with the town's population being comprised mostly of Chinese miners. In 1877, when surveyor George Dawson passed through Rock Creek, he reported that there were only about 15 Chinese working there, making wages of about $1.50 per day.

Around 1885, Henry White opened a general store. White, who was destined to discover the famous Knob Hill mine at Phoenix in 1891, supplied all the prospectors and ranchers in the Okanagan and Boundary. Another old pioneer of the district was Charlie Dietz. He was with the Fraser River miners when they stampeded to Rock Creek in 1860. Unfortunately, by the time Dietz reached Rock Creek, all the best claims were taken, so he returned to the Fraser River and Cariboo.

In the fall of 1886, White, Dietz, J. Cooper and F. Deitch located White's Bar on Rock Creek, and in three seasons they recovered some $50,000. At one time they had 12 men working for them on the claim and were taking out pay averaging $20 a day to the man. Ironically, a miner from Spokane had prospected the bar a few days before White and his partners staked it, and had sunk several test holes. Even though some of the holes were very close to where gold was later discovered, they proved barren, and the frustrated miner posted a notice on a tree that the bar was worthless. The same fall White's Bar was discovered, J. Morgan, G. Young, M. Hotter and C. Winkler discovered a bar three miles further up the creek and took out good pay the next season. In 1887 several claims were opened up on both branches of Rock Creek, and the Denver Company made good returns from a bar located between White's and Hotter's.

White, Dietz and the others were working their claims in the spring of 1887 when Fred Rice, Alfred McKinney, William Burnham and Edward Lefevre passed through the area in search of Rock Creek's mother lode. Their discoveries eventually gave rise to Camp McKinney.

During 1889 there were about six white and 20 Chinese miners recovering small wages at Rock Creek. That same year the Laura Hydraulic Mining Company spent about $15,000 getting their claims into production, but were prevented from doing a clean-up because of a severe early frost. They were more successful in 1890, recovering $10,000 over expenses. Production declined in 1891, with the total output from all Rock Creek claims yielding between $5,000 and $6,000. On December 22, 1891, when surveyor J.P. Burnyeat passed through Rock Creek, he noted that it had a population of 15 to 20, with one hotel and two stores.

The hotel mentioned by Burnyeat was the Rock Creek Hotel and stables owned by Malcolm McCuaig and James

G.B. Taylor. After his unsuccessful attempt at operating a general store in Rock Creek, he returned to Greenwood and became active in politics, becoming an alderman there from 1921-29.

Haddican, then the only hotel in the entire Boundary district. It was an old log building that contained a barroom, store and post office. The two stores mentioned were probably owned by Chinese. When the first issue of the Midway *Advance* made its appearance on April 26, 1894, it carried ads for the Lum Kee General Store and the Ah Kee General Store at Rock Creek. Both stores provided Chinese food and mining supplies. In addition, the Laura Hydraulic Mining Company operated a sawmill, and had erected a large bunkhouse and office building at the mouth of Rock Creek. These were destroyed by fire in 1894.

In 1894, Harry Pittendrigh purchased the Rock Creek Hotel from McCuaig and Haddican. The following year Pittendrigh contracted Albert Madge, the only carpenter in the area, to build a new hotel of lumber. When completed, the two-story building contained living quarters for the family at the west end, with the dining room, sitting room and centre kitchen located at the back, overlooking the Kettle River. The barroom was at the east end. Bedrooms for the travelling public were located on the upper floor. These could be rented for 50¢ to $1 a night, or room and board could be had for $30 per month. The verandah that completely surrounded the building gave it a good overall appearance. In September, 1894, a new business was established at Rock Creek when Ingram & Burber, "general teamsters and freighters," set up shop. A year later the business was owned by Conkle & Donald.

In 1896, the five claims on White's Bar produced a paltry $700 in gold, a far cry from its peak years. For the Ah Mat China Company, operating at the mouth of Rock Creek and on Rock Creek itself, it was a different story. Their group of five claims yielded $6,000. Some of the shareholders were so pleased with this result that they promptly sold their interests and went back to China. Despite their departure, however, the Chinese community at Rock Creek must have remained relatively substantial, for, on February 6, 1897, the Boundary Creek *Times* reported that Chinese New Year had been celebrated "with the usual accompaniment of firecrackers and rockets."

Prior to this, the history of Rock Creek had taken a new direction. Hard rock mines were being discovered throughout the Boundary and attracting new settlers and businessmen. In 1894, a wagon road had been completed from Penticton to Grand Forks. It passed through Rock Creek, and for a time it appeared that Rock Creek's future as a major stopping place was assured. Certainly the government thought so, for in April, 1897, the *Times* announced that a 160-acre parcel of land to the east of Rock Creek, much of which had been occupied by Chinese vegetable gardens for years, had been reserved as a government town-site. By June, Charles deBlois Green had begun surveying the town, and in August the government began advertising that the

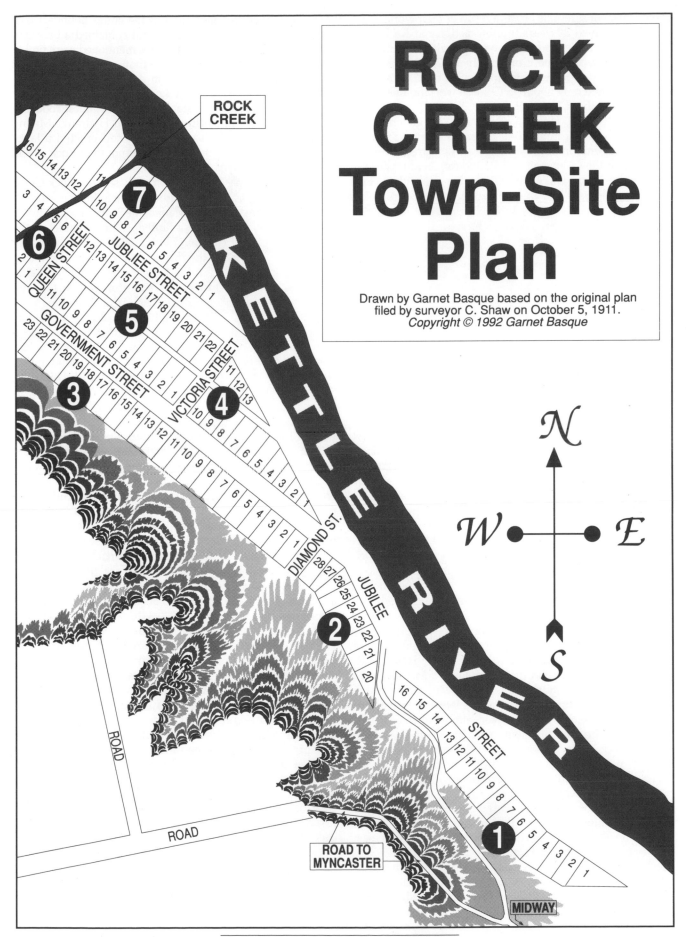

ROCK CREEK

ROCK CREEK Town-Site Plan

Drawn by Garnet Basque based on the original plan filed by surveyor C. Shaw on October 5, 1911.
Copyright © 1992 Garnet Basque

KETTLE RIVER

QUEEN STREET

JUBLIEE STREET

GOVERNMENT STREET

VICTORIA STREET

DIAMOND ST.

JUBILEE

STREET

ROAD

ROAD

ROAD TO MYNCASTER

MIDWAY

N
W • • E
S

This photo of Rock Creek shows a number of freight wagons heading east. Although the photograph is undated, we know that it was taken after 1899, because the Rock Creek Trading Company, shown in the foreground, was not established until May of that year by Olson & Phelan, of Greenwood. Although the two other buildings are not identified, the one in the distance was probably the Rock Creek Hotel, owned by Harry Pittendrigh.

sale of lots by auction would take place on September 23. "The town-site," wrote the *Times*, "is one of the prettiest and best suited in the district and the lots should command a good figure." However, on September 27, the *Advance* reported that government agent Leonard Norris had only been able to dispose of four lots.

One businessman who believed in the potential of Rock Creek was G.B. Taylor. In April, 1897, Taylor and Arthur Rendell, both of Greenwood, entered into a partnership and opened a general store. Unfortunately, the anticipated business did not materialize, and in late November, after only six months in business, they closed their doors. During the same time, the Rock Creek Hotel was being "overhauled and enlarged in readiness for the summer's travel." In May, Malcolm McCuaig, who had previously owned a hotel in Rock Creek, formed a partnership with Samuel Larsen and established the Riverside Hotel. Business proved to be so good that in September McCuaig sold his interest in the Boundary Hotel in Midway and moved to Rock Creek. Unfortunately, McCuaig's latest venture in the hotel business lasted only one year, almost to the day. On May 4, 1898, he died of pneumonia. McCuaig, one of the early pioneers of the province, had been born in Glengarry, Ontario in 1842. Before settling in the Boundary Country, he had participated in the Cariboo gold rush. He was buried at the Midway Cemetery.

After Taylor & Co. closed their general store, it was another 18 months before other businessmen decided to gamble on Rock Creek. This time it was Olson & Phelan, who operated the White Front Store in Greenwood. Fortunately, their Rock Creek Trading Company, which advertised a full line of supplies for prospectors, as well as hardware, groceries, boots and shoes, furnishing goods, etc., did enjoy better success.

Unlike other Boundary towns, Rock Creek never experienced the boom and bust cycle, with the possible exception of a few months back in 1860. There was no tremendous inflow of residents, no major business activity, and no railroad construction or hard rock mining to stimulate its economy. It seemed perpetually to fluctuate between a couple to a few businesses, 50 to 100 residents, and little else. Small wonder, therefore, that Rock Creek did not receive much press throughout the Boundary and elsewhere.

But, in July, 1899, a dramatic stagecoach hold-up just outside town temporarily threw Rock Creek into the headlines. The incident occurred about 2 o'clock on Saturday afternoon, July 6. The Snodgrass Stage, driven by Joe Snodgrass, had just left Rock Creek with four passengers en route to Penticton. As the stage was ascending the steep grade near Kennedy Creek, two masked men emerged from behind a large tree on the bank overlooking the road and ordered the driver to stop. Snodgrass, thinking it was a joke, initially ignore them. When the bandits repeated their demand a second time, however, Snodgrass realized that each man had two revolvers pointed at him. Bringing his team to a halt, Snodgrass inquired as to what they wanted. One of the robbers, who had moved to the roadway to the right of the stage, ordered Snodgrass to throw out the express box. Upon being told that the stage did not have an express box, the outlaw demanded that Snodgrass hand over the mail bags. After several heavy mail bags were turned over, Snodgrass was ordered to drive on with all due haste.

Eventually the stage met up with Phil Hickey, who was travelling from Camp McKinney to Greenwood. Hickey was informed about the robbery, but thought those on the stage were joking, that is, until he reached the scene of the robbery and saw the mail sacks scattered all over the road.

Hickey promptly rushed to Rock Creek and spread the alarm.

When the robbery scene was examined more closely, it became apparent that the robbers had not been very thorough in their search for funds. According to the *Times*, some of the mail sacks "had been left untouched while others had been cut open. The robbers did not even handle the registered mail very carefully. One letter which was cut open had $25 between its pages which were unmolested by the highwaymen." This caused the paper to conclude that the culprits "appeared to be novices and were apparently quite nervous about their desperate undertaking. One, a tall man, had a mask which covered only the upper portion of his face, while the other a stouter man was masked in a sheepskin which came down to his chest."

Unfortunately, with the international boundary only three miles away, and with the district's only policeman in "foot" pursuit, the robbers had little difficulty in making good their escape.

That same week the Rock Creek Hotel was broken into and some bottles of liquor were stolen. This time, however, the authorities were more successful, and the next day a man named P.J. Kelly was arrested. After a preliminary hearing at Greenwood, Kelly was ordered to stand trial at the next Vernon Court of Assize. On October 30, 1899, the *Advance* reported that Kelly had been found guilty and had been sentenced to three years in the B.C. Penitentiary.

With this crime "wave" behind it, Rock Creek settled back into its regular doldrums, all but forgotten about by the local papers. A brief item in the *Advance* on June 18, 1900, noted that William Meadows, formerly of Cascade, had purchased the Rock Creek Trading Company from Olson & Phelan. A month later the same paper stated that H.A. Green was building a blacksmith shop. During 1900, a school was established at Rock Creek for the first time. The first schoolhouse was an old, small frame building that stood on the hill overlooking the Rock Creek Hotel. Harry Pittendrigh, who donated the building and property it stood on, became a trustee. The first teacher was a man named F.W. Barton, followed the next year by Miss Mills. There were 14 students in attendance when the school inspector visited Rock Creek on October 18, 1900. In those days, with no gas or electric heat, parents were asked to contribute fuel for the stove. Even drinking water had to be hauled from the Kettle River. A new school was constructed by Albert Madge in 1912, which continued to be used until 1948. This building still stands across the road from the Gold Pan Cafe.

All was quiet and peaceful in Rock Creek until late May, 1901, when the town suddenly made headlines once more. Ironically, as it had two years earlier, it took a daring hold-up to focus attention on the small community. Remarkably, judging from the descriptions given, it appears that the same outlaws were involved in both robberies.

The incident occurred in the Riverside Hotel on the evening of May 18. Proprietor Sam Larsen, an employee named M.W. Bresser, and blacksmith H.A. Green were sitting in the bar talking when two masked men, armed with revolvers, entered the room and instructed the three men to hold up their hands. At first Larsen and his companions thought the two men were joking, "but the robbers informed their victims that they were in earnest and that if there request was not immediately complied with, they would use violence in carrying out their evil intentions. All hands were held up and one of the men went through the pockets of the three men while the other guarded the door.

The robbers evidently knew that both Larsen and Bresser had considerable money on them, and they also knew exactly where it was kept. The man that did the searching immediately placed his hands on Larsen's wallet, "which contained $450 in bills, besides a number of cheques. The hired man had his money in two pocket books, which were kept in separate pockets, and the two men were also aware of this fact as the one doing the searching put his hand only in the two pockets containing the two pocket books, which together contained $95 in cash."

The robbers then told Larsen that since "the cheques were of no use to them, they would be left at the road side about three hundred yards from the hotel, where he would find them the following morning, and they were as good as their word for the pocket book containing the cheques were found exactly where they agreed to leave them.

"No description of the robbers can be given beyond that one of them was a tall man while the other was much below the average height."

The Riverside Hotel was located nearly a mile from any other building and its isolated position made it an easy target for the robbers. Provincial constable George Cunningham was promptly assigned to the case, but, as in the stagecoach robbery two years earlier, the culprits were never caught.

The next several years were tough times for towns throughout the Boundary Country. Already a number of prominent towns, some boasting populations 20 times greater than Rock Creek, had died, while others were clinging tenaciously to life. Perhaps Rock Creek's diminutive size and stature was a blessing in disguise, for it seemed to venture forward as it had always done. On June 30, 1905, an ad for J.S. McLean's Iona Hotel, located "at the crossing of Rock Creek on the main road to Osoyoos," began to appear in the *Times*. In November of the same year, the *Times* announced that Sam Larsen had installed "a gasoline lighting system" in his Riverside Hotel. The same brief item pointed out that Thomas Hansen had made an excellent choice when he decided to establish a general store at Rock Creek. "He began here with a small stock of merchandise, but strict and obliging attention to business has resulted in surprising growth. Not long since he doubled the capacity of his store and today has it filled with a $10,000 stock of well assorted merchandise."

Of all the ghost towns and mining camps whose histories appear in this book, only two, Rock Creek and Greenwood, have survived to the present day. Rock Creek was never a major centre, nor is it ever likely to be, at least not in my lifetime. Neither, however, is it destined to die. In September, 1958, as part of the B.C. Centennial program, a memorial cairn was dedicated at Rock Creek, on the bank of the creek first made famous by miners seeking gold. It contains a time capsule that will be opened in 2058. I predict the town will still be in existence then. ✤

Camp McKinney

(Above) A group of unidentified miners pose for a photograph in front of the Cariboo mine's bunk and boarding house..
(Below) Lack of transportation to and from Camp McKinney curtailed early mining activity. Although the situation was greatly improved after a wagon road was constructed in 1894, as this 1895 photograph shows, it still left much to be desired.

CAMP McKinney is located on the eastern slope of the range of mountains dividing the Kettle River and Okanagan valleys, at an elevation of some 4,500 feet above sea level. The first interest in the immediate area occurred in 1884 when F.W. Goericke, a Rock Creek placer miner, discovered an outcrop of gold on the mountain slope about 10 miles from the mouth of the creek. Goericke named his claim the Victoria, the first mineral claim to be located in the district. Unfortunately, the total lack of transportation in those days practically precluded the working of a mine, and the site was virtually abandoned.

In the spring of 1887, Fred Rice, Alfred McKinney, William Burnham and Edward Lefevre left Spokane to prospect for quartz in British Columbia. When they reached Rock Creek they found Charlie Dietz and other placer miners on White Bar on the north fork of the creek. After visiting at Dietz's placer camp, they started to look over the ridge of country lying between the two forks. They passed the Victoria claim, and pushed on some 2,000 feet higher up the mountain. At it was late spring, the mountains were still covered with snow. This made prospecting almost impossi-

ble except upon some exposed ridges from which the wind had swept the snow. On May 2 they came upon an open bare spot overlooking a nice little creek flowing southward towards Rock Creek. The next morning, close to where the campfire had been built, McKinney discovered an outcrop of gold. That day, after a little work revealed the richness of the vein, Rice and McKinney located the Cariboo mine while Burnham and Lefevre staked the adjoining claim, the Amelia. On May 9, the adjoining Okanagan, Alice and Emma claims were recorded.

Although there were comparatively few prospectors in the country at the time, the news of the strike quickly spread and soon some 30 to 40 prospectors were camped around the lucky discoverers. After viewing McKinney's samples with "the quartz literally hanging to the gold," the newcomers staked claims in all directions.

Encouraged by this re-newed activity, Goericke took in Judge C. Haynes and C.B. Bush as partners and tried to develop the Victoria, sinking an incline shaft to a depth of 110 feet. According to the Boundary Creek *Times;* "Assays from the best ore ran $44 to $480, with very little silver, and the poorest was $7 to

$12; one sample sent to San Francisco carried telluride. In 1887 the claim was patented by Messrs. J.C. Haynes, F.W. Goericke and C.B. Bush."

On August 18, 1887, Gold Commissioner Tunstall, then at Granite Creek, wrote to the Minister of Lands and Works in Victoria requesting that 74 acres of "land situated about 800 yards south of the McKenneyville quartz camp in the Rock Creek district" be reserved for a town-site. The town, which the miners requested be named "McKennyville" in honour of the discoverer, was situated on a level plateau convenient to wood and water.

Surveyor-General W.S. Gore agreed and, within weeks, instructed a surveying firm to subdivide a town-site into blocks and lots. He instructed them to confine their survey to the mapping of a single street: others were to be "merely projected on paper" for the time being. "McKinneyville" (as it was properly spelled) was accordingly subdivided and registered that November.

Unfortunately, because the mines were more than 200 miles from railroad transportation, the only means of reaching them was by wagon from Spokane to Marcus, and thence 100 miles on horseback up the Kettle River Indian trail. However, despite the obvious difficulties of transportation and the consequent high prices of provisions, prospecting and development work was carried on vigorously during 1887, not only on the Cariboo and Amelia, but several of the adjoining and outlying claims. However, by 1888 many of the claim owners had to face the harsh reality of trying to obtain working capital. Quartz mining in B.C. at the time was unknown, and it was next to impossible to get capital to invest. In addition, the camp was practically inaccessible; all supplies being packed in over a mountain trail, and mail service was only once a month. "Under such circumstances," reported the *Times*, "it is not surprising that the majority of the miners were compelled to abandon their properties, however unwillingly, and seek more favorable localities."

In 1888 Gold Commissioner Walter Dewdney visited the new camp and was impressed by what he saw, particularly the New York-owned Douglas mine. In a subsequent report to his superiors, Dewdney stated that the government, at a cost of $1,915.51, had "build a first-class trail from the Indian village, In-ka-neep" through Camp McKinney to Rock Creek. "Freighters and others pronounced this a good trail," he wrote, "and far more convenient, as it shortens the route to the mines by about 15 miles."

On August 9, 57 men living at Camp McKinney signed a petition recommending that Stephen Tanner be given a license to operate a hotel and dispense "spirits." The license was granted and Turner arrived later that winter, although no record appears to have survived describing the type of establishment he might have erected or where it was located. The same winter the government trail was widened to a sleigh road, replacing teams of pack horses with teams of horses hauling boxes on runners.

In 1889, with about 25 properties being worked in the area, the prospects for Camp McKinney appeared bright. Transportation, however, remained the pressing problem. Reporting on the situation, Dewdney advised Victoria that a road was vital to Camp McKinney's future. "It is a moral impossibility to ship either ore or heavy machinery." Camp

McKinney's inaccessibility soon had its effect when the manager of the Douglas mine, after an investment of $30,000, ordered all work to cease. He then travelled to New York in an effort to convince the shareholders of the need for more machinery. The mine, like several others, had tons of ore ready for shipment but no means of getting it to market.

In his year-end report for 1891, Commissioner Dewdney reported that the Camp McKinney mine owners remained deadlocked for want of a road. The outlook for Camp McKinney looked even bleaker in the spring of 1892 as miners lost their sleigh road with the melting snow, leaving only trails east and west. With only assessment work being carried out, and most of the inhabitants abandoning the town, the post office was moved to Fairview, which had recently been connected to Penticton by a wagon road.

Meanwhile, the Cariboo mine had undergone some changes in ownership. When discoverers McKinney and Rice lacked the financing to develop the mine, they borrowed money from George B. McAuley. However, by 1888, despite being urged by McAuley to hang on, McKinney and Rice had grown discouraged and wanted to sell. McAuley was offered the opportunity to purchase the mine, but was in no condition financially to handle the prospect. Instead, McAuley persuaded Phil O'Rourke, of Bunker Hill and Sullivan fame, and Jack Hanley, to accompany him in an examination of the property. However, after O'Rourke and Hanley carefully looked over the ground, they decided not to invest in it. McAuley, however, was impressed by what he saw, and upon returning to Spokane he persuaded James Monahan and Clement King as to its viability. On April 29, 1888, McKinney and Rice sold the Cariboo to the group for a small outlay. (The exact amount is unknown, but it was estimated to be $7,000.) The Cariboo Mine and Milling Company was subsequently formed with 800,000 shares being issued. The group also acquired an interest in the Amelia at about the same time.

The opening up of the vein on which these claims were placed was slow, mainly due to lack of capital, but also because of the inaccessibility of the district at that time. In 1892 the B.C. *Minister of Mines* report stated that "nothing more than assessment work has been done in this camp during the season — owners are awaiting the construction of a wagon road across the mountain to Kettle River, when machinery can be brought into camp and work be commenced at once." Throughout 1893 the Cariboo was the only mine being worked seriously. Investing $1,000, the owners employed six men to sink a 61-foot air shaft. The other mines, meanwhile, accomplished little but assessment work.

By 1894 the Cariboo-Amelia properties had become camp leaders. That February, with snow still four feet deep on the trails, the owners had laboriously packed in a steam engine, boiler, assay outfit and a 10-stamp mill. The equipment had been bought from the abandoned Rainbow mine of Golden, Washington. The duty on the equipment, which totalled $880, was delayed by permission of the Deputy Collector of Customs. According to the B.C. *Minister of Mines* report, the mill began operating on May 1, and by November 1 "it had worked 163 days, milled 3,100 tons of ore, which produced gold to the value of $34,750, and about

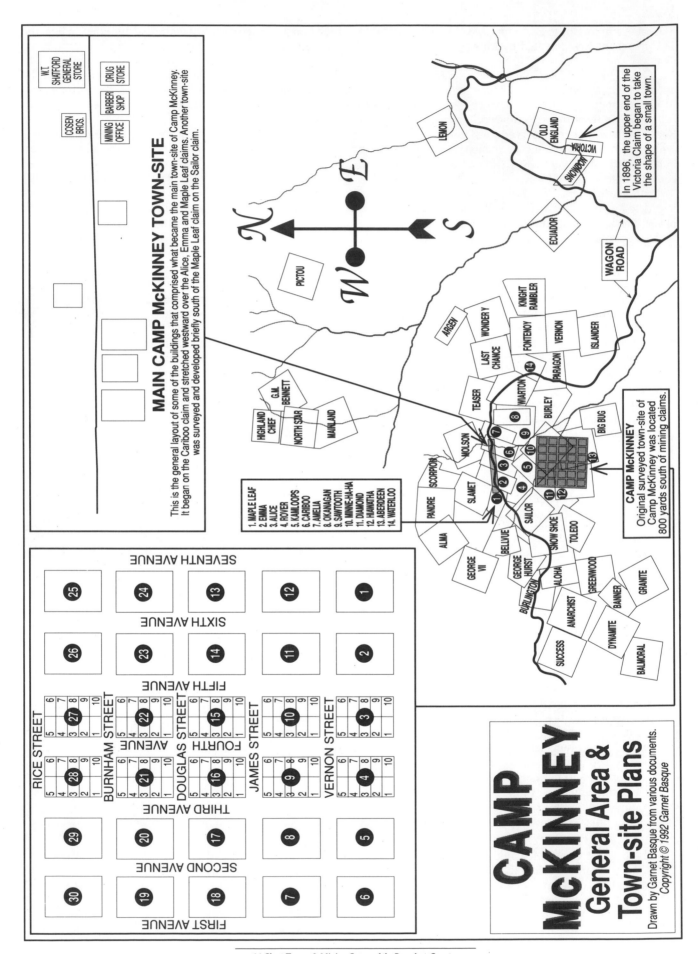

MAIN CAMP McKINNEY TOWN-SITE

This is the general layout of some of the buildings that comprised what became the main town-site of Camp McKinney. It began on the Cariboo claim and stretched westward over the Alice, Emma and Maple Leaf claims. Another town-site was surveyed and developed briefly south of the Maple Leaf claim on the Sailor claim.

W.T. SHATFORD GENERAL STORE

COSEN BROS.

MINING OFFICE

BARBER SHOP

DRUG STORE

In 1896, the upper end of the Victoria Claim began to take the shape of a small town.

WAGON ROAD

CAMP McKINNEY
Original surveyed town-site of Camp McKinney was located 800 yards south of mining claims.

1. MAPLE LEAF
2. EMMA
3. ALICE
4. ROVER
5. KAMLOOPS
6. CARIBOO
7. AMELIA
8. OKANAGAN
9. SAWTOOTH
10. MINNE-HA-HA
11. DIAMOND
12. HIAWATHA
13. ABERDEEN
14. WATERLOO

CAMP McKINNEY
General Area & Town-site Plans

Drawn by Garnet Basque from various documents.
Copyright © 1992 Garnet Basque

Two views of Hugh Cameron's Camp McKinney Hotel. The much travelled Cameron first arrived in Camp McKinney in 1887. In 1894 he and Malcolm McCuaig built the hotel seen in the top photo. It was situated on the Cariboo claim, and the Cariboo mine's cook house can also be seen in the picture. However, Cameron was forced to move his hotel from the Cariboo property, so it was dissembled and rebuilt on the Teaser claim. The lower photo was probably taken there, as there are some improvements to the front and an extension has been added..

60 tons of concentrate."

In the spring of 1894 there were about 70 people living and working at Camp McKinney, but there were no business establishments to cater to their needs. Although beef for the camp was supplied from Hosier's Ranch, most of the remaining supplies were obtained from Fairview. In mid-May, for example, 20 Indian pack horses left Elliot's General Store at Fairview for the mines.

Naturally, as the mines became more productive, some businessmen began to establish themselves at Camp McKinney. One of the first was Henry Nicholson, who arrived from Fairview on April 22, 1894, and established himself as a notary public and mining agent. Prior to this, Hugh Cameron and Malcolm McCuaig, both longtime pioneers of the district, had started construction on the log Camp McKinney Hotel. By the end of May, three men were erecting a boarding house for a man named Hughes, and a sawmill was running full blast cutting lumber for the stamp mill at the Cariboo mine. Before the construction of the stamp mill, the stamps had "been working on an unprotected foundation in the open air." By June a 56-name petition had been sent to the authorities requesting that a post office be re-established at Camp McKinney. The previous post office had been closed in 1892 and transferred to Elliot's General Store in Fairview. This request was granted in January, 1895, although postmaster Henry Nicholson was not appointed until October of the following year.

In 1895, during its first full year of operation, the Cariboo Company's small mill processed ore in excess of $100,000 from the Cariboo and Amelia mines. In 1896 their operation yielded $131,000.

The original Camp McKinney town-site, surveyed in 1887 some 800 yards south of the Cariboo claim, had apparently never been developed to any great degree. Instead, by 1894, a new town-site was beginning to take shape alongside the wagon road that passed through the Cariboo, Alice, Emma and Maple Leaf claims. However, despite the construction of buildings and the establishments of businesses, no town-site had been surveyed and not a single lot had been purchased by those involved. Most people preferred to live and conduct business on the various claims.

The Camp McKinney Hotel, for example, was situated on the Cariboo claim. Like the others, Cameron and McCuaig had apparently established their hotel without permission from the owners of the claim. This turned out to be a costly mistake when, in October, the mine owners ordered them to remove it from their property. Cameron was apparently able to delay the inevitable until October of the following year, when the premises was re-established on the Teaser claim. In the meantime, McCuaig apparently sold out his interest to Cameron.

On July 1, 1895, W.T. Shatford, who already had general stores in Vernon and Fairview, decided to open a branch at Camp McKinney. For the previous year a representative of Shatford's Fairview store, Mr. Cosens, had visited Camp McKinney on a weekly basis. Apparently he conducted enough trade to warrant the establishment of a branch store. In November another new business opened its doors when J. White established a butcher shop.

All these businesses, as mentioned were established along the wagon road that cut across claims from the Maple Leaf to the Teaser. However, this was not the only location being given town-site considerations. When ownership of the Victoria claim passed into the hands of capitalists from Victoria, they began work in earnest. In its October 17, 1896 issue, the *Times* noted that 20 men were "busily engaged building houses, making roads, etc., preparatory to the development work to follow. Already a good sized store and dwelling house, faced by four miners' cabins, with a

The hoist of the fabulous Cariboo mine at Camp McKinney. The inset photo shows miners posing beside a large ore bucket in the Cariboo-Amelia mineshaft. Over $500,000 in dividends were paid out by the Cariboo during its brief career.

blacksmith shop near by, give the upper end of the old Victoria claim the appearance of an embryo town." Thus, at this period of its life, McKinney was sprouting roots in two different locations, three miles apart, and was truly more of a "Camp" than a "Town."

Some chose to establish businesses even further away from the general mining scene. G.P. McCuddy, for example, had preempted land for a ranch to the west of Camp McKinney in 1893 when the wagon road was being constructed. Realizing its potential as a stopping place, McCuddy erected a hotel. In the fall of 1896 he added a two-story addition and applied for a liquor license. The ranch also included a large bunkhouse and a stable that could accommodate 100 horses.

On February 13, 1897, the *Times* published a brief description of what was the main business section of Camp McKinney, on the Cariboo claim: ". . .there are two general merchandise stores in the camp — that of Mr. W.T. Shatford, with Mr. A. Cosens in charge; the other owned by Mr. H. Nicholson, who is also postmaster, mining agent and notary public, and knows every claim in the neighborhood. The hotel is owned by Mr. Hugh Cameron, one of the kindest and best-known of the fast-dwelling army of old timers; making no pretentions to architectural beauty or interior lavish display, this night station is always a welcome sight to the weary traveller, and nowhere will more effort be made to make him comfortable. The (Cariboo) company's boarding-house, blacksmith and workshops, miners cabins and the stage buildings make up the rest of the settlement."

Two weeks later the *Times* predicted that a town-site would be surveyed at Camp McKinney in the near future. It also noted that Nicholson had ordered a large stock of general merchandise and was "enlarging and re-arranging his store in anticipation of a brisk trade in the spring."

That September, a contract was awarded to Joseph Frank for the erection of the Camp McKinney schoolhouse on a site donated by Hugh Cameron. Miss Blake, who had charge of the Anarchist Mountain school in 1896, was hired as the first teacher. Camp McKinney fell on hard times in 1898, the population decreased and the school closed. But by the summer of 1898 several families had moved back into the locality, and in August, a petition for the reopening of the school was forwarded to Victoria. In August, 1899, the school reopened with Miss Ray, of Kelowna, in charge. In all, there would be a total of nine different teachers in the Camp McKinney school from the time it first opened until it closed permanently in 1904.

Other improvements to the "town-site" in 1897 included a new hotel being erected on a fractional claim lying between the Cariboo and Minnehaha claims. The contract for construction of this new hotel, to be called the St. Louis, had also been awarded to Joseph Frank. The proprietors were Frank and Thomas Donald, who applied for a liquor license in November.

Although Camp McKinney was never a wild, wide-open town, it did have its exciting moments. The first trouble occurred back on August 18, 1896, when George McAuley was held-up by a lone robber while transporting three gold bars from Camp McKinney. The robber made his escape, but a miner named Matthew Roderick was suspected. He was later killed by Joseph P. Keane while, some believe, returning to Camp McKinney to recover the hidden gold. A coroner's jury brought in the verdict of "justifiable homicide," exonerating Keane of all blame in the death. However Dep. Att.-Gen. Arthur Smith, upon reviewing the evidence, ordered the arrest and prosecution of Keane for

(Above left) Camp McKinney had a number of hotels during its history. This is the St. Louis, which was built by Joseph Frank for the Donald brothers in 1897. This hotel was probably the most notorious in the various town-sites that are collectively referred to as Camp McKinney, changing hands many times. Since the man standing to the far left is James Lynch, who owned the hotel from January 1899 to May of that year, this photograph was probably taken during that time.

(Above right)The Sailor Hotel, constructed in November, 1899, for Paquette & Alkeidt, was located on the Sailor claim. It contained 12 rooms.

(Below) A general view of the main business area of Camp McKinney around the turn of the century. Despite competition from town-sites of several other claims in the area, this was the main Camp McKinney town-site.

murder. This charge was later reduced to manslaughter, to which Keane was found guilty. (Full details of this incident in Camp McKinney's history can be found in *Lost Bonanzas of Western Canada*.)

In mid-December, 1897, a barroom brawl occurred at Camp McKinney between Alex Ramage, George Taylor and Mike Dooley. Ramage was hit on the head by Dooley and received knife wounds to the head and neck from Taylor. Taylor succeeded in crossing the border into Washington before he could be arrested: Dooley was not as lucky. Arrested, Dooley put up $120 in gold dust for bail, then forfeited it when he fled to the states. Ramage, who was the instigator of the row, and who was on the receiving end of most of the punishment, was fined $20 and costs.

The Donald brothers had only been operating the St. Louis Hotel for a couple of months before their activities drew the attention of authorities. On March 5, 1898, three charges were laid against the pair. First, on January 1, Frank was accused of selling liquor to an intoxicated person. On February 6, Frank was accused of allowing an employee to sell liquor to one H. Douglas on Sunday. Finally, both Frank and Thomas were accused of keeping a betting house.

On the first charge against Frank, a lot of contradictory evidence was given. However, justices of the peace R.G. Sidley and Henry Nicholson held that the charge was proved, and Frank was fined $20 and $9.50 costs. Frank was also found guilty of the second charge and again fined $20 and $9.50 costs. In the third case, Regina vs Frank Donald and Thomas Donald, Sidley and Nicholson offered the following written judgement on March 5:

"In this case the defendants were charged with keeping a disorderly house, by keeping a room in which gambling was going on for gain. Now to come within the statute, it must be kept for the purpose specified, and this has not been shown. It must be a principal and essential part and not merely subsidiary and for the recreation of the guests. All the enactments against gambling are for the purpose of preventing diverse idle and evil-disposed persons from congregating together and playing for excessive sums of money. If the guests of an inn call for dice or cards, and for their recreation play with them, it is not against the statutes. A gambling house is a nuisance at common law, being detrimental to the public, as it promotes cheating and other corrupt practices, and incites to idleness and avaricious ways of gaining property. To make an hotel keeper liable for keeping a gambling house, it must be shown that he makes a gain by it or that he allows cheating to go on or excessive sums of money to be played for. As none of these have been proven, the case is dismissed."

It is unknown if these charges had any affect on their decision, but in October, 1898, the Donald brothers sold the St. Louis Hotel to James Lynch. Lynch then promptly sold a half interest to Thomas Humphrey, and the two partners immediately made plans to enlarge the premises.

That same fall, the Cariboo Consolidated Gold Mining and Milling Company, with headquarters in Toronto, and a capitalization of $1,250,000, assumed ownership of the Cariboo-Amelia mine. Five additional mines were acquired by the new firm: Alice, Emma, Maple Leaf, Saw Tooth and Okanagan.

Perhaps bolstered by this purchase, a syndicate of men comprised of George Naden, Thomas McDonnell, R.M. McIntire and Nels Leplant, of Greenwood, and a Mr. Ceperley, of Vancouver, decided to have the Sailor property laid out as a town-site. Sydney Johnson was hired to do the survey and he was soon busy subdividing the ground, which was described as "level, centrally located, and adjacent to the Cariboo." On October 21, Cosen Bros. of Fairview decided to open a general store in Camp McKinney alongside Shatford's. That same month Hugh Cameron was named mayor of the camp, although it is uncertain if this was merely an honourary title or if he was actually elected.

By early December the plan for the new town-site had been completed by Johnson, and lots were placed on the market. "The demand for real estate in the new town is something enormous," reported the *Times*. "Lots were eagerly sought before the plot was subdivided. The townsite on the Sailor is exceptionally well situated. The main street is level from end to end. The lots are 35 feet wide and 100 feet deep." A week later the newspaper reported that a large number of lots had been sold.

Camp McKinney now had three separate town-sites, stretched over six claims, competing with one another. One area of development, which never really amounted to anything, was on the Victoria claim. The newest "embryo" town-site, as mentioned, was on the Sailor claim. This was only a short distance to the west of what must be considered the main town-site, which was established on the Cariboo claim, and stretched eastward on the Amelia claim, and westward on the Alice, Emma and Maple Leaf. As new businesses moved into Camp McKinney, it is sometimes difficult to know precisely where they were established.

McDonnell and McIntire, two of the Sailor town-site partners, who had a real estate and mining office in Greenwood, established a branch on the Sailor town-site in early December, 1898. W.M. Law & Co., from Greenwood, started a branch of their general merchandise business at Camp McKinney the same month. However, since this business was established in a building rented from Hugh Cameron, it was probably located on or near the Teaser claim.

In January, 1899, an ad in the Midway *Advance* indicated that the St. Louis Hotel had changed hands yet again. The new proprietors were James Lynch and D. McDuff; Thomas Humphrey having apparently sold out his interest.

When Percy Godeneath, the travelling correspondent for the Spokesman *Review* visited Camp McKinney in March, he said: "Camp McKinney is booming. The stages are crowded and many private rigs are being brought into service to carry the visitors there." March indeed appears to have been a busy month. J.P. Flood and King Rees decided to open a "butcher's establishment"; Dr. Gordon of Toronto, appointed surgeon to the mines at Camp McKinney, opened a drug store and was making plans for a small hospital, and Charles deBlois Green, provincial land surveyor, had also opened an office.

Dr. Gordon was the first physician to establish himself at Camp McKinney. He was succeeded by Dr. R.B. White in 1900. When Dr. White decided to take a trip back east in the winter of 1900, his practise was taken over by Dr. Boyce of Kelowna. Upon his return, Dr. White maintained his Camp McKinney practise until 1903, when he moved to Penticton.

Dr. White's residence and office on Cariboo Avenue, Camp McKinney. Prior to establishing a practice at Camp McKinney, Dr. White operated a drugstore at Fairview. He is seen in the inset photo seated in front of his Fairview store.

By April, 1899, work in the camp was reported to be in full swing, with over 100 men on the different payrolls. "The large increase in the population of the camp," reported the *Advance,* "has induced the residents to ask for an appointment of a police constable." By mid-month, W.J. Snodgrass & Sons' stage was offering daily service between Camp McKinney and Greenwood. On April 8, the Cascade *Record* reported that the Sailor town-site had been sold to Toronto capitalist who planned to invest $30,000 "in waterworks and other improvements." In its April 15 issue, the *Record* reported: "Camp McKinney is putting on metropolitan airs — it will have a weekly newspaper in the near future." Unfortunately for posterity, this latest bit of optimism seems not to have borne fruit.

In May the *Record* reported that another claim, the Kamloops, was also to be subdivided into town-site lots and placed on the market. There is no evidence to indicate this was ever done, however. By the middle of the month, the *Advance* reported that Charles Winters, provincial police constable, had been appointed to Camp McKinney. In its May 29 issue, the *Advance* recorded yet another change of ownership in the St. Louis Hotel; now McDuff had bought out Lynch and would continue the enterprise alone. Of all the Camp McKinney hotels, the career of the St. Louis appears to have been the most beleaguered, for, only a month later, it was burglarized by P. Murphy and Doc Elwood.

Business activities in Camp Mc-Kinney continued unabated during the summer of 1899. In June, W.T. Shatford & Co. began construction "of an enormous store at Camp McKinney, the size being 28x60 feet, two storeys, and a warehouse attached and a cellar 20x28 feet." This expansion was necessary to enable the firm, with branches at Fairview, Vernon and Slocan City, to carry a larger selection of goods. Mr. G.E. Sanborne was in charge of the new store. The site was on the Cariboo claim.

By the end of July, the Columbia Telephone Company had completed their line into town. A week later telephone connection with the outside world was established. By that time, John Love and E.F. Scott, who operated a drug and book store in Fairview, constructed a branch across the street from Shatford's general store. Alongside of them, Joe Morgan opened a barbershop. A short distance up the street, Hugh Cameron's Camp McKinney Hotel was being extensively improved with paint and paper inside, and a

new addition was being added. Describing the improvements of the Camp McKinney Hotel, the Greenwood *Miner* wrote that it was "a different looking hostelry altogether. The bar has been placed in the new addition, and the old barroom has been converted into sleeping apartments."

With all this construction going on, the main town-site of Camp McKinney seemed to be firmly entrenched along this section. But the Sailor town-site was apparently not about to give up without a fight. In its November 17, 1899, issue, the *Miner* reported that: "A new hotel is being erected on the Sailor townsite by Paquette & Alkeidt. It will be a comfortable, well-furnished, 12-room hotel." Although the hotel's name went unrecorded, this was undoubtedly the Sailor Hotel. A month later the *Miner* added: "About 60 lots have already been sold (on the Sailor) and a number of buildings are going up.

During the winter months, most communities in the Boundary Country formed hockey teams. Camp McKinney was no exception, and despite lacking an ice rink in which to play or practice, the Camp McKinney squad was still able to give a good account of itself. At a match placed in Greenwood during the middle of January, 1900, they skated to a 3-2 victory. Unfortunately, Camp McKinney's hockey prowess was short-lived when the team amalgamated with Greenwood to form a stronger team known as the Boundary Hockey Club. This new hockey club joined the B.C. Hockey League and participated in games for the championship.

Construction activity continued throughout the winter of 1899. In late January, 1900, architect Robertson prepared plans for Alexander McAuley & Henry Rose for their proposed hotel at Camp McKinney. "The building will be a two-storey frame structure 44x50 feet in size," reported the *Times.* However, everyone, it seems, did not share the optimism in Camp McKinney's future. In its December 22 issue, the *Miner* reported that D. McMillan & Co. had moved their stock of goods from Camp McKinney to Greenwood.

One thing Camp McKinney still lacked, however, was a jail. Back in the fall of 1899, the residents of Camp McKinney had tried to induce the government to build a lockup. Without one, the Miner wrote: "it is impossible to maintain order, and deal with the drunken disturbers of the peace as they should be dealt with."

Even the Vernon *News* saw the pressing need for jail facilities, and in January that newspaper wrote: "One of the crying necessities of Camp McKinney is a lock-up. The constable there has no place at his disposal in which to keep prisoners, and much inconvenience is thereby experienced. Sometimes he is compelled to take them to a hotel, and sit up with them all night, and in any case a great deal of trouble is occasioned through this lack. Camp McKinney is a rapidly growing mining town, and the request recently forwarded to the government for a suitable building of this description should meet with a prompt and favourable response."

Despite the lack of a jail, church and bank, these were heady times for Camp McKinney. And if all the construction and mining activity was not enough to bolster its thoughts of permanency, in September, 1899, railway surveyors were working in the area for the third time. This prompted the *Record* to speculate that it "believed that route will be followed when the (rail)road is built from Midway to Penticton." This never happened, of course, but for a time the area was certainly buoyed by the possibility.

Meanwhile, the mines were very productive. The *Record* reported on September 23, 1899, that "in 63 days, 12 gold bricks, worth $5,940 were turned out of the mill of the Camp McKinney Mines, Ltd." In its February 10, 1900, issue, the same paper disclosed that a "$2,000 gold brick was the result of the last clean-up, of the Waterloo mine. . . ." Even the Phoenix *Pioneer* was paying attention to the bustle around Camp McKinney, writing in its February 17 issue: "There are said to be about 175 men working in Camp McKinney and the population is about 450. There is considerable building in progress." The *Pioneer's* population figure appears to have been too optimistic, however, as most records seem to indicate the total never exceeded 250.

On May 11, 1900, the new two-story frame Hotel Cariboo, situated on the Cariboo claim and owned by McAuley & Rose, opened with a big ball. It was completely furnished with furniture purchased in Greenwood and stocked with the best of everything. Two weeks later, on May 24, Camp McKinney residents celebrated the Queen's birthday. On May 26, the *Times* reported on the festivities:

"Her Majesty's birthday was fittingly celebrated here today with athletic contests, horse racing and a ball. The sports started shortly after the noon hour, when a large crowd had gathered along Cariboo avenue, in front of the Hotel Cariboo. The avenue had been laid out for a quarter of a mile as a track. Here was held the athletic sports and horse races. These concluded, the crowd moved off to the St. Louis Hotel, opposite which the tug-of-war was contested. Again the scene was shifted for the drilling contest, which was held opposite that famous old hostelry of mine host Hughie Cameron. Hughie had gone to pains to have his place decorated in evergreens, flags and bunting. From the flagstaffs on his two buildings floated to the breeze the Union Jack and the Stars and Stripes. . . . In the evening the prizes were distributed at the Sailor Hall, followed by a dance. Never in the history of the camp has a holiday passed off so successfully as that of today. Those having the affair in charge and to whom the credit is due for the way in which it was carried out were Messrs. Nicholson, Betts, Miles, Cameron, Winters, Welmhurst, McLean, Sanburn and Dr. White."

This festive occasion would appear to have marked the highlight of Camp McKinney's checkered existence. Cracks, ever so imperceptible at first, were beginning to appear in its make-up. In August, 1900, the St. Louis Hotel changed hands yet again. This time V.J. Rose and I.H. Deerdorf leased it from McDuff. A short time later it closed. On May 11, 1901, precisely one year to the day since its grand opening, McAuley & Rose dissolved their partnership in the Hotel Cariboo, McAuley continuing on alone. Then, just over one year later, the building was destroyed by fire.

On June 4, 1902, shortly after 2 a.m., the guests were aroused by smoke coming from the basement. Reporting the incident, the *Times* wrote that "the progress of the fire was so rapid that few escaped with little more than their night clothes, some being rescued by getting out of the front windows by means of a ladder. One man in jumping out broke a small bone in his foot. There was much clothing and considerable money lost."

The fire apparently started in the basement, where the furnace was located, although McAuley told the newspaper that the furnace had not been going since 5 o'clock that afternoon, and everything was alright when he went to bed at 10 p.m. Fortunately, there was little wind at the time, or the fire could have wiped out much of Camp McKinney's business section. "Mr. McAuley is a heavy loser," reported the *Times*, "the building being insured for only $2,500, while the cost of it and furniture amounted to $9,500. A large quantity of liquor was also destroyed."

On Monday, June 16, Lee Way and Yee Lee sold their store and business in Camp McKinney to Tow Dan. That trend continued a week later when W.T. Shatford disposed of his business in Camp McKinney to the Cosen Brothers, having decided to concentrate on his store in Fairview. "The Messrs. Cosens," reported the *Advance*, "will have in addition to their large stock of goods, Mr. Shatford's stock, which they will move into their own store, it being their attention to dispose of the building formerly occupied by Mr. Shatford. This is a large and commodious building, and with some necessary alterations, would be well adopted for a hotel, it being most centrally situated." This acquisition gave Cosen Bros. most of the general merchandise trade of Camp McKinney.

The reason for the decline of Camp McKinney was its mines. Unfortunately, throughout 1902 mining was restricted chiefly to the Cariboo, which had processed 15,616 tons of ore and yielded 8,400 ounces of bullion worth $112,300. Average number of men employed during the year: 50. Such a small workforce could not support the established businesses, and one by one they closed and moved away.

On January 10, 1903, Camp McKinney flickered briefly to life when the St. Louis Hotel, which had been closed for about two years, was reopened. W.E. McBoyle and Gorman West leased the premises and immediately applied for a liquor license, which was granted about two weeks later. Although the hotel was newly furnished and the bar was stocked with only the best wines, liquors and cigars, it apparently was not enough. In its June 13, 1903 issue the *Advance* reported that McBoyle had opened a hotel at Osoyoos. Although it is uncertain if West continued the venture for a time alone, it really did not matter, for in January, 1904, the Cariboo mine closed down. For all intents and purposes, Camp McKinney was dead.

(Above) A logging scene at Camp McKinney in later years.

Reporting on the closure in its January 14 issue, the *Advance* wrote: "The Cariboo mine is closed indefinitely in response to instructions from Toronto, and the whole crew has been laid off. The ore has been pretty much worked out down to the 600 ft. level, which forms the deepest workings. During 1903 the mine milled about 15,000 tons, which ran considerably less than $10 in values. The mine showed a little profit during the year, and is credited with between $50,000 and $60,000 cash on hand. There is mine equipment that cost $50,000 on the property."

There was still a slim hope for the mine, for, although some of the stockholders wanted to wind up the affairs of the company and disburse the assets, others were in favour of spending the cash in the treasury to developing the property at depth.

Three weeks later, however, the *Times* printed the worst possible scenario. The shareholders, at their annual meeting, decided to pay themselves a dividend of four per cent. "The disbursement takes about $50,000 out of the treasury and leaves a sum estimated at about $5,000 as a reserve fund. Now, with no ore in site to justify operations, the mine will remain closed indefinitely." Cariboo stock, which had once reached a high of $1.70, plummeted to a cent a share.

It did not take long for the remaining businesses at Camp McKinney to fold their tents and move away. Before the end of February, 1904, Cosen Bros. were in Greenwood, looking for new opportunities to engage in the general merchandise business. By early March they were moving their merchandise to Greenwood where they planned to open a store. But in Late June, James McNicol, a Midway general merchant, purchased the entire Cosen Bros. stock and hauled it by Myerkoff's freight teams to his Midway store.

For the next two-and-a-half years, nothing was heard of Camp McKinney. In the interim, its businesses and most of its residents had long since scattered. However, despite the gloomy future, one man's faith in Camp McKinney never faltered. That man, Hugh Cameron, continued to operate his Camp McKinney Hotel for the trickle of transient customers that passed through the area. His confidence appeared to have been rewarded when, on November 10, 1906, the *Pioneer* printed the following headline:

"CARIBOO HAS BEEN LEASED." The story that followed explained how a syndicate of Phoenix businessmen had leased the property, machinery and stamp mill of the Cariboo mine at Camp McKinney after several months' negotiations. "A force of men has already been sent to the property, to put the machinery in order and to begin pumping out the mine, preparatory to active operations."

A week later the *Pioneer* reported that de-watering of the Cariboo had begun. By April 13, 1907, the de-watering had reached the 400-foot level. Finally, on May 25, the Cariboo actually commenced mining activities once again. By mid-June 10 stamps were working, and a month later 10 more stamps were being repaired and readied for service.

By early July, 15 men were employed at the Cariboo. In early August, when treasurer A.B. Hood visited the mine, the force of men had been increased to 20 and the mill was "now running steadily on double shift." A week later half a dozen machinist were added to the payroll, and a week after that the work force was increased to nearly 30. Said the *Pioneer*, "it begins to look like old times in Boundary's oldest mining camp."

But the anticipated resurgence was not to be, for, on September 6 the *Times* noted that the isolation of Camp McKinney "appears to get on the nerves" and makes "it difficult to secure and retain a full force of men." Two weeks later the *Times* reported: "Hugh Cameron, for many years Mayor of McKinney, has abandoned the camp, and will no more dispense drinks for the boys." By the end of November, only three men were still employed at the Cariboo.

There were attempts made to mine the area in 1917, 1918, 1929, 1934, 1939, 1950 and 1960. Some were dismal failures, some partially successful, and one ended tragically when two miner were overcome by gas fumes and died. However, as these have little to do with the original Camp McKinney town-site, they will not be covered here.

As for the remaining buildings of Camp McKinney, many vanished during a forest fire in 1919. In 1932, most of the historic buildings that had survived the forest fire were intentionally burned to the ground by West Kootenay Power to lessen the threat to their power lines.

Today, very little remains to indicate what activities took place at Camp McKinney nearly a century ago. The most visible sign of activity is the head-frame over the shaft of the Cariboo-Amelia, but this dates only back to the 1960s. There are also two small log cabins, a slag pile, a few open shafts and some scattered debris. Camp McKinney also has a small cemetery, but only one headstone has survived fire and neglect. It is that of Jennie Skulagat Copeland, "born 1860 at Kitkargas, Skeena River, died May 13, 1903."

No real information is known about her. However, it is assumed that she was the Indian wife of James Copeland. James Copeland was a true Boundary pioneer, having first come to Rock Creek from the Fraser River in the rush of 1860. He is listed as a resident of Camp McKinney in the 1903 British Columbia *Gazetteer*, and was living in Bridesville as late as 1910 and was still a "sprightly youth in appearance" despite being over 70 years old. Although contemporary newspaper accounts, which cover his career in Omineca, Cassiar, Stikine, Boundary and Similkameen districts, do not mention a wife, it is assumed he met and married Jennie while in the north.

Although it cannot be verified by headstones or grave markers, a number of other individuals are known to be buried at Camp McKinney, or can be accurately assumed to be buried there.

The first person to have the dubious honour of being buried there was 20-year-old Victor Engston. On June 18, 1898, only two days after being employed as a mucker in the Cariboo mine, Engston was killed in an accident while coming up in the cage. Engston, who had apparently fallen out of the cage as it was being raised, plummeted 200 feet to his death.

On March 18, 1899, Mrs. Frank Kelsey's sister died of an attack of typhoid fever. The funeral services were held in the schoolhouse at Camp McKinney, and was largely attended.

On March 25, 1900, Pat Symons, a well-known prospector, choked to death while he was eating his supper at Hosier's Ranch, a few miles from Rock Creek. He was buried at Camp McKinney two days later.

Pat Symons was one of the old prospectors who joined the memorable gold rush to California in 1849. When the great placer excitement was on in the Cariboo he was one of the first, in 1864, to make a stake. In 1884 he went to Granite Creek, and in 1888 he joined the crowd who went to the Rock Creek placers. He was an interesting character, and at the time of his death, was one of the last pioneers that remained in the Boundary district.

On September 9, 1900, 23-year-old Robert Graham died in an accident at the Cariboo mine. About 11:30 in the afternoon, Graham was at the bottom of the 300-foot level, and after putting a quantity of steel into the bucket and mounting the cage, he gave the signal to hoist and the cage started on its upward journey. The weight of the steel, which projected over the bucket, was sufficiently great to overturn the cage, the narrowness of the shaft being all that prevented it from doing so, but when the drift at the 200-foot level was reached the cage, which was securely fastened to the cable, capsized, throwing Graham down the shaft and causing instantaneous death. The body was frightfully mangled.

On June 5, 1901, Andrew Kirkland was killed while driving a four-horse stage from Camp McKinney to Midway. On the fateful Wednesday morning, about five miles from Camp McKinney, the stage started to make the descent down the long and winding hill into the canyon of Jolly Jack Creek. Before Kirkland realised what was happening, the horses began to pick up speed and the stage was soon out of control. At the bottom of the hill, the road turned almost at a right angle to the bridge. The stage was going at a tremendous speed by the time this point was reached, and horses and stage could not negotiate the curve. The stage flipped over as it flew through the air, landing on the opposite bank upside down. Kirkland, whose neck was broken, lived only for a few minutes. There were three passengers in the stage: two received minor injuries and the third escaped without injury. The funeral of Kirkland took place on Friday, June 7.

In September, 1901, Cecil Nicholson, Camp McKinney's provincial police constable, died of typhoid fever in the Camp McKinney Hotel. He was 26 years of age.

On October 29, 1902, William Edwards burned to death in his cabin. Edwards was a Camp McKinney old-timer, having lived there since 1887. An original Cariboo gold miner known as "English Bill" or "Red Dog Bill," Edwards had apparently been drinking heavily the night before, and it was assumed that when the fire broke out, he was too intoxicated to awaken. His charred body was not found until October 30. The remains were buried at Camp McKinney the following day. The funeral was attended by old-timers from all around the district.

A closer examination of old newspapers will undoubtedly turn up more people whose final resting place is Camp McKinney. In 1990-91, the Oliver Heritage Society received a B.C. government grant of $1,100 to protect the Camp McKinney cemetery with fencing and identify the site with a plaque.

Although they are not buried there, three other Camp McKinney residents deserve a final word. The first is Alfred McKinney, discoverer of the Cariboo mine. Although McKinney sold out to others, he continued to live in the Boundary. In the spring of 1907, thanks to a subscription raised mostly in Phoenix, McKinney went back east for treatment of cancer of the face. When he returned that October, however, he was little better off. "The case is an aggravated one," reported the Pioneer, "his entire left check being eaten away."

After his return from eastern Canada, McKinney went to the Similkameen, where he was found nearly dead in the Hope Mountains. He was sent to stay with his daughter in Abby, Washington, where he succumbed to the cancer.

George McAuley, who was a driving force behind the Cariboo mine for many years, died in July, 1904, while on a wedding trip to Scotland.

Finally, Hugh Cameron, Mayor of Camp McKinney and referred to by many as the "Father of Camp McKinney," maintained his faith in the camp almost to the end. Originally from Cape Breton, Cameron arrived in B.C., via California, in 1873. His early activities included the Cariboo placer camps before finding his way to Rock Creek and Camp McKinney. In September, 1907, possibly because of ill health, Cameron left Camp McKinney and moved to Victoria. A year later, on November 12, the 69-year-old pioneer died of heart failure. His remains were buried at New Westminster. His death marked the final link to the town of Camp McKinney. ❀

Boundary Falls

(Above) *Like Rock Creek, Boundary Creek was the scene of placer gold mining. This photograph shows an early mining operation on Boundary Creek not far from Boundary Falls.*
(Below) *A rare photograph of George Arthur Rendell in 1898. Rendell operated the first general store in Boundary Falls and later went on to become a prominent Greenwood businessman.*

GOLD was first taken out of Boundary Creek on September 4, 1860, by Henry Sudbrinck, the first prospector on the creek, and his partner Dutch Bill. Owing to the lateness of the season, how-ever, very little mining was done that year. During the summer of 1861, 68 men were working on the creek. The best location was called the Norwegian claim, as it was worked by four Norwegian sailors who had jumped ship at San Francisco. (This was where John "Jolly Jack" Thornton operated for many years, and not far from where the remains of his crumbling log cabin can still be seen.) Overall, however, the gold was not as plentiful as Rock Creek, and by the fall of 1861 all the white miners had returned to Fort Colville, their abandoned claims being taken over by the Chinese.

Although Boundary Creek was worked sporadically over the next 15 years, it was not until 1887 that the area gained prominence once more. That summer five prospectors, L.M. McCarren, Tom Jones, Tom Morgan, and men named McLeod and Hart, came into the area. The five operated a placer claim on Boundary Creek, from which they cleaned up over $3,000 in less than a month. After the diggings were exhausted, the partners decided to prospect for

quartz. They soon made a discovery near Boundary Falls, and that winter a tunnel was run in 30 feet, which showed quartz assaying up to $200. Three years later the partners divided their properties, Jones, Morgan and the others taking claims at Camp McKinney, while McCarren received all interest in the Tunnel mine.

The area surrounding McCarren's claim was a natural prospector's headquarters. The open hills provided food for their horses, even through the winter, and it was the nearest point of entry to the mining camps in the hills that were starting to draw attention throughout the district.

According to the available information, the first businessman to establish himself at Boundary Falls was W.W. Gibbs. Although the precise date he opened his assay office is unknown, it was advertised in the first issue of the Fairview *Advance*, which made its appearance on April 26, 1894. Two weeks later Thomas Hardy opened the Boundary Falls Hotel, which offered the "best of liquors and cigars." At the same time, four carpenters were busy constructing a livery stable for Conkle and Donald, while two more were building a residence for Mr. Thomet. The sawmill,

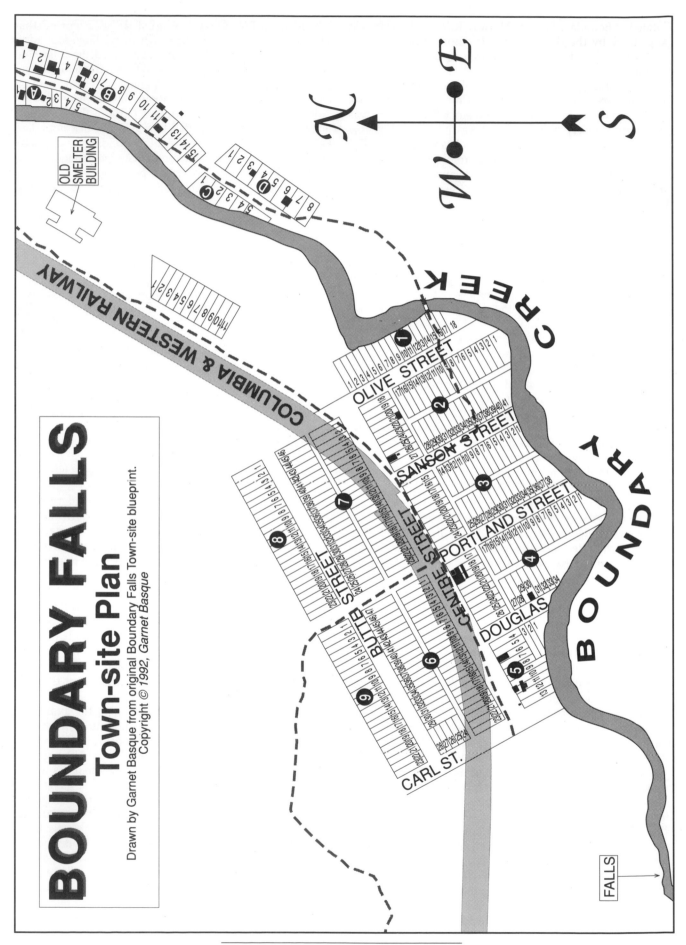

BOUNDARY FALLS
Town-site Plan

Drawn by Garnet Basque from original Boundary Falls Town-site blueprint.
Copyright © 1992, Garnet Basque

OLD SMELTER BUILDING

COLUMBIA & WESTERN RAILWAY

CREEK

BOUNDARY

OLIVE STREET

SANSON STREET

PORTLAND STREET

CENTRE STREET

DOUGLAS

BUTTE STREET

CARL ST.

FALLS

located at Boundary City, as Midway was first known, was kept busy by the flurry of construction, prompting the *Advance* to predict that Boundary Falls would enjoy a lively season.

Suprisingly, no one had yet established a general store, with the exception of the two small Chinese stores at Rock Creek, anywhere in the Boundary district. The country was then very sparsely populated and was inhabited by few prospectors and a still fewer number of ranchers. Although Boundary Falls, centrally located among the Boundary Creek mining camps, was now the principal stopping place, most of its supplies were ordered and generally packed in on horses from Marcus, Washington.

This situation changed at the end of June, 1894, when George Arthur Rendell opened a general store at Boundary Falls, offering "a full line of dry goods, groceries, and miners' supplies." However, the difficulties that beset Rendell, in getting his first consignment of goods, received via Penticton, is worth relating. According to the Boundary Creek *Times:* "It happened just at the time when the Okanagan River changed its bed, and consequently the goods had to be kept at Penticton until a ferry boat was built — a matter of a month. Then, as the road through Camp McKinney was not completed, the unlucky shipment had to be piloted around by Osoyoos, through the Colville reservation to the mouth of Rock Creek, a charge of $15 being made on every wagon for the honor of enjoying the escort of the U.S. customs officer while passing through U.S. territory. Arriving at 'Ingram's' it was found that the bridge had gone out, without the slightest regard for the travelling public, and a ferry had to be called into requisition. The river was at flood, running like a mill race, and a very enjoyable and exciting time was spent in conveying the goods across. At last the caravan arrived at Boundary Falls, a little the worse for wear and tear, which nevertheless did not affect the sales. Shortly afterwards, in November, 1894, a fairly good stage road from Penticton to Grand Forks was constructed, and the pack train is now almost a thing of the past — a reminiscence of the good old times when the bucking cayuse saved the grocer the labor of mixing sand and sugar in scientific proportions."

In September, 1894, James and Robert Kerr, who already had a butcher shop in Midway, decided to open a branch store at Boundary Falls. The following December, Thomas Hardy built a dance hall, and the dance held there on Christmas eve was well attended by visitors from throughout the district. In February, 1895, Hardy erected a two-story, 30x40-foot addition to his hotel. This was used partly as a stable and partly as an ice house. On February 14, R.W. Jakes, M.D., built an office and residence, and two weeks later a stage arrived with the materials necessary to establish the Boundary Falls post office.

March brought the addition of two new businesses. One was John A. Coryell, "Civil and Mining Engineer, Provincial Land Surveyor and Draughtsman," who erected an office and residence. The other was the Boundary Falls Livery, Feed & Sale Stables. Owned by Henderson & Martin, it included a stage line that ran between Boundary Falls and Marcus twice a week. They also provided saddle horses for prospectors.

On April 22, the Midway *Advance* (the newspaper had moved from Frairview in August, 1894), reported that Thomas Hardy was erecting a two-story, 35x40-foot addition to his hotel. The building, completed the following October, contained "some sixteen to twenty rooms of a commodious character." A Grand Opening Ball, held there on October 31, was attended by about 100 people, including "some thirty ladies from different parts of the neighborhood." Two weeks earlier the *Advance* noted that Boundary Falls had "doubled the number of its buildings and inhabitants since 1894." That same month, George Rendell moved his general store into a new, larger building.

Up to this point Boundary Falls had expanded rapidly, considering the small population that resided in the district. The construction to date appears to have all taken place on the east side of Boundary Creek along the wagon road. (See blocks A, B, C & D on the town-site plan.) What arrangements had been made between the businessmen and McCarren, the property owner, is not recorded. However, as yet, no town-site had been surveyed. In fact, it was not until the middle of March, 1895, that McCarren decided to have a 10-acre section of his ranch subdivided into 25x100-foot lots. John Coryell, hired to perform the survey, began on April 18 and completed the job the following November. By this time, C.A.R. Lambley was a part-owner of the town-site.

But the future of Boundary Falls, which had once looked so promising, was about to experience a dramatic downturn. Twin stars were rising three miles to the east, and they would soon outshine all other towns in the Boundary Country. Closer and more central to the mining camps than Boundary Falls, Anaconda and Greenwood would prove to be an irresistible magnet, drawing businessmen and entrepreneurs from miles around.

The first to leave was John Coryell, who moved to Midway only two weeks after completing the town-site survey. In March, 1896, W.W. Gibbs moved his assay office to Anaconda. In late April, Kerr Bros. closed their butcher shop. In late May, Thomas Hardy moved to Anaconda and erected the Palace Hotel. That same month George Rendell established a general store at Greenwood.

The news for Boundary Falls was not all bad, however. For a time, McDowell and Nelson operated a butcher shop after Kerr Bros. left. Unfortunately, they moved to Anaconda in June, 1896. Likewise, Boundary Falls was not without its hotel and general store: Thomas Hardy rented his establishment to James J. White, of Fairview, while Rendell kept his Boundary Creek store open. In June, 1896, Boundary Falls received a little good news when the firm of McKenzie, Burns & Mitchell set up shop. They were bricklayers, stone masons and plasterers, although, with so little construction activity, it is difficult to understand how they obtained work.

On October 1, 1896, White hosted a dance in the Boundary Falls Hotel, which the Boundary Creek *Times* rated as a great success, attracting "a larger gathering, probably, than have yet been assembled at one time on any previous occasion, festive or otherwise, in Boundary. Estimating roughly, between 150 and 160 guests from all parts of the district were present. Dancing commenced about nine o'clock, and was kept up to a violin and banjo orchestral accompaniment until early morning. The partition dividing

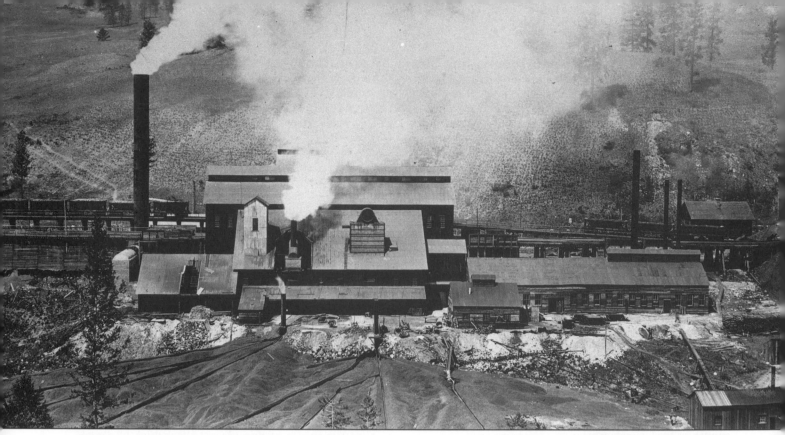

The ill-fated Boundary Falls smelter. From the very beginning there was one problem after another. After the original Standard Pyritic Smelter failed to get off the ground, the Montreal & Boston Copper Co. purchased it and made some major renovations, including new furnaces that were larger than those of the Greenwood or Grand Forks smelters. But problems continued to plague the operation, and in 1907 it was shut down permanently.

two large rooms on the ground floor had been removed during the week, thus extemporising a capital dance-hall, the walls being further decorated with evergreens."

White, a native of Ontario, was well known throughout the district. Over six feet tall and weighing 250 pounds, the 45-year-old White had arrived in B.C. during the Canadian Pacific Railway construction boom. After living on the coast for some time, White moved to Fairview where he farmed and mined until he rented the Boundary Falls Hotel.

White's tenure as a hotel operator lasted only one year. In May, 1897, Thomas Wake, a well-known old-timer, purchased the premises from Thomas Hardy. A month later, on June 17, White was killed in an accident. Driving a rather spirited team of horses, White lost control of them while descending a steep hill leading into Midway. Witnesses reported that "White had lost control of the lines and was clinging to the seat. Shortly afterwards he was thrown over the dashboard. Mr. Glaze and others who ran to his assistance found him unconscious. A front and hind wheel of the heavy wagon had evidently run across his head and neck."

White was immediately rushed to the Greenwood Hospital where he was attended to by Stephen Taylor, Dr. Jakes being absent at Vernon. Taylor did everything possible for White, but he died without regaining consciousness. He was the first person to be buried in the Boundary Falls Cemetery.

Although Boundary Falls had been stagnant for some time, Thomas Wake had faith its fortunes would turn around. Following his purchase of the hotel, in anticipation of a busy summer, he had given the establishment a com-

plete overhaul, the interior having been "rejuvenated" by a small army of painters and paperhangers.

With one hotel, one general store, a few homes and very little else, Boundary Falls was quiet and peaceful. The only minor incident to date reported by the Boundary papers occurred in March of 1897, when O. Sandford was charged for assaulting Ah Sing, a cook at the hotel. Reflecting the racist attitude of the day, the *Times* wrote: "As the evidence was conflictory and it was shown that the Heathen was an 'aggravitin' beggar,' the case was allowed to be settled out of court, Sandford paying costs."

On January 22, 1898, the *Times* reported that J.B. Ferguson, of Boundary Falls, had received a letter from James Punch, manager of the Boundary Falls Mining Co., promising to erect a mill at Boundary Falls "as speedily as possible" to treat ore from its mine. The principal shareholders of the company were members of the William Hamilton Manufacturing Co., a well known machinery firm. Unfortunately, nothing else was heard of the venture.

On May 21, 1898, the *Times* advised its readers that: "In all probability the Boundary Falls townsite, owned by Messrs. McCarren and Lambly, will change hands in a few days. Mr. Lambly, when seen regarding the sale, stated that they had an offer from the Milburn syndicate, but that the deal was not completed. Mr. Hankey, of Nelson, representing the syndicate, was in Greenwood on Thursday and discussed the matter with Messrs. McCarren and Lambly. The townsite is 320 acres, known as the McCarren pre-emption. The Boundary Falls water-power is also claimed by Messrs, Lambley and McCarren under an old record and one secured in January '97."

There was little new to report in Boundary Falls for the remainder of 1898, 1899 and most of 1900. The Boundary Falls Hotel was still the only licensed establishment, and Rendell & Co. operated the only general store. But, by the fall of 1900, the future of Boundary Falls began to improve noticeably. By mid-October, some 40 men were employed in the construction of the Standard Pyritic Smelter. "The mason work has been commenced," reported the Phoenix *Pioneer*, "and an order for 300,000 feet of lumber has been placed with McPherson Bros." The main smelter building was completed in just over a month, and on November 24, the *Pioneer* described the works: "Facing the north on the east end is the sampling department. There will be installed the following machinery: Two 36 and two 48 automatic samplers; one 7x10 Blake crusher, two sets 12x20 rolls, and two belt elevators. East of this department are located the bins for the sample discard. Next comes two parallel rows of storage bins, each one being 16x16 feet in size, with eight bins in a row. To the east again are lime and storage bins. All these bins are situated practically in the centre of the building, and overhead crossing the ore bins are double rows of railway track. Next comes the furnace floor department, with a floor running east from the stone retaining wall 60 feet with a length of 140 feet. The walls for the dust flue are finished, as also the concrete base for both the stack and furnace. . . . The metal smokestack when set up will tower 112 feet above its base. Its diameter is 9 feet 6 inches."

Naturally, where there is activity, businessmen are sure to follow. The Lewis brothers were quick on the scene and established the Pyritic Smelter Hotel. On New Year's eve, they celebrated the opening of their new hotel with a ball. Providing the entertainment was the four-piece band from Midway.

By mid-January, Mgr. Andrew Laidlaw was predicting that the smelter would be in operation by the first of February. "The mile long flume is finished," noted the *Pioneer*, "and 80 feet of the 100 feet of 9 foot 6 inch steel stack are up, on the 20 foot brick foundation. All of the machinery is on the ground and one of the side tracks, of which there will be 4,500 feet, is laid. The trestles are being built, and every part of the work is moving smoothly. Mr. Laidlaw says that he expects no trouble in securing whatever ore he may need to keep the smelter running when once started."

On April 27, 1901, the Greenwood *Miner* carried this brief, but fascinating piece of news: "Rendell & Co. have closed their branch store at Boundary Falls. The stock has been sold to Xeith & Co., who are now moving it to Rendell, (a new town-site) on the West Fork of Kettle river, where they intend operating a store."

Now, upon first reading, it appeared strange that, just when Boundary Falls was on the verge of apparent prosperity, its pioneer merchant decided to sell out. However, the June 2, 1902, issue of the *Times* explains the apparent paradox.

The Standard Pyritic Smelter had been completed more or less on schedule in February or March, 1901. Unfortunately, however, its furnaces were not blown in. An explanation was provided by Supt. E.J. Wilson, who reported that, not only would certain alterations have to be made in the plant, but the company's mining properties were not sufficiently developed to insure a steady supply of ore. At this point, Price Brothers, of Quebec, the principal shareholders, decided "to go no further and took possession of the smelter and mines under a mortgage for large sums of money advanced by them."

Meanwhile, a new player was about to enter the picture. In 1897, W.L. Hogg, of Montreal, had bonded four claims in Deadwood Camp, about two miles from Greenwood. The Sunset, Crown Silver, C.O.D. and Florence Fraction were afterwards organized by Hogg under the Montreal, Boundary Creek Mining Company. In 1901 the group was acquired by the Montreal & Boston Copper Co. Ltd. (M&B).

With such a group of mines, the M&B was naturally justified in having a smelter of its own. Having ample capital, the company was contemplating the erection of its own smelter when the Standard Pyritic Smelter got into financial difficulties and was offered for sale. The M&B engaged H.C. Bellinger, a famous smelter expert, to thoroughly examine the smelting plant and report as to the feasibility of converting it into a modern up-to-date smelter. When Bellinger reported that the plant could be made into a first-class smelter, the M&B purchased it from Price Brothers.

Albert Goodell of Colorado was appointed superintendent, and under his guidance, additional machinery was ordered and alterations were made in the buildings, ore bins and railway tracks. On March 15, 1902, the *Pioneer* reported that the sample mill of the smelter was "being dismantled, preparatory to putting in a larger plant. A No. 5 Gates rock crusher and a Bridgeman sampler have been ordered and a larger engine than the one previously installed has been purchased, and, with the other new plant, will shortly be received at the works. Much of the sampling plant at first put in will be used, but it will be supplemented by the heavier machinery.

"Nothing definite has yet been announced in regard to the furnace already built, but it is anticipated that whatever betterments are required in this department of the new smelter will shortly be taken in hand. Alterations and extensions of the buildings and the erection of additional ore bins are among the improvements that will be made. With so much to do to get the works in proper shape for continuous smelting on a sufficiently large scale to make it pay, it appears unlikely that the furnace will be blown in before next June."

On March 28, the *Times* reported: "A large gang of workmen have been employed now for the past four weeks getting the plant in shape. Labourers, carpenters, machinists, electricians have been working hard to get everything in readiness for early April smelting. It is only a question of a few days now until the mammoth furnace will be glowing and the molten ore pouring out in continuous stream."

Despite the optimism, however, the Sunset Smelter was not blown in until mid-June. The *Times* noted the importance of the event by devoting the entire front page of its June 20, 1902, issue to the Sunset mine and the Sunset Smelter. Describing the smelter itself, the paper said:

"The main building at the smelter is 182x120 and 80 feet in length. On the west side is the sampling department which has been greatly improved. Originally there was in this department two 36 inch and two 48 inch samplers, a 7x10 Blake Rock crusher, and two sets of 12x20 rolls and two belt elevators. East of the sampling mills were placed the bins for the sample discard, next were located two parallel rows of ore storage bins, eight in a row and each bin 34x10 feet; south of these for storage of lime and coke, the whole group of bins occupying the central portion of the building north and south. By the new management the sampling mill building has been enlarged, a No. 5 Gates rock crusher and a Bridgman sampler have been added. More storage bins have been added on the west side of the building and the railway tracks extended to the southern ends of the works. The whole has been arranged so that there is no handling of ore from the time it leaves the railway until it enters the furnace. The ore passes directly from the cars into the bins underneath the track. From here passes directly into the crusher to storage bins alongside the furnace. The furnace floor has a length of 140 feet. From here to Boundary Creek there is ample room for a slag dump. The dust flue of stone walls with brick roof is 200 feet in length and connects with a steel smoke stack 112 feet high. The furnace is larger than at either the B.C. Copper or Granby smelters. It has a nominal capacity of 300 tons but with the self-fluxing character of the ores here, this should be increased to at least 400 tons. The additional machinery comprises two 80 horse power engine and a 250 light dynamo and engines for sample mill and crusher."

The next day the *Pioneer* noted that both hotels had had their liquor licenses renewed, thus assuring that thirsty workers would not run out of liquid refreshment. In another article entitled NEW SMELTER HAS STARTED, the newspaper said: "Another important epoch in the progress of Boundary mining and smelting was marked this week, Wednesday, when the single furnace of the Sunset smelter at Boundary Falls, three miles below Greenwood on Boundary creek, was blown in."

But the problems facing Boundary Falls and its smelter were far from over. This time the problem was external, and affected the B.C. Copper Smelter as well. Due to a miner's strike in the Crowsnest Pass, coke shipments had been curtailed. Thus, less than a month after it was blown in, the Sunset smelter ran out of coke and had to shut down. Shipments of ore from the Sunset mine to the smelter were discontinued, although the 35 men employed at the mine were retained.

Fortunately, the coke problem was soon corrected and the furnace was blown in again. The following month the *Pioneer* reported that an additional furnace was about to be installed at Boundary Falls, "thereby increasing the capacity of the plant to 500 tons daily. The new furnace will measure 40x176 inches in size, and will be of standard water jacket construction. The smelter is reported to have been running smoothly and making a little money."

On November 5, the Anaconda *News* reported that enlargement and improvement of the Sunset smelter was being pushed. "A new engine room is being built; it will be 130 feet long and 40 wide. The walls are of thick stone masonry and one will serve as a retaining wall for the ore bin level. One end of the building will hold the blowers, the central part is for electric light and the large engine, while the boilers will have the remaining space." Other construction included two new coke ovens, each with a capacity of 300 tons each. These were located between the tracks on both ends of the main building.

In mid-November, two M&B directors, J.N. Greenshields and A.A. Munroe, spent several days at Boundary Falls. Impressed by what they saw, they issued instructions to secure a third furnace as rapidly as the Union Iron Works of Spokane could manufacture it. The second furnace, manufactured by the same Spokane company, had just been shipped. "Two furnaces will be running by the new year," noted the *Times*, "and the third should be in operation by March 1st. These two furnaces will bring the capacity of the smelter up to about 1,000 tons a day."

On Saturday, January 10, 1903, the Sunset smelter recorded its first accidental death. The victim was 21-year-old James Laidlaw, who had been employed at the smelter for about six months. According to the *Advance*, Laidlaw had been working on the night shift in the sampling mill, and had gone to the upper floor to soap a belt that had been slipping. "Twenty minutes afterwards another of the men found a mitt and part of a boot on the lower floor, and went up to see what had happened. He found the body of Laidlaw entangled in a four-foot pulley and being carried around with the wheel. The wheel was at once stopped and the body removed, but life was extinct. It is supposed that the man's hand was caught between the belt and the pulley and the deceased drawn in. The body must have been whirling about for half an hour before the fatality was discovered. The deceased's limbs were broken, his skull crushed and flesh cut and bruised, showing the violence attending the death of the unfortunate man."

Laidlaw, described as "a steady and industrious young fellow," had worked more than two years at McPherson Brothers' sawmill at Boundary Falls until it closed down in 1902.

At the end of January, the *Pioneer* stated that a post office was "to be established at Boundary Falls in the near future." According to the pamphlet *British Columbia Post Offices*, however, the area had a post office as early as January 1, 1894. This first post office, officially listed as Boundary Creek, closed on November 1 of the same year. Then, on March 1, 1895, the post office was reestablished as Boundary Falls. It finally closed in 1942.

In early March, 1903, another coke shortage forced the Sunset smelter to close down. This permitted management an opportunity to install some new machinery, and two months later the two furnaces were again in blast. This encouraged the construction of several new buildings. One new business was the Boundary Falls Mercantile Co., which was ready for business in early July, offering a "full line of general groceries, with a bakery in connection." The building was a two story structure with a hall above the store.

On July 15, the *News* announced that a third furnace was being installed at the smelter. "The foundations for the blower are completed. It will be a large one, and will supply two furnaces. The furnace foundations are under construction and will be ready for the furnace in a short time. The old engine room has been taken down to make room for the third furnace. The main building will cover the entire space being occupied by the engine room.

"The slag pots for taking out hot slag are here and that method will be employed as soon as the locomotive arrives." By this time 80 men were employed at the smelter, and the future for Boundary Falls never looked better, despite the fact that a week later one furnace had to be temporarily closed down again for lack of coke.

On September 19 the locomotive for the slag railway arrived. A short time later the tracks were completed and, on September 29, the locomotive ran for the first time.

The town-site of Boundary Falls, too, was enjoying new growth. Several new buildings were being built, including a three-story addition to the Smelter Hotel. Two months earlier, S. Barry Yuill and Charles Dempsey, of Greenwood, had leased the Boundary Falls Hotel. Business was lively at both general stores, the hotels were busy, and with the smelter running full blast, it looked as if Boundary Falls was going to have a boom.

On October 30, the *Times* announced: "Boundary Falls is now on the map. The platform that was called a 'station' by the CPR is roofed in and a comfortable waiting room added, also benches for passengers to sit on."

But, just as the small town was starting to make real progress in development, the bottom suddenly fell out, when, on December 18, the Times announced that the Sunset smelter had closed down.

According to the newspaper, the M&B had decided to suspend its smelter operations temporarily because the Snowshoe mine had shut down, leaving the smelter without sufficient ore to keep the furnaces running. Company officials would not discuss future operations, claiming negotiations were underway "for the purpose of combining with large and important mining interests." The company was confident these negotiations would be "successfully terminated in a few days," resulting in the smelter obtaining "an almost inexhaustible supply of ore." In the meantime, however, all employees were paid off.

This had an immediate impact on Boundary Falls when John McMillan, who had applied for a liquor license for a new hotel to be called the Union Hotel, withdrew his application.

Two months later the *Times* speculated that James Breen, "one of the best known and most successful smelter men on the continent," might purchase the smelter. Breen was in the Boundary Country "making arrangements to either purchase or build a smelter. . . ." A few years earlier, Breen had secured control of the Dominion Copper Company (DCC) and spent considerable money in developing its properties. Breen planned to erect a smelter for the treatment of DCC ores, and secured an option on a smelter site at the mouth of Eholt Creek, about one and a half miles above Greenwood. After discussing the project with officials of the company in Toronto, however, plans for a smelter were dropped, so Breen turned his attention to other interests and the mines of the company remained idle for some time. When the Boundary Falls smelter closed down it was announced that the DCC was negotiating to secure the Boundary Falls smelter and consolidate the interests of the M&B with those of the DCC. However, if the negotiations failed, the DCC had decided to resume operations at its mines and Breen would go ahead with the erection of a smelter.

On April 15, 1904, based on information learned from the east, the *Times* announced that an agreement had apparently been reached between the DCC and the M&B, and predicted that operations would resume in early May. In its May 13 issue, the *Times* reported that H.T. Pemberton, representing the M&B, had arrived in the Boundary and confirmed that a deal had been struck.

"Yes, it is true we have succeeded in effecting a merger of the interests mentioned. Our properties now, in addition to the Sunset, include the Morrison in Deadwood camp, a three-quarter interest in the Emma in Sunset camp, the Athelstan and Jack Pot in Wellington camp, and the properties of the Dominion Copper Company in Phoenix. You may say that the smelter at Boundary Falls will blow in just as soon as we can land ore at the smelter. The various mines included in the deal will immediately be opened up, and the work of unwatering the Phoenix properties will begin in a few days. Arrangements have been made for the erection of the third furnace at the Boundary Falls smelter the installation of a fourth furnace, as well as the erection of a convertor plant, at an early date. We expect to have the smelter at Boundary Falls running full blast before the end of the present month."

Despite Pemberton's optimism, however, the smelter did not resume operations until some four months later. On September 23 the *Times* announced that Munroe & Munroe (M&M) had acquired the assets of the M&B. A.A. Munroe, who was in the Boundary, told the newspaper that the smelter would be blown in the following Thursday.

Although the actual start-up date was not reported in the local papers, it would appear that operations resumed more or less on schedule, and Boundary Falls began to prosper once again. A schoolhouse had been built in 1903, and when the inspector of schools passed through the district in early December, it had 10 students. The inspector's

John Casselman at the switchboard of the Boundary Falls hydro-electric power plant, downstream from the falls, c1916-17.

report was far from flattering, however. "No advanced pupils; fair work in reading and number; little attention to training in language; writing poor; intermediate grade to have oral history and geography; more teaching to be done."

Another sign of prosperity was the construction of Boundary Falls' third hotel, the Queens. Sometime the previous summer, C.A. Dempsey and Alex McPherson had purchased or leased the Boundary Falls Hotel. But when the liquor licenses for the three hotels were renewed in January, 1904, Dempsey was the sole proprietor of the Boundary Falls Hotel. McPherson had apparently sold his interest, then, with a new partner named Wellwood, built the Queens. The Smelter Hotel was now being run by Thomas Wake. Another business was established the following April when Fred Hilbert, one of the first barbers in Greenwood, opened a shop in Boundary Falls.

But the beleaguered smelter continued to dominate the news of Boundary Falls when, in February, 1905, M&M ran into financial difficulties and were forced to liquidate their interest in the M&B to the Guggenheim Exploration Co. But operations had resumed for less than three months when both smelter and mines were again closed down. In a statement to the Times on May 26, Mgr. H.T. Pemberton said all operations had ceased on "telegraphic instructions from New York, which ordered the closing down of the mines and 'blowing out' of the smelter, pending the reorganization of the company."

However, W.T. Smith, a heavy shareholder in the DCC, and one of the best known operators in the Boundary district, told the Times the shutdown was "due to gross incompetency on the part of the management." Smith went on to charge the M&B with "non-accounting for ores," and claimed that the shareholders of the DCC were entitled to $100,000 which should have been paid over by the M&B.

"Nearly a year ago the Dominion Copper Company entered into an agreement with the Montreal & Boston Consolidated for the sale of all its properties in Phoenix camp for $480,000, being on a basis of 15 cents per share, on 3,200,000 shares of stock. Under the terms of the bond the purchasing company was to pay $12,000 per month, and two dollars per ton on all ore shipped from the Phoenix mines to the company's smelter. Settlement for this ore to be made every 30 days and the proceeds applied to the bond. So far only 96,000 has been paid on the bond, and no settlement made for some 50,000 tons of ore shipped during the past 90 days. In other words the Dominion shareholders are entitled to the distribution of at least $100,000. James Breen, who owns 1,000,000 shares is now in the east demanding for the local shareholders, an accounting of the ore treated. He is the heaviest individual shareholder.

"Regarding the re-organization scheme I believe it is for the express purpose of paying off the bond of the Dominion Copper Company, as I notice by the eastern financial press that the directors of the Consolidated propose issuing $700,000 of six percent mortgage bonds. This cannot be carried out until we are paid up, and they obtain legal title to the mines."

Reverting to the serious charge of incompetency in the smelting department, White continued: "It is the same old story of the directors sending out a manager with no practi-

cal experience in mining or smelting. H.T. Pemberton is not, in my opinion, a qualified man. I don't believe he ever saw the inside of a copper smelter before he took charge of the plant at Boundary Falls. This gross incompetency has resulted in a direct loss of thousands of dollars in copper matte, which even the veriest novice could ascertain for himself by an examination of the slag dump."

In his defence, Pemberton issued the following statement regarding the allegations made by Smith:

"The charges made by W.T. Smith about slag losses is a malicious falsehood which may be proven by an examination of the company's monthly statement on file at New York and open to the inspection of any shareholder of my company. Mr. Smith has seen fit to bring me personally into this matter but his motive is beyond conjecture. The issues he mentions regarding non-payment for ores smelted are a matter for settlement between the directors of the two companies and have no bearing upon the local management.

"Instructions were received from New York to close down pending the re-organization, and for this reason only were operations suspended. I cannot too strongly refute the allegations made by Smith which will be proven on examination to be without foundation."

While the latest charges, counter-charges and back room manoeuvring created intense interest in Boundary mining circles, the shutdown had far greater impact for the 250 employees who had been paid off.

Elsewhere in the same issue of the Times, details of the re-organization revealed that the DCC had acquired 2,600,000 shares in the new company at $1 each. The new company would "start off with its properties fully paid for, and about $250,000 cash in its treasury." With the smelter and mines finally owned by a strong syndicate of mining men, the prospects for the company looked bright. However, instead of starting up, the DCC announced that smelter operations would remain suspended while its capacity was "increased from two to four furnaces, which will give it a capacity of 1,000 tons per day."

As many employees sought work elsewhere, depriving the small town of much of its population, businessmen soon felt the pinch. On June 17, the Pioneer noted that the Boundary Falls Hotel had the only liquor license in town. The other two hotels had either closed down or not bothered to apply. A week later the Boundary Falls sawmill was dismantled and shipped to Slocan Lake.

For the remainder of the summer and fall, nothing is heard of Boundary Falls. Obviously, the town was in a very depressed state of affairs as it waited for the smelter to resume operations. That finally occurred on November 29, 1905, and only two days later the Times noted: "Boundary Falls is once more a hive of industry, vacant houses are now filled and those who remained in the little smelter town, trusting that the close-down was only temporary are now wearing a happy smile while at work."

Up to this time, tiny Boundary Falls had been a one-industry town, and the history of that industry had been anything but stable. Now, with a strong management team, sound financing, and ample supplies of ore, the Sunset smelter was running smoothly, bringing prosperity to Boundary Falls. Then, on May 11, 1906, the new town received more good news when the Times announced that

Boundary Falls school class c1919. Back row, left to right: George Swanlund, Armand Anderson, John Morris, Harold Folvich, Sylvester McDonald and Elizabeth McDonald. Front row: Annie Swanlund, Annie Casselman, Caroline Casselman and Mildred Cruise.

the power plant. From the power house a stand pipe will be run up the side of the hill and connected with a reservoir which will be constructed on a level with the top of the dam after it has been raised the necessary six feet. The object of the stand pipe and reservoir is to regulate the water power and to safeguard against accidents.

"The power house will be 26x40, constructed of brick on strong foundations. The initial equipment will consist of one generator of 150 KW (200 horse power) three phase, producing 4,400 volts. This will be directly connected to a 200-horse power impulse water wheel, regulated by a needle nozzle. The governor, a most important part of the machinery, will be manufactured by the Lombard Governor Co. of Ashland, Mass., and will be known as the Lombard governor, recognized as one of the very best available today. This piece of machinery, which is small compared with some of the largest parts, will cost over $1,000. The power house is designed to allow for the installation of more machinery when this becomes necessary.

"At present Alex Robinson, who has the contract for rock work, has several men at work preparing for the laying of the pipe line and the construction of the dam. Considerable rock will have to be blasted out and some deep gulleys filled up. The work, including the building of the power house, will occupy the entire summer, but the company expects to have everything completed by the autumn."

Meanwhile, in its May 26, 1906 issue, the *Pioneer* printed a glowing report on the progress of the smelter under the DCC. Both furnaces were now in blast, treating about 600 tons of ore per 24 hours. The smelter currently employed 110 men, but that number was expected to increase as soon as expansion of the works was completed. A new 35x75-foot machine shop had been completed, and the CPR had constructed a 1,000-foot spur for handling matte that was being shipped to the B.C. Copper Company's smelter at Greenwood for processing.

The prosperity of Boundary Falls continued throughout 1906 and most of 1907. Then, on October 15, 1907, the bubble burst when, in addition to closing down its smelter, the DCC shut down operations at the Rawhide and Sunset mines, throwing a total of 208 men out of work. When interviewed by a *Times* reporter, Mgr. W.C. Thomas said that the closure came "as a bolt from the blue on instructions from the president of the company, Senator Warner Miller, of New York, who had wired to cease all operations until his arrival." Thomas, who speculated that operations were being suspended because of a combination of extremely low copper prices and very high operating costs, predicted the closure was only temporary. A month later, H.H. Melville, vice-president of the DCC, arrived in the

the Greenwood Electric Company (GEC) was commencing work on an electric power plant at Boundary Falls. "The contract for the rock work has been let to Alex Robinson and he has several men at work there. E.G. Warren spent Tuesday at the Falls taking levels and making other preparations for the construction of the dam. Preparations are now under way for the opening of a road leading to the plant site. This will be necessary for traffic and for the handling of building material and supplies."

When completed, the *Times* advised its readers a week later, "Greenwood's busy suburb will have one of the most up-to-date producing stations in the country." Some years earlier Robert Wood and C. Scott Galloway had tried to establish a power plant at Boundary Falls. Considerable construction work was undertaken at that time. A dam was built some 300 feet above the falls and a shelf was blasted out of the face of the cliff directly over the falls and some trestle work constructed to carry the pipeline. Part of these works were now being utilized by the GEC. The old dam, which was still in perfectly solid condition, was being raised six feet higher to increase the storage capacity of the reservoir by several million gallons.

From the dam a 30-inch wood stave pipe was being constructed to carry the water 1,450 feet to the power line, 1,150 feet below the falls. "The intake of the pipe line will be at the top of the present dam, so that when the work is finally completed there will be a body of water six feet deep above the pipe, supplying a powerful stream of water to the power plant below. The line will be carried along the edge of the cliff on the shelf of rock already blasted out and will follow the contour of the hill side without passing over the old trestle. After covering about half the distance it passes over the top of the hills and follows a straight line down to

Boundary with M.M. Johnson. Accompanied by local company officials, they inspected the Rawhide, Brooklyn and Sunset mines and examined the smelter. On November 15, Johnson told the *Times* it was unlikely that operations would resume until "the market straightens out." In the meantime, the mines were being kept in excellent shape.

Ironically, a Miner's Union Hall and reading room had been completed at Boundary Falls only a week earlier. It opened with a ball on November 6, although, with the current state of affairs, the mood must have been sombre.

For the next six months, except for the occasional rumour, nothing was heard of the DCC operations. Then, in April, 1908, the Boston *Commercial* reported: "Dominion Copper is said to be badly in need of money. It is claimed that the $400,000 which the company had in its treasury a year ago was used to buy new properties, to purchase mining equipment and reconstruct and enlarge its smelter. A fair scale of production had barely been reached when copper became unsaleable and declined severely in price. The low prices recently recorded for Dominion Copper bonds raise the question as to whether the coming interest will be met. Its mines are said to have been examined a few months ago by Granby interests."

Throughout the following months rumours persisted that the DCC was about to resume operations, and when asked to comment on the situation, Manager Thomas replied: "Everything is looking much brighter now. The money necessary to meet the interest on the bonds, which come due on June 1st, has already been paid over. We are still keeping all the mines in shape and have several thousand tons of ore, enough for about five days at the smelter, as well as a large supply of coke."

"Mr. Thomas continued to say that as yet no word had been received giving him instructions to resume, but this might come at anytime, and that when it does come, the smelter can go into commission almost as soon as a force can be gathered to operate it."

Sure enough, on June 5 the *Times* announced that the DCC would resume operations in 10 days. "The smelter of the company will open with two furnaces, employing over 100 men. At the mines there will be work for over 200 men." Once again the beleaguered smelter was blown in; but operations had barely got back to normal when the smelter closed down again less than two months later. This shutdown, according to the *Times*, was due to a shortage of coke. However company officials expected regular shipments to resume the following day, and said the smelter would be blown in again four or five days after that. Unfortunately, the smelter was dealt another blow two days later.

Around 9:30 p.m. on August 13, a disastrous fire engulfed and totally destroyed the 30x100-foot frame structure that housed machine and blacksmith shops, entailing a loss estimated at $25,000 to $30,000. Only the energetic efforts of employees, and an excellent water supply, prevented the entire smelter from being destroyed. Fortunately for the financially troubled DCC, the building was insured.

On August 28 the first shipment of coke, and a dozen ore cars, arrived at the smelter, and operations were expected to resume at the beginning of September. But, although the coke problem had apparently been resolved, the DCC's financial situation had not improved. By November the company was in receivership, and in December the *Commercial* reported: "It would appear, that in addition to bonded indebtedness of $800,000 and accrued interest there are outstanding claims for about $75,000, inclusive of wages for August and September, aggregating $20,000. The miners have filed liens against the properties.

"Pending sale the receiver has been authorized to borrow $20,000 in priority to the trust mortgage securing the bond issue to defray expenses of the receivership, the principal item being cost of power and labor in keeping the mines pumped out. The receiver estimates that his expenses will aggregate $4,000 per month.

"It is not possible to say what time will be required to bring the properties to sale."

Meanwhile, the *Times* reported that the Granby Consolidated Mining, Smelting and Power Co., of Grand Forks, had offered the DCC "$300,000 for its properties, including the smelter, which has recently been equipped at an expense of $300,000.

"The B.C. Copper company, the third producer of importance in the Boundary district, has also made an offer to the Dominion companies for its properties, but this, we understand, was not sufficiently large to consider."

By February, 1908, a reorganization committee had been formed of the leading bondholders and stockholders in an effort to purchase the assets of the DCC at the foreclosure sale. These plans failed to materialize, however, and on March 26, 1909, the *Times* announced that the properties of the DCC were to be placed on the open market and sold under the mortgage held by National Trust. On June 11, 1909, the *Times* reported that the assets had been sold at auction to a syndicate of New York capitalists for $261,500. The purchaser planned to form a new company called the New Dominion Copper Company, and resume operations of the properties. The smelter, however, was never to resume operations.

Boundary Falls had never been much of a town. For a brief period it boasted three hotels, two generals stores, a barber, a stage line, and possible a few other businesses. Its history was irrevocably locked into the success of its smelter and the town lived and died with it. After the final closure of the smelter in 1907, the town slid into oblivion. For a time some businessmen and residents held on, fervently believing that the smelter would rebound once again, as it had done so many times before. But eventually the truth, or economics, forced the remainder to leave. In June, 1907, the Smelter and Boundary Falls hotels were still dispensing liquid refreshments to its guests. In December, 1908, the school teacher, Mr. S. Moore, had resigned, probably for a lack of students to teach, although the school itself did not close until 1946. By January 15, 1910, only one hotel remained in operation at Boundary Falls, and it had been refused a liquor license.

Today, except for some ruins of the electric power plant at the scenic Boundary Falls, some massive slag piles, part of the stone retaining wall and some scattered ruins, nothing remains of the former town. Perhaps even more tragic, few photographs, except for the smelter, have survived. There is little of interest to view today, except for the beautiful falls themselves, of which few people are aware even exist. ✤

(Above) The Kettle River at Rock Creek in the fall of 1984. Although the history of Rock Creek dates back to 1858, it still retains its rustic charm and tranquility.

(Left) A coloured postcard of a placer mining operation in British Columbia. Although this photo was not taken at Rock Creek, it does depict the typical mining that was carried on there for so many years. Yet, despite having been mined extensively from 1860 onward, there is no record of anyone having reached bedrock, where the richest quantities of gold are known to accumulate. Perhaps Rock Creek will one day witness a resurgence as miners try to get at this elusive treasure.

(Above) *This assay shack at Camp McKinney was probably built in the 1930s. When photographed in 1987 there were core samples all over the floor.*
Left) *Chinese placer mining on McKinney Creek, then known as the South Fork of Rock Creek. The Chinese, being thorough miners, piled the overburden rocks out of their way and formed ground sluices. Some of these trenches are up to eight feet deep.*
(Below) *This painting by the author shows Camp McKinney during its prime.*

(Above left) *Various treasures unearthed at Camp McKinney by Gary McDougall in 1987. They include an axe head, Chinese jug, hand blown bottles and many square nails, all of the 1890s vintage.*

(Above centre) *Remains of boiler used to life ore buckets from mines at Camp McKinney. The doors and other parts were dynamited off during World War II for scrap metal.*

(Right) *One of the numerous old mine adits at Camp McKinney. This one is approximately 20 feet deep and is currently filled with water. These shafts are dangerous, and should be avoided.*

(Below) *Head frame and buildings dating from the 1950s was photographed in 1984. Today there are some new buildings on the site and the area is once again being considered for mining operations.*

(Left) Looking down on what remains of the dam at Boundary Falls in 1991.
(Above) A frontal view of the same dam.
(Below) A short distance below the dam, lies Boundary Falls, after which the town-site was named.

(Above) John "Jolly Jack'" Thornton's old log cabin on Boundary Creek. (Right and Below) Two views of old cribbing at Boundary Falls. The trestle on the right, which hugs the side of a cliff high above Boundary Creek, once carried a pipeline. The works below follow closer to the shore of the creek itself. It once carried a 30-inch wood stave pipe from the dam. Both are relics of the Boundary Falls hydroelectric project.

(Above) Part of an old boiler lays rusting at the site of the Boundary Falls smelter.
(Left) This old stone retaining wall was once a part of the Boundary Falls smelter.
(Below) Even after 80 years, little grows on the slag heap of the Boundary Falls smelter. This view is looking east. The original four blocks of the Boundary Falls town-site were located to the left, across Boundary Creek. All three photos were taken in 1991.

THE ANACONDA HOTEL.

MAXIMICK ©

One of three painting by Bill Maximick especially for this book, this scene shows Anaconda in its early years, probably 1897 or 1898.

(Above) The B.C. Copper Co.'s smelter was actually built at Anaconda, not Greenwood as is commonly believed. The manager's house (red roof) however, was in Greenwood. It still stands today.
(Right) Clumps of hardened slag, shaped like a bell, litter the smelter site today.
(Below) A 26-ton slag pot pouring molten slag.

(Above) *This original Anaconda building can be seen along the main highway just before you enter Greenwood.*

(Right) *Sign at the corner of 3rd. St. and Tacoma Ave., Anaconda, in 1991.*

(Below) *A general view of the Anaconda town-site in 1991, photographed from the road leading to Deadwood.*

(Opposite page) Touted as the highest smokestack in the province, the B.C. Copper Co.'s smelter chimney at Anaconda consists of nearly 250,000 bricks. It is 120 feet high and had an inside diameter of 12 feet. Note the workers atop the inset photograph.
(Below) The original Greenwood fire hall. Built prior to 1900, it was dismantled in 1964.
(Right) The fire bell from the original Greenwood fire hall. It can be seen in front of the Greenwood City Hall.
(Bottom) A coloured postcard of Copper Street, Greenwood. The second building on the right is the Commercial Hotel. The photo was taken c1900.

(Above) This was once the residence of Ralph Smailes, who was the mayor of Greenwood at one time. It is located on Government Street, almost across from the post office. Photo was taken in 1991.
(Opposite page) The Catholic "Church of the Sacred Heart," Greenwood, 1991. Construction began in March 1898. The first service was held in the still unfinished church on June 26, 1898, by Father Palmer.
(Below) Copper Street, Greenwood, in 1991. The Greenwood Inn was originally the Windsor Hotel, erected in 1896. The white building on the right was originally the Pacific Hotel, which opened for business in 1897.

Two views of the interior of the Provincial Court House at Greenwood. The court house is located on the top floor of the Greenwood City Hall building, shown in the photo on the right. The top photo shows the judges's bench, with the lawyer's desk in the foreground. The judge's chambers were in the back. The lower photo, taken from the open doorway of the above photo, shows the jury box on the right and the spectator balcony at the rear of the court room.

Anaconda

A street scene, with freight wagons, in Anaconda, probably in 1897 or 1898. This is the only good photograph of Anaconda to have survived, and it was used as research for the full colour painting on pages 40-41.

SITUATED on Boundary Creek, at the mouth of both Lind and Copper creeks, the history of Anaconda dates back to June, 1894, when John W. Lind preempted approximately 300 acres of land in the area. The log cabin built by Lind was not only the first residence in the future town-site, but it was probably the first building of any description to be erected anywhere in this part of the district.

For over a year there was little development in the area. Then, in September, 1895, Robert Wood purchased Otto Dillier's Ranch, which adjoined Lind's property, and immediately took steps to lay out a town-site. Although the record is not clear, it appears that Lind's Ranch had been considered as a potential town-site prior to the purchase of Dillier's Ranch. In any event, Ewing Keithley, Fred Keffer and Lewis Hind acquired 50 acres of land from Lind to the east of Boundary Creek in the fall of 1895, and by December eight blocks had been plotted into town lots.

Due to the lateness of the season, it was not until the spring of 1896 that Anaconda began to flourish. The first frame building to be erected was occupied by the Graham Restaurant. In March, W.W. Gibbs, formerly of Boundary Falls, moved to Anaconda and established an assay office.

The following month A.R. Tillman established the Anaconda Sawmill. It had a daily capacity of 20,000 feet of lumber, and provided shingles and mouldings in addition to rough and dressed lumber.

By early May a half dozen carpenters were putting the finishing touches on the Anaconda Hotel, a large two-story, 35x75-foot building owned by Mark & Tholl. By this time the town-site had been surveyed by Charles Green, and the streets were being cleared and graded. "The owners of the Anaconda townsite are evidently of a literary turn of mind," noted the Midway *Advance* on April 27, "judging from the names that have been given to several of the streets. Shakespeare, Shelly, Byron, Milton, but not Austin, streets appear conspicuously in the place, while the cross streets are appropriately named after the great smelting centers, as Butte, Tacoma, Everett and others."

By the middle of May, Anaconda's second hotel was fast nearing completion. Owned by Thomas Hardy, formerly of Boundary Falls, the two-story, 40x60-foot Palace Hotel was apparently appropriately named. In October, the Boundary Creek *Times* pronounced it as far superior to any hotel built in Greenwood, Boundary Falls or Midway. "The addition of a handsome verandah has further improved the appearance of the exterior of the premises, and appliances are now being put in position to heat the rooms with hot air from a furnace in the basement."

In June, two general stores opened for business. One was owned by James McNicol, who also had a store at Midway, while the other, the Anaconda Mercantile Co., was operated by F.J. Miller and W.M. Law. Later that same month. E.W. McDowell moved from Boundary Falls to establish a butcher shop in Anaconda.

On July 6, ads for the Anaconda Bakery began to appear in the *Advance*, owner A. Widmore offering the town's inhabitants fresh bread, cakes and pies. The same issue of the newspaper carried an ad for Armstrong & Lawder, "the hardware, tin and stove men" of Anaconda. They offered "McLary Steel Ranges, wood and cook stoves, parlor stoves, box stoves, miner's camp stoves or any other stove you want. Silverware, graniteware, crockeryware, glassware, woodenware, tinware of all kinds. Toilet seats, hardware of all kinds, cutlery, forks and spoons, daisy churns, new Williams Sewing machines, wringers, washers, window shades. New Chatham wagons and trucks."

In August, H. Wright, "boot and shoe maker," opened for business. That same month Mark & Tholl dissolved their partnership in the Anaconda Hotel; Nicholas Tholl was now the sole proprietor. In September, when the first issue of the *Times* appeared, it reported that J.P. McLeod, a barrister and solicitor from New Westminster, had opened an office in Anaconda. It also noted that a man named Casby had acquired the building that had recently housed the Graham Restaurant, and that he was converting it into a stationery and fruit stand.

In October, A.H. Lawder decided to retire from the hardware business and sold his interest to L.Y. Birnie, who had been in charge of the store. The new partnership was known as W.J. Armstrong & Co. That same month, Keithley, Keffer and Hind filed an application for the incorporation of the Anaconda Townsite Company, with a capitalization of $10,000.

On November 1 a post office was established, and on November 14, the Anaconda Commercial Club (ACC) was organized with a membership of 21. The objects of the association was "the furtherance of the commercial and social interests (of Anaconda), and for the advancement of all enterprises having for their object the benefit of town and vicinity." In late November a contract was awarded to Mark Kay and John Blough to build a bridge across Boundary Creek. By mid-December, George Rankin was building a large two-story building on Butte Avenue, the bottom of which was to be a blacksmith shop. A week later G.A. Ford opened his barbershop in the Palace Hotel. At this point in its brief history, Anaconda was already larger than Midway, which had been established much earlier.

On New Year's eve, the ACC sponsored a dance in their hall on Butte Avenue which was well attended by about 35 couples. "The hall was tastefully decorated with evergreens and bunting and lighted by Chinese lanterns"; wrote the *Times*, "the floor was in admirable condition and the music good. Supper was served at the Palace hotel at midnight, after which dancing was resumed the party not breaking up until 5 a.m. The dance committee are to be commended upon the success that attended their arrange-

ments for the occasion. The dance was in every way well-conducted, and the 'rough' element was notably absent."

By mid-May, 1897, the bridge over Boundary Creek had been completed and tenders were being considered for the construction of a road connecting it with the Deadwood Camp road. Business had picked up since the first of May, with the stores, particularly the Anaconda Mercantile Co., doing an excellent trade.

On June 12, the *Times* announced that a 75 percent interest in the Anaconda town-site had been purchased by T.A. Garland, of nearby Greenwood, for $10,000 and other considerations. Col. John Weir currently held the remaining 25 percent.

On July 1, Anaconda celebrated Dominion Day with considerable enthusiasm. The festivities began with horse races at 10 a.m., followed by a baseball game against Greenwood's finest in the afternoon. This was followed by a drilling contest, marred, unfortunately, by an accident to one of the participants. The first contestants, Dennis Clune and Jack Sullivan, drilled together for 15 minutes "without a hitch, without a mishit and without any delay to mar the uniformity of their work." The men were loudly applauded when it became known they had drilled 31¼ inches.

J. Hoffstetter and McDowell, their opponents, had never drilled together before and had only entered to make a match against Clune and Sullivan. They made good headway for the first three minutes, although Hoffstetter had missed the drill several times. Then in his excitement, Hoffstetter missed the drill altogether and struck McDowell's wrist with full force. "A big piece of flesh was torn from the wrist, which bled profusely," causing the contest to be abandoned. Dr. Jakes attended the wounded man, but it would be some time before he would have use of his arm.

Following a tug-of-war, just barely won by the Anaconda team, the celebration was brought to a close by a grand ball and banquet in Wilson's hall.

Anaconda had been established as a town before Greenwood, about one mile to the northeast. However, although starting in second place, Greenwood quickly forged ahead of its rival as the main town along Boundary Creek. The two towns were so close, that as each expanded towards the other, it was soon difficult to distinguish where one ended and the other began. This is particularly true even today, as residences of both towns are side by side.

As Greenwood began to outstrip its rival in growth, most of the new entrepreneurs established themselves there. This also led to some of the Anaconda businesses relocating to Greenwood. This may explain why W.J. Armstrong & Co. sold their entire stock of hardware, stoves, tinware and crockeryware to Thomas Hardy in September, 1897. In November, G.H. Ford moved his barbershop and bath house from the Palace Hotel, Anaconda, to Copper Street, Greenwood. This trend continued in February, 1898, when the Anaconda Mercantile Company partnership between F.J. Miller and W.M. Law was dissolved. Miller retired, and Law moved the stock to the Barrett block in Greenwood, where he continued the general merchandise trade.

But not everyone had lost faith in Anaconda. Back in October of 1897, Rosie McLeod had completed a substantial and roomy dwelling house, and H.J. Homan had estab-

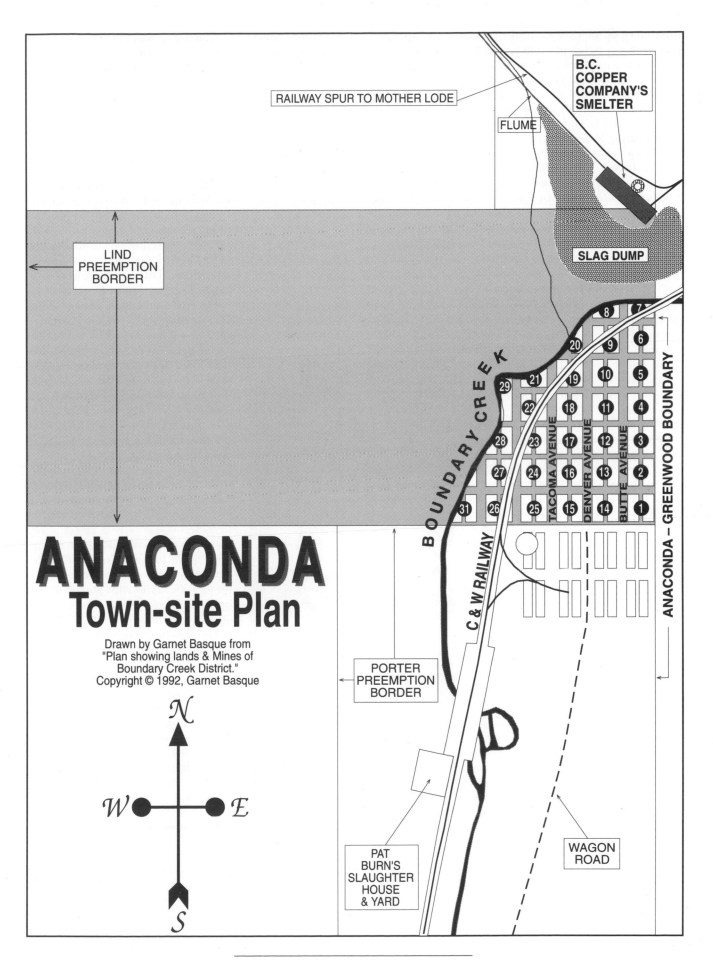

RAILWAY SPUR TO MOTHER LODE

B.C. COPPER COMPANY'S SMELTER

FLUME

SLAG DUMP

LIND PREEMPTION BORDER

BOUNDARY CREEK

ANACONDA – GREENWOOD BOUNDARY

TACOMA AVENUE

DENVER AVENUE

BUTTE AVENUE

C & W RAILWAY

ANACONDA
Town-site Plan

Drawn by Garnet Basque from
"Plan showing lands & Mines of
Boundary Creek District."
Copyright © 1992, Garnet Basque

N
W E
S

PORTER PREEMPTION BORDER

PAT BURN'S SLAUGHTER HOUSE & YARD

WAGON ROAD

lished a small lumber business. By April, 1898, part of the town-site was being cleared in anticipation of the boom that would accompany the construction of the Canadian Pacific Railway. In October, Thomas Hardy rented his Palace Hotel to S. Snodgrass, W. Curtis and J. Philips and moved to Greenwood. Beyond that, however, little was written about Anaconda until January 28, 1899, when the *Times* said that, "Owing to the large number of people coming into the district the vacant houses in Anaconda are being rapidly tenated." Even this, however, was a reflection of Greenwood's prosperity, not Anaconda's, the paper stating that it was "almost impossible to get house or rooms to let in Greenwood."

In mid-February, 1900, with the situation at Anaconda remaining stagnant, 46 Anaconda real estate owners signed a petition asking Greenwood City Council to extend its municipal boundaries to embrace the Anaconda town-site. With this in mind, Alderman Sharpe introduced a resolution in favour of the petitioners, which was carried unanimously. Reporting the event on February 13, the *Times* favoured the amalgamation: "Anaconda will be a welcome addition to the City of Greenwood."
However, two days later, when the *Times* covered the subject in greater detail, it attitude toward the merger was changing:

"Anaconda is a suburb of Greenwood. It is no longer a distinct and separate town. Greenwood has grown until there is no area of unoccupied land separating it from Anaconda. This being the case there can be no objections taken to including Anaconda within the corporate limits because it is Anaconda. But the resident of Greenwood and those of Anaconda should seriously consider the matter before voting for the extension of the city limits. Generally speaking, neither a city nor those brought within the municipality are benefitted or satisfied by such an extension. Their reasons of this dissatisfaction are many. Increased municipal area carries with it increased expenditure on streets, police and fire protection, and in connection with all other matters which the ratepayers naturally expect from a municipality in return for taxation. It is impossible to satisfy the outlying portions of a city in this respect. The business portion of the city usually receives the greatest attention, and by the time such improvements are made that will meet the requirements of the business centre, there is little if any money left for the outskirts. There is consequent dissatisfaction. The ratepayers demand in the way of expenditure what the municipal council is unable to give.

Boundary Creek pioneer Thomas Hardy established the first hotel at Boundary Falls. When Anaconda emerged on the scene, he moved there and built the Palace Hotel. He later leased the premises and moved next door to Greenwood, where he was elected mayor (18991900). From there he moved to Phoenix.

"The *Times* will welcome Anaconda into the municipal fold if the electors decide upon such a course, but it desires to caution its residents, and those of Greenwood, against acting hastily in the matter of increasing the municipal area. The municipal boundaries today include too large an area for its population; the evils will be aggravated by a still further increase."

To understand the *Times'* sudden shift in opinion regarding the merger, one must look at the political situation. When Thomas Hardy was elected the mayor of Greenwood in January, 1899, he still owned the Palace Hotel in Anaconda. Now it could be argued that it was mere coincidence that the month following his election the 46 petitioners had presented their merger proposal to Greenwood City Council. But it appears likely that this conflict of interest was at least part of the reason why the newspaper was trying to foster a growing resistance to the amalgamation.

On June 19, 1900, when the *Times* published its strongest opposition yet against annexation, it charged that the merger bylaw had been railroaded through council without first being voted on by Greenwood City ratepayers. The *Times* went on to warn its readers that the bylaw was "a cunning and well devised plan to perpetuate municipal mismanagement and boss rule."

"In the year of grace 1899 the management of municipal affairs passed under the control of what is popularly known as the Hardy faction. Since gaining control, those in power have revelled in saturnalia of municipal mismanagement and of loose and illegal expenditure of public money without commensurate results. They have heaped exorbitant taxes upon the ratepayers and have landed the city in courts with the result that heavy judgements are now pending against the city, with more to follow.

"The ratepayers of Greenwood are slow to take an interest in what vitally concerns the future of the city, but a year and a half of the sort of thing described above has had its effect upon public opinion, and there is a strong probability that unless drastic measures are taken, the reign of the present powers that be will shortly close."

Although the newspaper did not specifically mention Hardy's potential conflict of interest, it obviously had him in mind when it added: "Those who lived in Greenwood in the early days can well remember there were grave doubts as to whether Greenwood or Anaconda would attain supremacy and it was only by an organized and persistent effort on the part of the people of Greenwood that the business became centered here and Anaconda became a suburb of the larger town. But those who made the struggle and were defeated have not forgotten nor forgiven, and they are now taking advantage of certain peculiarities in connection with municipal government in Greenwood to endeavor to regain some of their lost prestige."

The newspaper continued its battle against the merger on June 20, when it claimed that the bylaw authorizing the extension of the city limits by including Anaconda was illegal under the Municipal Clauses Act, which stated that "the limits of any incorporated city or town shall not be extended unless the consent of the owners of more than one-half in value of the land to be included within the boundaries of the proposed extension affected thereby, and who are entitled to petition for incorporation as a municipality under this act, has been first obtained at a poll to be held for that purpose."

Since "No such petition was presented to the council in reference to the annexation of Anaconda," continued the *Times*, "the by-law is consequently illegal, and even if it now receives the assent of the ratepayers can have no affect."

One Greenwood City alderman, D.J. Sullivan, took exception to the articles published by the *Times*, and in a letter to the newspaper he suggested the editor should "confine himself to the facts." Sullivan claimed that the annexation of Anaconda had not been rushed through council but had been under consideration for at least two months. He then went on to state: "Such rot as that the people of Anaconda are to be benefited to the detriment of the people of the upper end of town (Greenwood), is not worthy of consideration, as there are no arguments adduced to support this illusion, for the simple reason that there can be none put forth." In closing, Sullivan said that the Greenwood property owners would decide the matter.

This they did, and on June 22, the *Times* announced

that the "ratepayers of Greenwood turned down the proposition to annex Anaconda by a vote of 93 to 43. Both sides worked hard but it was evident from the time the poll opened that a heavy vote would be polled against the scheme. Mayor Wood and Aldermen Sutherland, Sullivan and Sharpe worked hard to secure an endorsation of the by-law but their efforts proved fruitless."

Nothing noteworthy occurred at Anaconda during the next six months. Then, on December 10, 1900, the first issue of the Anaconda *News* made its appearance. Normally, the establishment of a newspaper in a town was a status symbol. However, the *News*, published by Robert Keffer, the young son of Fred Keffer, could hardly be considered a newspaper in the normal sense. Only 5½ inches by 8½ inches, the first issue was a single page comprising a grand total of only 70 words!

Although the age of Robert Keffer when he started the *News* is not known, he was probably no more that 11 or 12. This is suggested by the jokes that appeared in the paper, which would only be appreciated by young children, and by the fact that in 1908, after eight years of publication, young Robert quit to attend Washington State University. Upon leaving for that institution, he was still referred to as "master Robert" by the Phoenix *Pioneer*.

Although it began publication on December 10, 1900, there was nothing of interest in the "paper" until September 17, 1901. On that date the *News* recorded the fact that F.F. Travis was building two fine cottages on Tacoma Avenue. It also noted that Anaconda had two accountants, E. Jacobs and D.F. McCrea. It was over two months later before it next noteworthy event was recorded: "The new school house at Anaconda is under roof, and is a fine looking building."

In fairness to Keffer and the *News*, however, it should be pointed out that no other paper in the district published information concerning Anaconda during the same period.

(Right) A rare photograph of the Anaconda News *printing office. The quality is poor because the print was made directly off the newspaper's microfilm copy.*
(Below) Greenwood alderman James Sutherland fought hard to get Greenwood to amalgamate with Anaconda.

The town simply was not newsworthy. However, that situation changed on December 9, 1901, when the *Advance* ran a story about a serious fire at Anaconda.

About 4 a.m. on December 5, fire broke out in the Palace Hotel. A short time later the building and its contents had been reduced to ashes. "It is not know how the fire originated," wrote the *Advance*, "but it had gained good headway before being discovered."

Without an "effective water system," it was impossible to stop the fire's progress, and it was only through the efforts of a volunteer fire brigade that a neighbouring building, 30 feet away, was not also consumed, although its exterior was scorched. Hooper & Bell, the proprietors, estimated their loss on the contents at $2,500, $1,000 of which was covered by insurance. The building's owner, Thomas Hardy, now a resident of Phoenix, estimated his loss at $5,000, of which he had $2,800 insurance.

"The conflagration spread with such rapidity that the guests were unable to save but very little of their belongings," wrote the *Advance*. "A few weeks ago the hotel narrowly escaped being burned, owing to a defective flue, however, the flames were discovered and extinguished in time to prevent any serious loss. The Palace was built in 1896 by Thomas Hardy, since then the town has gradually grown towards Greenwood until it was poorly situated to do a large trade, so it is not likely to be rebuilt."

This was not the first fire to occur at Anaconda. On February 3, 1899, a fire ended in tragedy when John C. Lloyd, a well-known prospector, was fatally burned to death in his cabin. The weather was exceedingly cold at the time and when Lloyd retired for the night, speculated the *Times*, "it is supposed he filled the stove. The stove set fire to the cabin while Lloyd slept. About 6:30 o'clock Friday morning residents saw the cabin in flames. They rushed to the burning building and found Lloyd unconscious outside. He had evidently been awakened by the crackling of the flames and endeavoured to escape from the burning building. He was badly burned and although Dr. Oppenheimer did everything in his power to save his life, Lloyd died about Friday noon."

The 33-year-old Lloyd, a native of Iowa, had been a resident of Anaconda for about two years. His remains were buried in the Boundary Falls Cemetery.

In the spring of 1902, activity in Anaconda began to increase. By mid-March the foundations and framework for J.W. O'Brien's new three-story Hotel Vendome, on Butte Street, had been completed. After being "comfortably furnished throughout," the estab-

lishment was ready for occupancy in early May. Opposite the new hotel, a small building was occupied by a dressmaking establishment, while elsewhere on the same street, opposite Wilson's hall, another new building was being constructed. On March 16, the *News* announced that $500 was to be spent on improvements to the town streets. In May the Anaconda post office was provided "with glass-front boxes, neatly numbered in black," wrote the *News*. "The building is a real credit to the town, and also to the energy of Mr. L.A. Smith, the genial postmaster." The population of Anaconda at this time was 195.

Over the next 10 months, Anaconda was visited by fire on three separate occasions. The first incident occurred early in the evening of July 16, 1902, when the residence and office of Thomas Garland caught fire from a spark from a stove pipe in an adjoining building. Although a volunteer fire brigade was hastily organized, all they could do was save a portion of the furniture. The building, which had once housed the Graham Restaurant, was valued at $1,000 and was not insured.

Later that same evening, a vicious 30-minute windstorm swept through the valley, toppling large trees across telephone, telegraph and electric wires. The wind scattered

(Opposite page) Wilfred Hall, who now lives in Nelson, once lived in Anaconda, Boundary Falls and Greenwood.
(Below) Martin Anderson and Mr. Nelrud enjoy a drink of spring water at Anaconda, near the site of the old brewery.

the burning embers from Garland's office in all directions, and for a time the Hotel Vendome was in danger of being set ablaze. Fortunately, the gale was followed by a heavy rainfall which help combat the threat from fire.

The second fire occurred on October 21 when a small office building owned by John Lind was destroyed.

The third fire occurred about 11 p.m. on May 12, 1903, when a house owned by Thomas Webb was consumed by flames. At the time of the fire, the house was occupied by David Webb, who, although trapped in the burning building for a time and badly burned, eventually recovered.

Despite the fact that there was only one establishment licensed to dispense liquor in Anaconda by the spring of 1903 — the records do not indicate at which hotel — the town was never-the-less beginning to attract new businesses. One of these was Smith & McEwen, who occupied the old Anaconda Mercantile building and offered books, fancy groceries and miner's supplies. However, it was Pat Burns that created the greatest interest when he decided to move his stock and slaughter yard from Eholt Meadows to a five-acre site in Anaconda close to the railway.

Ignoring the fact that Pat Burns & Co. had moved to Anaconda, the *Times* described the operation as another Greenwood enterprise: "The improvements being made at the new site are the necessary buildings and yards for slaughtering purposes, buildings for storage of meat, erection of stock scales, installation of steam boiler for use chiefly in rendering down tallow, putting in a railway siding, and other works necessary for the establishment supplying practically the whole of the meat for the Boundary district trade, carload lots going hence to Grand Forks, Phoenix and other Boundary centres of population. Some seven men are regularly employed in connection with tending and slaughtering live stock and delivery of meat, so that the bringing near to Greenwood of this establishment gives it one more home industry to add to the building up of the town."

On May 20, the *News* ran a small article on Anaconda's "Soap Factory and Slaughter House: P. Burns & Co. have nearly finished their new slaughter-house in lower Anaconda. Everything is on labor saving lines. From the time a steer is killed until loaded in the railway car, it is not taken from the overhead hook on which it is dressed. This hook runs directly to the scales and car.

"Fire guards and a large tank with hose have been provided in case of fire. A flume from a mountain spring supplies the water.

"All fats will be converted into soap at the plant.

"This slaughter house will be the central plant for the surrounding country from Rock Creek to Grand Forks."

Anaconda's most famous industry, however, is one which has always been associated with Greenwood — the smelter. In late July, 1903, residents of Anaconda might have been forgiven for wishing the smelter had in fact been established elsewhere. On July 22 a tremendous windstorm ravished the area. Although it only lasted about 15 minutes,

the powerful wind toppled trees onto houses and across roads and the railway tracks. The most notable victim was the smelter's 90-foot smokestack. The top portion of the steel smokestack struck a rock ledge as it fell, completely closing it beyond repair. Soon black noxious smoke filled the town. Although the lower portion of the smokestack was also damaged, it was repaired and raised a week later. This steel smokestack served the smelter until a permanent brick one, which still stands, was later built.

In August, Nicholas Tholl, one-time owner of the Anaconda Hotel, began a small "sawmill" operation on the hill above Anaconda. Equipped with a "wood-sawing machine" mounted on a wagon, this unique sawmill could easily be moved to a new site when the wood supply in one area was exhausted.

The construction of the Anaconda smelter was revitalizing Anaconda with other businesses as well. The South End Grocery sold fruit, candy and groceries, while H.A. King & Co. offered cigars, stationery, confectionery and the latest periodicals.

On September 16, the *News* announced that the foundation for the new smokestack was completed. Work was also progressing rapidly on the excavations for the converter and the trestle for the slag railway. When the latter was completed, melted slag was carried from the smelter in cars fitted with bowls that held about 50 cubic feet (25 tons) of material.

In 1991, Wilfred Hall, then 86 years old, described the dumping of molten slag at Anaconda. Although Hall lived with his parents in Greenwood, he would frequently visit the home of his uncle, Thomas Coulson, in Anaconda. Coulson lived in a cabin about a half mile west of the smelter, and in the evening young Hall would sit outside and watch in fascination as the pots were emptied. "A little engine would push four or five cars along a track out of the smelter. Each car held a large cone-shaped bucket containing red hot liquid slag. Each bucket would be dumped one at a time, lighting the sky with a fiery glow. Some slag always hardened in the bottom of the bucket. To get it out a man would hit the bottom of the tilted bucket with a sledge hammer and after a few blows the core would drop out." What resembles huge German army helmets scattered over the slag pile today, is the hardened slag from these bowls.

As business continued to improve, J.H. McMannus, who had leased the Vendome Hotel from J.W. O'Brien, had to rent Mr. McKay's boarding house as an annex to accommodate all the guests.

On November 4, 1903, the *News* printed an update on construction activities at the smelter: "The iron trestle and fill for the slag railway are finished, and the track is laid as far as the fill. Work on the rest is being rushed. All will be ready to dump hot slag from two furnaces in a few days. Five slag cars are ready for business.

"The track up the hill to the railway has been rebuilt, in readiness to let down parts of the steel converter building.

(Above) Train of slag pots being loaded with molten slag at the B.C. Copper Smelter.

The stonework for the converter foundations is nearing completion.

"The brick stack is over half done, and will probably be finished in about two weeks, if the weather remains good. The brick building for the transformer is also about half done.

"A railway for hauling stone from the quarry back of the ore bins to the converter foundations has been in use for some time, and is a great convenience.

"The store house has been fitted with five rows of shelves for holding pipe fittings, bolts, etc. A nice office has also been put in."

On Wednesday, December 3, smoke was turned into the new brick smokestack for the first time. By this time, every house in Anaconda was occupied, and the *News* claimed that "more houses have been rented or sold during the past three months than in any other time excepting the early boom."

Evidence of Anaconda's newfound prosperity was demonstrated by the advancement of the *News* itself. During the first half of 1902, it was a mere two-page "newspaper." That October, a third page was added. By early February, 1903, it had grown to four pages. The paper remained at four pages until April, when the *Fernie Extra*, consisting of eight pages, was printed. Later in the year a fifth page was added, and in October, a sixth page.

In December, McMannus purchased the Vendome Hotel from O'Brien and was granted a liquor license. Two months later the *News* reported that a "new addition to the Victoria Hotel" was nearing completion. Unfortunately, it is unclear if this was a new hotel, or the original Anaconda Hotel under a different name.

In March, 1904, the Superintendent of Education issued his annual report on Anaconda's school: "Inspected Jan. 16, 1903; 29 students present. Commodious schoolhouse recently erected in this district; large dictionary and other books secured for use of school through the efforts of teacher.

"Inspected Mar. 15, 1904; 31 pupils. Condition of school much improved."

There was little news concerning Anaconda until the October, 1904, when Joseph Bauer purchased the Vendome Hotel. That same month, Thomas Webb, whose house had been destroyed by fire in May of 1903, built a new cottage on Butte Avenue. In November, the Smith & McEwen store was put on rollers and moved to Butte Avenue opposite the Vendome Hotel. The move was necessitated by the construction of the new road to Boundary Falls, which diverted traffic away from the old location. That same month, Louis Forsechner started construction of a brewery on Denver Avenue. "The building is good sized and of two stories," wrote the *News*. "It is situated very near Lind Creek so as to have the best water obtainable for use in brewing." When completed, the Silver Springs Brewery offered "fine lager beer and porter, etc., etc."

In March, 1905, in exchange for obtaining the water rights to Lind Creek, the City of Greenwood agreed to extend its waterworks and fire protection system to Anaconda. Greenwood's part of the bargain, reported the *Times* is as follows: "Provide and lay a 4-inch main along Second street from Everett to Tacoma avenues; 2-inch main along Tacoma ave from Second street to Fifth; 2-inch main along Fifth from Tacoma ave to Denver ave; 4-inch main on Denver ave from Fifth to Sixth street; 4-inch main on Sixth street from Denver ave to Everett ave; 2-inch main on Butte ave from Second to Sixth street; also install three fire hydrants; install key hydrants for domestic use at points along the above pipe lines where there are at least three applicants for same, not otherwise served; will connect said water system with the Greenwood system and will allow the residents of

Anaconda the use of said water free of charge for the term of one year from the date the water is turned on in the system; Greenwood fire brigade will respond to all fire alarms from Anaconda which will pay Greenwood $5 for each turnout and other actual expenses involved in said turnout."

On May 31, 1905, the *News* appeared looking like a real newspaper for the first time in its history.

In June, Hans Peter Thompson, the new owner of the Vendome Hotel, operated the only licensed establishment in Anaconda. A reflection of Anaconda's failing fortunes were echoed in the *News'* circulation figures at the end of 1905. Although its distribution had increased from 130 copies to 220, only 40 subscribers lived in Anaconda.

In its annual update, the *News* described the improvements made in Anaconda during 1905: "Most important is the new Lind Creek water system, which has now been in operation some three or four months. A reservoir has been constructed well up in Lind Creek gulch, is lined with concrete, and has a capacity of about 250,000 gallons. The reservoir is connected with the town by a six inch wood main. Mains have also been put down the more important streets of Anaconda (Everett, Butte, Denver and Tacoma Aves., and 2nd St.). Four inch mains are used on most of the streets. Fire hydrants have been in at three corners in Anaconda. Key hydrants have been put in for the use of a majority of the families, and water put in the houses of others.

"Several of the most important streets in Anaconda have been graded this fall, and their appearance greatly improved. Everett Ave. has been graded from the upper end at 2nd St. to its connection with the main road at 6th St. Butte Ave. had been still more thoroughly finished the same distance, and some work has been done on Denver Ave., 6th St., and 2nd. These will likely be completed next spring when the frost gets out of the ground. The CPR has repaired the crossing at Denver Ave., and will soon put in a crossing to connect with the new bridge to the west side built this spring. We would likely to get a CPR flag station in Anaconda if a petition signed by the residents was to be sent to the railway company. The new Silver Springs brewery, located on Denver Ave., was started up a couple of months ago.

"Considerable building will likely be done in Anaconda in the spring, as all available houses are now taken and surrounding industries continue to grow and employ more men."

But Anaconda's struggling economy continued to play havoc with the hotel business. In July, 1906, Mrs.

This postcard shows Nicholson Coulson and his wife standing on the porch of their home in Anaconda c1910. The present highway passes to the left of the picket fence. A three-story wooden building stood on the ground to the left of the photo. It was called the "Flop House" and, according to Wilfred Hall, was where the Hindu smelter workers lived.

Stanton leased the Vendome Hotel from Peter Thompson, had it thoroughly renovated, and opened under new management. Less than two months later, however, she disposed of her lease to a Mrs. Peterson. Then, as if economic factors were not enough to contend with, on October 11, the hotel was burglarized and $50 worth of liquor stolen. This was only five weeks since the last change of proprietors, but according to the *Times:* "At the time of the burglary there was a deal on for the transfer of the license from Mr. Thompson to Mike Chapk." This apparently fell through, or if completed, did not last long, for on June 21, 1907, the *Times* noted that Peterson had transferred ownership to Morris Van de Bogert. Amazingly, only three days later, the *Times* noted that the original owner of the hotel, J.W. O'Brien, had purchased the hotel, thus completing a full circle.

On February 1, 1908, the *Pioneer* announced that "Another Boundary weekly has gone into the journalistic boneyard." While the *News,* as noted, never officially became a true newspaper until May of 1905, it departure was never-the-less a sad loss for the "suburb" of Greenwood, as Anaconda was clearly becoming. As the years passed, less and less was heard about Anaconda as a separate entity. It became, for all intents and purposes, an extension of Greenwood, its booming, thriving neighbour. Anaconda suffered another blow to its independence on July 1, 1915, when the post office was closed. The school fared better, surviving until 1924, after which time the remaining children of Anaconda went to school in Greenwood.

Today, one can still walk along the slag piles left by the smelter, and view the crumbling brick chimney and other remaining foundations. Part of the town-site of Anaconda is still there, complete with streets and original homes. But, except for local residents of today's Greenwood and Anaconda, the town does not exist. Visitors passing through on the main highway assume that all the buildings and streets are part of Greenwood, but they are not, although it might be very difficult indeed to determine exactly where Anaconda ends and Greenwood begins. Certainly, however, Anaconda had a fascinating history in its own right. ❀

Greenwood

(Above) This photo is described as the first cabin built on the Greenwood town-site. However, the first two log cabins were built by Mr. Sutherland and Mr. Shonquist, and since the man in the photo appears to be Robert Wood, it seems more likely that this was his first home.
(Below) Robert Wood, founder of Greenwood.

ACCORDING to the dictionary, a ghost town is a deserted town, especially a former boom town now empty and decayed. By that definition, Greenwood is certainly not a ghost town. According to the 1989 figures compiled by the post office for household mailing, more commonly known as "junk mail," Greenwood had 56 businesses and 432 residences. This would put the current population at around 1,000, and it is not my intention to annoy them or belittle Greenwood by including it in this book. However, Greenwood certainly qualifies as a mining camp, and my own loose description of a ghost town is a town that is currently a "ghost" of its former self. In that regard, Greenwood qualifies yet again.

As mentioned above, the Greenwood of 1992 is a substantial community. But this was not always the case. In 1893, the future town-site was a wilderness of stunted pine trees and tangled undergrowth. A miserable trail that cut through the forest provided the only access with the various mining camps that were slowly beginning to attract attention in the area. In

August, 1893, Otto Dillier preempted several hundred acres of timber at the junction of Boundary and Twin creeks and erected a small log cabin. For the following two years the property remained virtually unchanged. Then, in September, 1895, Robert Wood, a merchant from Armstrong, British Columbia, visited Boundary Creek with his nephew. After they inspected the mining camps in the area, Wood became convinced that Dillier's Ranch, centrally located, was ideally suited for a town-site. Wood promptly purchased the property from Dillier and immediately set to work developing his town-site.

In October, Wood returned to Armstrong to finalize his business affairs and get his family. Prior to leaving, however, Wood hired a number of men to work for him. Some were employed in excavating the foundation for a store. Others were kept busy hewing logs for the building, constructing roads, clearing brush and making other general improvements. These men were camped in tents scattered all over the future town-site. Already two married couples, Mr. and Mrs. Sutherland and Mr. and Mrs. Shonquist, had purchased lots and erected Greenwood's first two log cabins.

By late November Mr. and Mrs. Woods returned to Greenwood, and a short time later Greenwood's first business establishment was open for business. Owned by Robert Wood and Ralph Smailes, of Vernon, the tin shop and general store was operated from a small log building. While their residence was being built, the Woods lived in the "roughest manner imaginable in a small room partitioned off" in the store.

In December, a partnership consisting of Wood, Hubble and Westel began construction of Greenwood's first hotel, the Pioneer. (See the inset article "Greenwood's First Hotel," on page 60.) Lumber was expensive and had to be hauled from the sawmill at Midway. This situation improved on January 20, 1896, when the Midway *Advance* reported that a foundation for a sawmill was being prepared at Greenwood. In production one month later with a daily capacity of 15,000 feet of lumber, the Greenwood Sawmill employed about 25 men in the mill and logging camps.

The availability of lumber spurred construction activity, and by the end of April Greenwood already had some 40 buildings erected or nearing completion. In addition to the hotel and general store, the mushrooming town could also boast of two assay offices, one run by Guess Bros., the other by Barrett & Hodgson; a laundry operated by Smith & Straight; Dinsmore's bakery; the Cafe Royal restaurant and the Fashion Livery, Feed and Sale Stables. Greenwood also had a mining engineer's office, a real estate office, a blacksmith and a carpenter. A contract had also been let for a 20x40-foot opera house.

Despite the rapidity with which his town was emerging from the wilderness, Robert Wood was apparently not satisfied. He employed a large force of men to construct a wagon road to join the main trunk road leading into Deadwood and Copper camps. "Together with the building of bridges, rock work and grading," noted the *Advance*, "the probably cost of the improvement will be $3,000." Later, Wood built a wagon road to connect Greenwood with Greenwood Camp, as Phoenix was initially known.

Road construction was generally a government respon-

sibility, and Wood was not relieving them of their obligations purely from the goodness of his heart. Greenwood and Anaconda had emerged upon the provincial scene within a mile of each other almost at the same time, with a slight lead going to Anaconda. In the beginning, both towns fought hard for supremacy as the leading town in the Boundary Country. Wood was a shrewd businessman who probably realized that if he waited for the government to build roads, he would have no control over where they would be established. However, if he constructed them himself, he could have them radiate out from Greenwood, thus giving his town a distinct advantage over its rival.

On May 1, 1896, Greenwood's second hotel, the Windsor, opened for the first time. George Seymour, one of the proprietors, was his own architect and hauled all the lumber for the building. Construction, which began in March, had been no easy task. When Seymour and his partner Sam Webb arrived in Greenwood they found that all the carpenters were employed with other projects, "consequently the building of the hotel was a slow process," reported the *Times*, "then there was very little lumber to be had, either for love, jawbone or money, and it was found necessary to purchase a team of horses and a wagon before the furniture could be brought in from Marcus; and to put a climax on their misfortunes a load of glass and china went over a bluff on the road, and the fragments that remained weren't worth much. At length the building was completed and opened on May 1, though the license was not obtained until July 1. Since then the proprietors have done a very profitable business, the Windsor Hotel being a very popular institution in Greenwood."

Later that month George Rendell, the Boundary Falls merchant, decided to open a branch store in Greenwood. Rendell entered into a partnership arrangement with Robert Wood and Ralph Smailes, and the new venture became known as Rendell & Co. The business was conducted in a new two-story, 30x45-foot building, the second floor of which was reserved for social gatherings or public meetings. Attached to the back was the original 30-foot-long general store that had been used by Wood & Smailes, which now functioned as a warehouse.

By the end of May, Greenwood could boast of three hotels, the newest addition being the International, owned by O.F. Mickle. In June, Miller Bros. started a watchmaking and jewellery business, W.D. Paton opened a furniture store and A.D. Worgan, formerly of Vernon, opened a photography shop.

One of the most important events in the early history of Greenwood, at least as far as posterity is concerned, occurred on September 12, 1896, when the first issue of the *Times*, with Harold Lamb as publisher and W.J. Harber as manager, made its appearance. Without the *Times*,

The first sawmill office in Greenwood, 1896.

and other frontier Boundary newspapers used as references, this book, in its present form, would not have been possible.

The first issue of the *Times* carried ads for most of the establishments already mentioned, plus many more. Among the new businesses were the following: C.A. Jones, sign and house painter; R.W. Jakes, M.D. (formerly of Boundary Falls); Kerr Bros., butchers; Greenwood Grocery (later known as the White Front Store), Olson & Phelan; Robert Buckley, harness & saddlery; A.B. Hart & Co., contractors and builders, and W.E. Meddill, plasterer, bricklayer and stoneman.

But booming Greenwood had more to offer than business establishments. On Wednesday, September 9, Miss Grace Thorber arrived by stage from Penticton to take charge of the Greenwood school. The first school was in a private building, but on September 26, construction of a new school was begun. The one-and-a-half-story, 22x35-foot building, constructed by A.B. Hart, included a 10x10-foot porch. The upper floor was fitted for living rooms.

Unfortunately, Miss Thorber's tenure as a Greenwood school teacher did not last long. On Monday, December 6, 1897, she died at the home of Ralph Smailes after a short illness. According to the *Times*, Thorber "contracted a severe cold which superinduced fever. The latter appeared to have settled in the head and despite constant attention from Dr. Jakes and those who watched by her bedside, she never rallied after the relapse on Saturday." She was only 19 years old.

Meanwhile, back in September, 1896, Robert Wood was financing another "more or less business venture" to attract "attention and trade" to Greenwood. Nevertheless, noted the *Times*, the construction of the first hospital in the Boundary district was a "real and permanent benefit to the entire community."

Constructed on the hillside overlooking the town, the Greenwood Hospital commanded "a picturesque view of the valley and the pine-clad ranges in the distance." The hospital, built at an estimated cost of $10,000, was placed under the charge of Dr. Jakes, and in mid-September he moved his family from Boundary Falls and took up residence in the institution. Two months later, on November 19, the hospital was almost destroyed by fire.

Dr. Jakes discovered the fire between the hours of one and two in the morning and immediately spread the alarm. However, before the volunteer fire brigade could arrive at the scene, flames were seen issuing from the roof of the building. "Fortunately the air was very still," reported the *Times*, "and this, together with the praiseworthy exertions of the volunteers, alone saved the building from total destruction. The damage to the roof and walls is estimated at $1,000, and furniture was destroyed to the value of $500. The origin of the conflagration is not known but it is attributed to a spark from a fire that had been left burning in the grate of one of the rooms on the second floor. Hart, the contractor, proceeded on the following day to repair the damage." By mid-December the fire damage had been repaired.

On December 19, the *Times* described the improvements made to Greenwood's third hotel, the International. "All the rooms are large and well lighted, and the barroom is supplied with a capital billiard table. Twelve bedrooms and a sitting room on the third floor have been plastered and kalsomined, and finished in natural woods, brilliantly polished. The furniture which arrived this week from Spokane, is of a very superior quality, the bedroom suites being particularly handsome. A layer of cement between the floors serves affectively to deaden any sound from below. The hotel is heated throughout with hot air, and the temperature in each room may thus be regulated at will."

GREENWOOD'S FIRST HOTEL

SOMETIME in December, 1895, Frank Wood, Robert Westel and a man known only as Hubble, formed a partnership and decided to erect a hotel in Greenwood. With the nearest sawmill located at Midway, and lumber costing $25 per 1,000 feet, the first "hotel" was necessarily small and primitive. Nevertheless, on December 31, a special dinner was given to celebrate the opening of Greenwood's first hostelry. A year later, the Boundary Creek *Times* published details of that less than memorable occasion:

"The guests partook of turkey, with oysters as the *piece de resistance* — the oysters, by the way, were also pioneers. It was remarked at the time that the guests, utterly disregarding all hygienic and gastronomic axioms with regard to the proper mastication of food, 'bolted' their dinner with indecent haste, no one waiting to hear the eloquent speeches that had been prepared for the occasion. The reason was obvious; The thermometer registered 12 degrees below zero and the hotel was made of green lumber, the wind playing high jinks through the cracks. Under these circumstances even turkeys and oysters cannot command the respect to which they are strictly entitled. No sooner, however, was the building knocked together than the proprietors, Messrs. Wood, Hubbell (sic) & Nelson (sic), were literally besieged with customers. The dining-room at meal times was a sight worth seeing; as many as 60 and 70 men sometimes crowding into the limited space, struggling for a place at the tables. When the more fortunate secured seats, they were urged in moving terms to lose no time in finishing their meal. Above the dining room was a loft or garret, wherein was placed six bunks supplied with straw mattresses. A man thought himself lucky then if he could call one of these luxuriant couches temporarily his own."

It should be noted that the *Times* was incorrect in listing John Nelson as one of the original owners of the Pioneer Hotel. The first crude building, which sat on lot 21, block 5 on Government Street, was erected by Wood, Hubble & Westel. On March 2, 1896, these three partners advertised that their enlarged premises, which now included lot 22, was "prepared to welcome guests and provide good accommodation." The 40x60-foot hotel contained nine bedrooms, an office, dining room and sitting room and included a first class livery stable in connection. What had been the original hotel, was now the barroom in the new building.

The partnership of Wood, Hubble & Westel remained in place until late July, 1896, when Hubble sold his interest to his partners and joined a former business associate in the hotel business in Rossland. About one month later, Westel disposed of his interest, and Frank Wood and John Nelson became joint owners. On November 12, Wood sold his interest to J.J. Caulfield, and the firm was then listed as Nelson & Co. This partnership continued until May 10, 1897, when it was dissolved and the hotel was then operated by Nelson & Tynan. This partnership was dissolved on November 17, 1897, after which the premises was owned by John and Susie Nelson.

That same week the newspaper noted that provincial constable F.R.M. Elkins, who had served for the North West Mounted Police for five years, had been transferred from Revelstoke to Greenwood.

By the end of December, 1896, some 300 town lots had been sold in Greenwood since March 1. From two small log cabins erected last Christmas, there were now nearly 50 fine business buildings alone, nearly every trade being represented in the town. Despite this phenomenal growth, or perhaps because of it, Government Street was described as an obstacle course: "there are certainly boulders innumerable, not to mention stumps, ups-and-downs, water holes and brush heaps."

In mid-December, Frank Wood had made arrangements with a Milwaukee firm to purchase a plant to produce soda-water. The machinery for the factory arrived on January 14, 1897, and was installed two days later. The plant had two 18 gallon fountains with a daily capacity of 6,000 bottles.

During the same week, Robert Wood sold a one-half interest in all the unsold lots in Greenwood to C. Scott Galloway, who also acquired "a half ownership in the Dillier pre-emption, adjoining the town, and in the property known as the 'Porter ranch' situated to the south of Anaconda, for the sum of $25,000."

By this time, Greenwood real estate was demanding high prices, the *Times* noting that an offer of $1,000 for a vacant lot next to the Pioneer Hotel had recently been refused. A week earlier, a lot on Silver Street that contained a small shack worth "perhaps $50 to $75 was sold for $450." In mid-February, J. Powell was offered $1,000

The Greenwood Hospital in 1900.

GREENWOOD HOSPITAL

The Boundary Creek *Times* described the Greenwood Hospital as "perhaps, the most pretentious building yet erected in the country between Vernon and Rossland. The building is three stories in height and has a basement beneath; it is 104 feet long by 56 wide. The outside is painted an olive green with old gold trimmings, and the roof a dull red relieved by a terra cotta belt-course." The basement contained the kitchen, store-rooms, laundry and morgue. "Here, too, is the large furnace, from which pipes running all through the building, maintain the atmosphere of any temperature that may be required. Through the main entrance one comes into a spacious hall, to the left of which is the doctor's consulting room, comfortably provided with a tiled fire-place and mantel, off from this is another small room, where, no doubt, many a nervous patient will tremulously await the physician's diagnosis deduced from the tell-tale evidence of a protruding tongue... To the right is the men's ward, a large, airy room with plastered walls, pleasingly tinted; partitioned off from the ward is the nurses' waiting-room, conveniently fitted with closets. The bath-room near-by, where an unlimited supply of hot or cold water will always be obtainable, is almost luxuriantly appointed and is a characteristic feature of the general idea which the architect has so successfully carried out.... Further on, in the left wing, is the ward for female cases. The room is like in size and appearance that on the other side of the building where male cases will be treated, but instead of being one large apartment, it is divided into several small rooms or cubicles. On this floor there is also the doctor's private parlor and dining room, and a ward dining room.

"Ascending the stairway with its balustrade of native tamarack, facing are two large rooms, one of which is to be called the guest chamber. On the left is a second bath-room, and turning to the right, with a view facing the town, are two handsome rooms intended for the private use of the doctor's wife. There is yet another flight to be climbed to the third floor, where the cistern is placed into which, until a regular water-works' system is carried out, a ram pumps a continual supply of pure water. The whole of this floor will be placed at the disposal of convalescent patients."

for two lots on Copper Street which he had purchased 10 months earlier for $100 each. During the first week of March, two vacant lots on Copper Street were sold for $850.

On February 9, the first bottles of "pop" to be manufactured in the Boundary Country went on the market in Greenwood. Local "connoisseurs" who sampled the contents, "passed a very favourable opinion." Frank Wood had apparently already received large orders for soda water from Carson, Grand Forks and other towns in the district. However, the rewards must not have been as great as first anticipated, for in April Wood sold the soda plant and went to Camp McKinney.

For those who preferred a stronger drink, the *Times* announced on February 28 that C. Scott was making plans to establish a brewery at Greenwood. Then, on March 13,

the newspaper reported that A. Smith, a brewer from Colfax, Washington, had obtained an acre of ground on the Dillier preemption to the north of town and intended to erect a brewery and manufactue beer. "Mr. Smith is now away, but is expected to return in a fortnight, bringing with him his plant, which has a daily capacity of 25 barrels. He is under contract to turn out 10 barrels, or 300 gallons, of beer per day. The brewery, which will be built at once, is to be a three-storey structure, 24x40 feet." On April 17, the *Times* announced that Otto Mangett, a brewer from Chewala, Washington, had let a contract "for the erection of a large building, to be used as a brewery, across Boundary Creek, on the Dundee addition to the townsite." According to the newspaper, the plant, with a 10 barrel capacity, was to be brought in at once and beer would be flowing by July 1.

Greenwood's first general store , owned by Robert Wood and Ralph Smailes, was the small log building seen in this rare photograph taken in 1897. When George Rendell decided to open a general store in Greenwood, he entered into a partnership with Wood and Smailes and constructed this larger, more appropriate building. The original store was then used as a warehouse.

For some reason, none of these projects appear to have been consummated, however. On July 17, the *Times* reported that Leibes & Forsechner, two experienced brewers, were waiting for their license and expected within the week to "supply a delectable fluid to satisfy the thirst of the most fastidious beer drinkers." This brewery was established in Anaconda. Finally, in November, Louis Blue visited Greenwood and made arrangements to establish a branch of the Lion Brewery. Based in Rossland, the Lion Brewery was one of the largest establishments of its kind in the province. The *Times* noted that the beer would be shipped from Rossland in carload lots and bottled in Greenwood.

Greenwood had expanded so much during 1897, that it would be impossible to record the numerous buildings that were constructed, or detail all the social activities that took place, in anything less that a book devoted entirely to the town. In April, electric street lights were installed in front of the Pioneer and Windsor Hotels. That same month, a telephone was established between Taylor's Drugstore and the hospital. Although these were only token efforts, they signalled Greenwood's progressiveness. In addition, through-

out the year streets were continually being cleared, graded and levelled, and some already boasted sidewalks. April also saw the establishment of a private banking business when the Bealey Investment Company was established.

By June, Greenwood was booming with summer trade. An example of this was the fact that during one two-day period, 23 freight teams delivered merchandise to the enlarged Rendell & Co. store alone. Even the *Times* was enjoying the prosperity. It had started as an eight-page newspaper, but had expanded to 12 pages in March. By the end of May it was 16 pages.

On the sport scene, a tennis club and baseball team was organized in June. In July, the baseball team played a match in Greenwood against a team from Nelson, Washington. "At the end of the fourth inning the score was even,"

A general view of Greenwood in 1897.

reported the *Times*, "but then the Greenwood team went to pieces and the match closed with a score of 35 to 17 in favor of the visitors. The big score was because of the rough ground, as it was almost impossible to field a ball among stumps and rocks."

Politically, the item of greatest importance during 1897 was the incorporation of the City of Greenwood on July 12, and the election of its first city council. The first mayor, elected by acclamation, was the town's founder Robert Wood. The first six aldermen were: John Hammil, George Rendell, Archie McKenzie, L.M. Barrett, M.J. Phelan and C.S. Galloway.

By October, surveyors for the Columbia & Western Railway had run a line through Greenwood, and by the end of the year, the City of Greenwood could boast of six hotels. But Greenwood's growth was attracting more that legitimate business enterprises. Some, whose public morals were best symbolized by the red curtains on their windows, were apparently becoming a particular nuisance, for, on November 20, the *Times* reported: "After considerable discussion the police officer was instructed to put the law in motion to rid Silver street of certain undesirable characters." Apparently Gold Street was another red light district.

In January, 1898, Robert Wood was elected to a second term as mayor, once again unopposed.

On April 26, Greenwood faced the nemeses of all frontier towns — fire. Smoke was first noticed coming from G.R. Naden's stable about 9 a.m. and the building was soon a mass of flames. "About 200 willing workers congregated and forming a bucket brigade succeeded in saving the valuable business houses in the vicinity. Rendell & Co.'s large store, the Bealey Investment & Trust Co.'s bank, Police Magistrate Hallett's office and Ald. Barrett's residence were in the most dangerous positions. In the stables was a quantity of baled hay and oats, which added fuel to the flames." Mrs. Naden's saddle horse was trapped in the stable, and it was only after considerable difficulty that the unfortunate animal was rescued. It had nearly suffocated from the smoke and was rather badly burnt.

"The wind in the morning was shifting and treacherous. It came up in

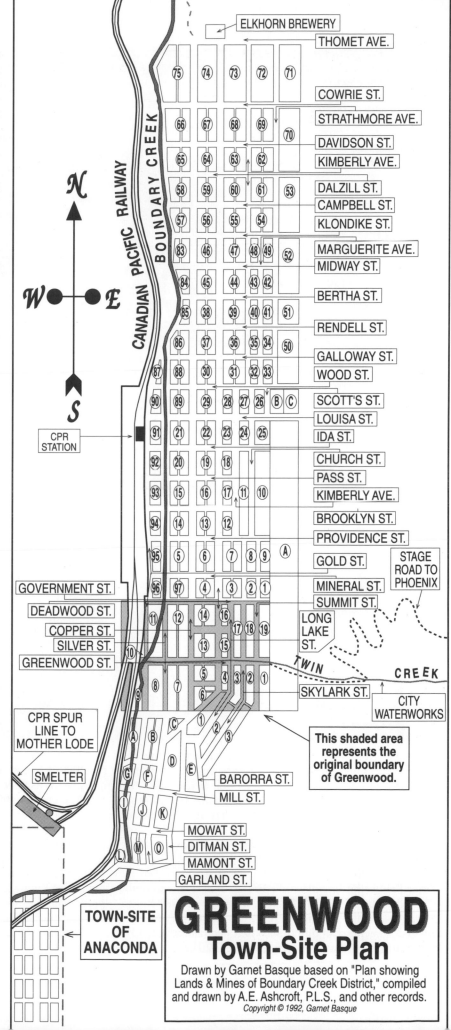

GREENWOOD
Town-Site Plan

Drawn by Garnet Basque based on "Plan showing Lands & Mines of Boundary Creek District," compiled and drawn by A.E. Ashcroft, P.L.S., and other records.

Copyright © 1992, Garnet Basque

Two general views of Greenwood's Copper Street. The above photo was taken in 1899, the peak year of construction. The three-story building on the left is the Windsor Hotel, which still stands in Greenwood today. This building was quite an improvement over the primitive building seen on page 65. The bottom photo, taken a couple of years later, shows the same Windsor Hotel with its bay windows. Opposite the Windsor is the now completed Commercial Hotel. On the same side of the Commercial Hotel, the spire of the Rendell Block can be seen.

fierce gusts from every quarter, driving the flames towards Mayor Wood's and Mr. McMann's residences, then towards Ald. Barrett's and again towards Rendell & Co's. and the bank." It looked for awhile as if Alderman Barrett's fine new residence was going to burn up like its predecessor had in October of 1897, "but the bucket brigade did effective work under the guidance of Capt. Nelson and the other officers of the Volunteer Fire Department."

On June 26 a dedication ceremony was performed by Father Palmer for Greenwood's first church. Plans to build a catholic church had first been formulated by Father Rivers in August, 1897, during which time Robert Wood had donated an acre of land and $600 had been contributed by the faithful. Constructed by Derosier & Bourke at a cost of

$1,800, the Church of the Sacred Heart was 25x50 feet in size and 91 feet in height from the ground to the top of the cross. With its galleries, it had seating capacity for 500 people. The church still stands today on the hill overlooking Greenwood. (*See colour photo on page 47.*)

On September 10 and September 24, the *Times* ran separate articles on Greenwood's "building boom." In fact, there was so much new construction and additions being built that Greenwood carpenters were stretched to their limit. One thing Greenwood sorely needed, it seems, was a proper jail, the building now posing as a lock-up, according to the *Times*, was totally inadequate.

"Hugh McCallum, arrested last week charged with theft is now a free man. McCallum walked through the jail.

This was not a difficult thing to do as it was built on plans furnished by the late government. The jail building is deficient in everything except ventilation. There is plenty of that. The fresh breezes from the hills, the dust from Government street and everything else that floats through the air passes in and out through the cracks in the walls." This escape scenario would be repeated on other occasions.

Despite this particular irritant, the renewed activity soon drew the attention of the banking fraternity, and on November 2, the citizens of Greenwood arose to find not one, but two new banks in their midst. Reported the *Times:* "On Wednesday morning the Bank of British North America had a hastily prepared sign stretched across the Le Plant building on Copper street — a sign which announced in brief terms that this strong financial institution was ready to do business in Greenwood. Around the corner on Greenwood street, the Cosmopolitan restaurant building was also decorated with a similar sign. It told the surprised residents of the city that the Bank of Commerce was doing business.

"The Bank of British North America officials had been in the city for a few days and most of the people knew that they were sizing up the situation but few expected that they would open a branch for some time. The Bank of Commerce people did not arrive until Tuesday afternoon and scarcely any one knew they were in the city until they saw

Louis Blue, 1899

the sign on Wednesday morning. They went to work immediately upon their arrival, secured a building and were doing business sixteen hours after their arrival in the city.

"When it is considered that both institutions are backed by millions of paid up capital and take a leading place among unbreakable chartered banks of Canada, their Greenwood offices on the day of opening were amazingly plain as far as their interior fittings went."

In fact, a *Times* reporter was astonished to see W. Godfrey, manager of the Bank of British North America, "cashing a cheque on the billiard table in the Leplante building, receiving money on deposit, and opening accounts with merchants." The Bank of Commerce enjoyed slightly better arrangements, conducting business from the counter of the Cosmopolitan Restaurant.

Now it may seem odd that these two financial institutions opened for business in such a disorganized and primitive manner, which was not the original intention. The first bank to express an interest in Greenwood was the Bank of British North America. Back in September, 1897, bank inspector H.B. McKenzie had visited Greenwood with J.D. Sword. At that time the *Times* reported that McKenzie was impressed by "the substantial business appearance of Greenwood," and it expected a branch would be opened there before too long.

The Elkhorn Brewery, located north of the Greenwood city limits, c1899. When this photo was taken the brewery was owned by the Portman family. In the foreground is Mrs. Portman, Mr. Portman, John Portman and C. Thomet.

Next to express an interest was the Bank of Montreal, the *Times* reporting back on August 20, 1898, that officers of that bank had determined that Greenwood was the financial and commercial centre of the Boundary district, and they planned to open a branch "in a few weeks."

But nothing substantial occurred until Sunday, October 30, when W. Godfrey and W.T. Oliver, representing the Bank of British North America, arrived from Rossland accompanied by James Martin, MPP. After acquainting themselves with the local businessmen and visiting some of the mining properties, they realized Greenwood's advantages as a banking centre. Accordingly, Godfrey sent a telegram to Vancouver and soon received permission from the directors to establish a branch. Godfrey and Oliver then started to make arrangements to open in a few days, and intended to "furnish the building with the usual elaborate fittings." But on Tuesday afternoon, November 1, H.H. Morris and Mr. Scott, representing the Bank of Commerce arrived in the city. They must have learned about the plans of the Bank of British North America, for they immediately rented the Cosmopolitan Restaurant and began making preparations to open the following morning. When this information reached Godfrey, he had little choice but to open the same day in any manner possible, or be known as Greenwood's second bank.

Surprisingly, a week later Greenwood could boast of its third bank. On Wednesday, November 9, G.A. Henderson, manager of the Bank of Montreal in Vernon, and Mr. Seymour, arrived by the Penticton stage. Henderson had undoubtedly heard about the two other banks being established a week earlier, and he moved rapidly to protect the interests of the Bank of Montreal. He immediately leased the building previously occupied by Pat Burns & Co. and hired carpenters to make the necessary renovations. Although it opened a week behind the others, the Bank of Montreal had the advantage of conducting business among old clients, since most of Greenwood's businessmen previously had accounts with the Vernon branch.

In an attempt to be the first bank to open in Greenwood, the first Canadian Bank of Commerce operated from the counter of the Cosmopolitan Restaurant before occupying their own premises. The Boundary Creek Times *occupied the left half of the building.*

All in all, 1898 had been another banner year for Greenwood, with $14,000 spent on grading and improving the streets and $11,000 being expended on constructing waterworks. Greenwood, with a population of about 1,200, now had eight general stores, six completed hotels and two under construction, four lawyers, four assayers, four barbershops (six barbers), three banks, three doctors plus several stationery stores, livery stables, bakeries, harness shops and blacksmith shops and a number of other businesses. Greenwood also had a school, hospital, church and brewery, and an ice rink was under construction. During 1898 alone, nearly $70,000 had been spent in new construction. (*See Greenwood Building Improvements in 1898.*)

In January, 1899, because of his many business interests, Robert Wood decided not to run for mayor. Two men contested the position. Ralph Smailes, a partner of Robert Wood, was one of the first residents of Greenwood. His opponent, Thomas Hardy was one of the earliest pioneers of the Boundary district, having first established a hotel at Boundary Falls, then later at Anaconda, before moving to Greenwood. Thomas Hardy won the election by 21 votes, 81 to 60. Hardy was also reelected the following year.

In January, 1899, the city got its second newspaper when the Greenwood *Miner* made its appearance. This year would prove to be one of record-breaking growth for Greenwood. (*See Greenwood Building Improvements in 1899.*) From January 1 to mid-June, according to the *Times,* some $203,400 worth of construction had been completed. Perhaps the most surprising aspect of this new construction was the "substantial character" of some of the projects.

From an architectural standpoint, Rendell & Co.'s three-story block on the corner of Copper and Government streets was probably the handsomest building in the city. Built at a cost of $20,000, it had a 50-foot frontage on Copper Street and ran along Government Street for 75 feet.

Then, On June 18, a serious fire threatened the total destruction of Greenwood's business section. At 2:30 Sunday morning, a night watchman named McKenzie saw flames underneath the Clarendon Hotel (previously the Imperial), and immediately spread the alarm. The fire was soon working its way along the walls of the building, and by the time the volunteer fire fighters reached the scene the entire structure was a mass of flames. Although a hose was run from the fire hydrant above Government Street, and a stream of water was kept continuously on the flames, the fire had gained too much headway. A small frame building, used as an assay office by J.C. Luckenbel, stood on a lot between the Clarendon and International hotels. It was soon a mass of flames and served as a connecting link between the two establishments. For a time there was fear that dynamite had been stored in the assay office and spectators were ordered back to a place of safety. Fortunately, however, this proved not to be the case. After the Clarendon Hotel was consumed by the flames, the firemen switched their attention to the International Hotel, trying in vain to save it from destruction.

Between the International Hotel and its next intended victim, the Arlington Hotel, stood a vacant lot. The fire was raging with such intensity that, for a time, it appeared that the flames would bridge this gap and continue out of control through the entire business district. From the Arlington Hotel to Government Street there was no vacant lot, and businessmen fearing the worse were hastily removing merchandise from their stores, which they were certain would perish in the conflagration. The heat was so great that A.H. Sperry & Co.'s store, across the street from the Clarendon Hotel, caught fire. This was quickly put out by the firemen, however, and wet canvas was then spread over the roof to prevent a reoccurrence.

Despite the fact that the firemen had only one hose, they were successful in halting the fire's advance at the International Hotel. Although only three buildings were destroyed, the losses were rather substantial. The Clarendon Hotel had been elaborately fitted up and carried a large stock of the very best liquors and cigars. The day before the fire a carload of supplies had arrived and been stored in the hotel. The loss of building and supplies totalled $11,000, of which $4,500 was insured. E. Escalet, who operated the Clarendon Cafe in the hotel, lost an additional $2,500, none of which was insured. The loss to the assay office and supplies totalled $900, of which $250 was insured. The International, owned by Louis Bosshart, was one of the oldest hotels in Greenwood. Its value is not recorded, but it was insured for $4,000. Although the cause of the fire was not learned, arson was suspected.

Less than two months later, Greenwood was hit by another fire. This one was first detected between two and three o'clock on August 3 by officer Lawder, who first noticed flames under Heaton's barbershop in the Pacific Block and spread the alarm. Volunteer fire fighters responded immediately and this time they had two streams of water to apply to the flames. Despite this, however, it was impossible to save the Pacific Hotel, so firemen directed their attention in trying to saving nearby buildings. In a short time the Windsor Hotel on the

The Rendell Block on the corner of Copper and Greenwood streets was constructed in 1899 at a cost of $20,000. The top floor of the building was removed in the 1940s, but the rest of the building still stands in Greenwood today.

GREENWOOD BUILDING IMPROVEMENTS IN 1898

During 1898 a large number of business blocks were erected. It is difficult to give an exact estimate of the cost of the buildings erected, as no record was kept, and many small residences were built in all parts of the city. The cost of each is small but the total is quite a large sum of money.

Below is a detailed statement of the building operations during 1898. Several small buildings may have been missed, but it will give a fairly good idea of the value of improvements during 1898:

Business Establishments Value

Barrett Block, Copper Street	$ 6,000
Barrett residence, Government Street	4,500
Windsor Hotel, Copper Street	2,600
Flood Block, Copper Street	2,500
Greenwood Hotel	2,500
Pioneer Hotel, additions	2,500
Cohen building	2,000
Rendell & Co., Greenwood Street	2,000
Keough building	1,900
McKague Block, Copper Street	1,800
Roman Catholic Church	1,800
St. Charles Hotel, Copper Street	1,700
Barnard store, Government Street	1,700
Bannerman Bros. store, Copper Street	1,500
Bealey-Flood basement	1,500
Ottawa House	1,200
Sperry & Co, store, Copper Street	1,200
Miller Bros., drugstore, Copper St.	1,000
S. Shaeffer building	1,000
Barnard residence, Long Lake Street	900
Barnard basement	900
G.H. Collins residence	900
Rendell & Co., bonded warehouse	850
Butler, harness shop, Copper Street	800
G.B. Taylor residence	800
Hardy building, Copper Street	800
R. Wood, residence addition	750
Elliot residence	700
L. Ostroski residence	700
Burn's building, Copper Street	700
Restaurant and barber shop	700
A.N. Other residence	650
Weldmark residence	600
Edwards residence	600
Palmer residence	500
P. Burns & Co. meat market	500
Campbell & Cropley store	500
Porter residence	450
McKenzie residence	400
Thomas Miller store	400
Restaurant, Greenwood Street	400
Assay Office, Government Street	300
Rendell & Co., Inland Revenue Office	300
Sundry small residences	10,000
Repairs and excavating	3,000
TOTAL	69,000

south, and Hallet & Shaw's law office on the north of the Pacific, were also in flames.

Although firemen were able to save the shell of the Windsor, the interior of the hotel was totally gutted. Valued at $15,000, it was only insured for $3,500. Hallet & Shaw's building, valued at $2,000, was also destroyed. Henton's barbershop and contents, where the fire originated, was valued at $1,200, of which $500 was insured. Henry Sauve's loss amounted to $200, and the Greenwood Trading Co. lost $200 in damaged goods. The heaviest losers, however, were

GREENWOOD BUILDING IMPROVEMENTS IN 1899

OWNER	DESCRIPTION/LOCATION	VALUE	OWNER	DESCRIPTION/LOCATION	VALUE
Rendell & Co.	50x75, 3-story block, corner Copper & Greenwood	$20,000	Caulfield & Lamont	25x50, 2-story building, Copper Street	$ 2,500
George Block	2-story, Copper Street	$18,000	H. Johns	residence	$ 2,500
J.P. Armstrong	60x90, 3 story hotel, cr. Gov't. & Deadwood	$18,000	Posty & Villandre	2-story hotel, Government Street	$ 2,500
Naden-Flood	50x85, 2-story block	$15,000	Swayne	25x75, 2-story block, Silver Street	$ 2,500
Alhambra Hotel	50x95, 3-story hotel & theatre, Deadwood Street	$14,000	W.S. Fletcher	stone foundation, corner Copper & Deadwood	$ 2,500
Grahame & Perry	3-story hotel, corner Copper & Deadwood	$12,000	Robert Wood	two residences, Kimberly Street	$ 2,300
Sperry & Co.	25x110, 2-story brick store, Copper Street	$12,000	A.T. Kendrick	2-story residence	$ 2,000
Guess Brothers	25x50, 2 story brick block, Copper Street	$10,000	Munroe	25x40, 2-story building, Copper Street	$ 2,000
Hunter-Kendrick	2 story brick store, corner Copper & Deadwood	$10,000	Pat Burns & Co.	warehouse & cold storage	$ 2,000
Louis Bosshart	50x65, 3-story store	$ 9,500	Smith & McRae	30x30 store addition, Copper Street	$ 2,000
New Pacific Hotel	50x75, 2-story, Copper Street	$ 9,000	W.E. Medill	residence	$ 2,000
Louis Forchner	3-story hotel, Government Street	$ 7,500	Mrs. Smith	2-story residence, Gold Street	$ 1,900
City of Greenwood	City Hall & Fire Station, Greenwood Street	$ 7,500	Thomas Hardy	residence	$ 1,800
Walter Waterland	50x80, 2-story hotel, Copper Street	$ 7,500	Dawson & Craddock	25x60, 1 story store, Copper Street	$ 1,500
Old Pacific Hotel	burned down in June, Copper Street	$ 6,000	I.H. Hallett	1½-story residence	$ 1,500
Andrew, Sater & Johns	25x75, 3 story hotel, Copper Street	$ 5,500	John Empey	office & residence	$ 1,500
David Manchester	25x70, 3-story hotel, Copper Street	$ 5,500	McMillan Brothers	25x60, grocery store, Copper Street	$ 1,500
International Hotel	alterations & additions, corner Copper & Greenwood	$ 5,000	Methodist Church		$ 1,500
Masonic Building	2-story store & hall, Government Street	$ 5,000	Dr. Schon	residence	$ 1,500
Robert Wood	2-story block, Government Street	$ 5,000	F.W. Hart	cottages	$ 1,200
Thomas Walsh	25x65, 3-story hotel, Copper Street	$ 5,000	Ford	25x49, 2-story store	$ 1,200
Miller & Wallace	3-story block, Copper Street	$ 4,500	White & Mitchell	25x40, store	$ 1,200
Barrett & Hodgson	alterations to hotel, Copper Street	$ 4,000	George Guess	50x150, skating rink	$ 1,200
Yale-Kootenay Lumber	offices & buildings, near CPR Depot	$ 4,000	D. McKinnon		$ 1,000
Robert Wood	alterations & additions, Government Street	$ 3,600	Stoeke	25x40, butcher shop, Copper Street	$ 1,000
Cooper & Seymour	25x57, 3-story hotel, Copper Street	$ 3,500	Williams	25x40, 1 story store, Copper Street	$ 1,000
Russell & Co.	2-story hardware store	$ 3,500	J. Sutherland	store, Silver Street	$ 800
City of Greenwood	2-story school, north end	$ 3,500	H.A. King & Co.	alterations to store	$ 770
CPR	freight shed & warehouse	$ 3,000	Mrs. O'Neil	25x40, 2-story restaurant, Copper Street	$ 750
Baptist Church		$ 3,000	Eles	residence, Long Lake Street	$ 600
Reneault & Gauvreau	hotel, Silver Street	$ 3,000	Bannerman Brothers	warehouse, near CPR Depot	$ 500
Thomas Walsh	2-story hotel (burned), Copper Street	$ 3,000	J.A. Russell	warehouse, near CPR Depot	$ 500
W. Kirkwood	2-story residence	$ 3,000	Miller Bros.	alterations to drug store	$ 500
J.H. McFarland	residence	$ 2,500	Sperry & Co.	warehouse	$ 500
R.J. Bealey	25x50, 2-story store, Copper Street	$ 2,500	Thomas Walsh	1-story building, Copper Street	$ 400
Butler	25x50, 2-story store, Copper Street	$ 2,500	Arthur Mowat	office, Copper Street	$ 350
			C.J. McArthur	residence, Kimberly Street	$ 350
			Wilson	residence, Silver Street	$ 225
			50 small residences	Throughout Greenwood	$10,000
			B.C. COPPER CO. SMELTER		
			B.C. Copper Co.	34x70 assay office	$ 2,600
			B.C. Copper Co.	45x100, boiler & blower house	$ 1,500
			B.C. Copper Co.	28x42, barn building	$ 600
			B.C. Copper Co.	16x32, office building	$ 500
			B.C. Copper Co.	16x50, foreman's office	$ 500
			B.C. Copper Co.	24x44, storehouse	$ 400
			B.C. Copper Co.	26x42, carpenter shop	$ 375
			B.C. Copper Co.	20x30, blacksmith shop	$ 250

Madden & Dallas, owners of the Pacific Hotel. Their building and contents were valued at about $14,000, only $4,900 of which was insured.

There were a lot of similarities between this fire and the one that had occurred back in June. Each was discovered in the early morning, and each began under a building. There was little doubt now that an "incendiary" was responsible. However, although an investigation was made, no one was ever caught.

Despite these two "fiery" setbacks, Greenwood lost barely a step. By September, the city had a new Baptist Church and a new Methodist Church. This was also the month that construction of the B.C. Copper Co.'s smelter at Anaconda began. At four o'clock Wednesday afternoon, October 18, 1899, Greenwood celebrated another milestone when the first train, "decorated with Union Jacks and Old Glories," made its way into Greenwood. In November, another big hotel opened its doors.

"Greenwood can now boast a really first-class hotel," reported the *Times*. "The hotel Armstrong has been elaborately furnished and is now prepared to welcome guests. The hotel from the kitchen to the attic shows that a master hand had direction of the furnishing. Nothing has been spared that would add to the comforts of the guests. The 54 bedrooms are all supplied with handsome sets and are carpeted and otherwise furnished in a manner that will satisfy the requirements of the most fastidious. The parlors, offices, bathrooms, etc., are all fitted on the same elaborate scale."

As 1899 drew to a close, the population of Greenwood stood at about 3,500. Although the pace of construction in the last six months of the year slowed somewhat over the first six months, there was still an impressive $320,000 in new buildings for the year. However, Greenwood was not all happiness and prosperity. Like most towns and mining camps in the Boundary district, serious crime was seldom a problem in Greenwood. However, there was always the minor disturbances; drinking, gambling and prostitution. The city made an honest effort to eliminate all three, but, as today's law enforcers are well aware, prostitution is difficult to eradicate.

Since it was considered a blight on the town, prostitution was seldom mentioned in the local press. But at the end of October an incident occurred in a house of ill repute that made front page headlines in the *Miner*. It appears that Annie Moore, one of the soiled doves of Gold Street, had an amorous suitor who desired more that the occasional quick fix. The man's name was David Bryant, and he was deeply in love with Annie. "It had long been his desire to sell his claims, and take her out of the life of shame she led, marry her and give her a home of her own. He was getting old, had had few of the pleasures of comforts of home life, and wanted to settle down peacefully for the rest of his days."

Annie confessed to having deep affections for Bryant, and might even have married him one day. However, Bryant was a jealous man who hated to see Annie talking to another man. Naturally, he would get rather upset when he paid her an unannounced visit and found her in the arms of a paying customer. Annie suggested that Bryant should stay away during her "working hours," but he never did.

Finally, the strain became too much for Bryant and he threatened to kill himself if his financial and love affairs did not improve. On the night of his death, he called on Annie several times, only to find her with other men. Each time he left, apparently in good spirits, he had a few drinks, then returned. The last time he returned, at 10:30 p.m., he was greeted by one of Annie's "hostesses," Jessie Montgomery. Bryant asked to see Annie and was sent to her bedroom. A few minutes later Annie appeared and, after a brief conversation, Bryant pulled a 45-calibre Colt revolver and pointed it at her. There was a brief struggle during which Annie tried to take the gun away from Bryant. Finally Bryant pushed Annie aside, put the weapon to his breast and pulled the trigger. The bullet tore through his heart and killed him instantly.

The mere fact that the death had occurred in a house of prostitution was enough to suspect foul play. However, the coroner's investigation concluded that it was a case of suicide over a love affair that had gone sour. It was a sad ending to the life of an old, and well-liked prospector.

As the new year dawned, Greenwood continued to move forward, and in February, 1900, the town was illuminated by electric lights. "The light is very steady," noted the *Miner*, "and gives excellent satisfaction. Street lights will be installed without delay." Less than a month later the same paper noted that 1,500 lights had been turned on and more were being added daily.

If 1899 could be noted for Greenwood's phenomenal growth, 1900 was probably best noted for crime. It began in February when four stores were robbed on four consecutive nights by what the *Times* described as "a gang of burglars."

The first robbery occurred on Wednesday, February 21, when G.S. Watson's small fruit and cigar store, adjoining the Pacific Hotel, was burglarized. Watson stated that his door was still locked the following morning, but since the lock was old, it would have been easy for "any professional burglar" to open. As the amount taken, "about $5 in cash in cigarettes," was small, it was not even mentioned in the paper at the time.

The following evening, the store of A.H. Sperry was entered and the cash register was relieved of its loose change, amounting to $19.10. Nothing else was taken.

Friday night the scene of operations shifted to Greenwood Street where the second hand store of A.L. White was broken into. This time the burglars appeared to be bolder, and actually lit several matches to enable them to be selective in their theft. They made off with four or five antiquated watches, three Clauss and one Hindu razor.

On Saturday night the robbers hit the store of the Greenwood Trading Co. on Copper Street. Like the previous night, entry was gained by cutting a glass panel out of the rear door. In addition to eight or nine dollars, the thieves stole "several pairs of boots and shoes, underclothing and some shirts. The goods on the shelves were considerably disturbed and it is impossible to say how much was taken."

A month later, Greenwood's tenderloin district became the source of irritation. Mamie Foster, a black prostitute conducting her trade on Gold Street, had been before the police on other occasions. This time she was charged by Hugh Sweeny of having robbed him of $40. Foster, of course, denied the charge, and the evidence presented by both sides was very contradictory. No decision was reported by the *Times*, but Police Magistrate Hallett instructed the police to warn the city's soiled doves that henceforth, any woman charged with soliciting would receive a prison sentence instead of being fined.

On June 30, crime took a major leap forward when Theo Moran was stabbed by a Frenchman named Roe. The incident occurred in the Alberta Hotel, and was precipitated when Roe, "under the influence of liquor," insulted Moran's wife. Moran beat Roe with his fists, and the matter should have ended there. But a short time later Roe obtained a knife and lunged at Moran, stabbing him near the heart and across the abdomen. Although the wounds were serious, Moran apparently recovered.

After the assault, Roe fled the premises, chased by an excited crowd. He was finally captured by the chief of police in the valley opposite the Miner's Hotel. Roe was then taken to the city lock-up, despite warnings that the culprit could easily escape from there. To prevent that from happening, the police took the extra precaution of applying heavy shackles. This, unfortunately, did not deter Roe. "His method of escape was simple in the extreme," reported the *Times*. "He went into an upper bunk in his cell, placed his feet against the ceiling, pressed against it and the plank was lifted, as it had never been nailed. It was then an easy matter to jump into the police court room and walk out into the street." Although a reward of $25 was offered for his capture, there is no record to indicate he was ever seen again.

Greenwood's first murder occurred on Wednesday evening, October 17, 1900, in a small shack about 200 yards from the CPR depot. The owner of the cabin, Manuel Poiston, arrived home from work at 6 p.m. and found the cabin door locked as usual. However, upon opening the door and lighting a candle, Poiston discovered blood on the floor and saw a hand sticking out from under the bed. Samuel Feora lived in a nearby cabin with his son, and upon discovering the grisly scene, Poiston ran from his cabin shouting "Sam, Sam," unaware that the man he was trying to obtain help from was actually the murder victim.

Joe Feora, the 19-year-old son of the deceased, was in the cabin preparing supper when he heard Poiston's shouts and ran outside. Poiston told Joe that he had found a dead man in his cabin, and the two men returned to the scene. Upon entering the cabin, Joe recognized the clothes worn by the victim as those of his father, and pulled the body out from under the

Left: One of Greenwood's finest hotels, the Leland was built by J.W. Powell in 1899..

GREENWOOD HOTELS

EST.	HOTEL	ORIGINAL OWNER(S)	LOCATION
1896	Pioneer	Wood, Hubble & Westel	Lots 21 & 22, Block 5, Gov St.
1896	Windsor	Seymour & Webb	Lots 31 & 32, Block 7, Copper St.
1896	International	O.F. Mickle	Lots 18 & 19, Block 7, Copper St.
1897	Greenwood	Torney & Moran	Lot 22, Block 7
1897	Rossland	Alfred Cameron	Lot 30, Block 12
1897	Pacific	Henry Madden	Lots 33 & 34, Block 7
1897	Commercial	Barrett & Hodgson	Lot 5, Block 5, Copper St.
1897	Imperial	Grahame & Parry	Lot 13, Block 12
	(later Clarendon — 1899)		corner Copper & Gov. St
1898	St. Charles	Bedard & Berger	Lot 25, Block 12, Copper St.
1898	Ottawa	A. Bourke	Lot 3, Block D, Sutherland add.
1899	Kootenay	Thomas Walsh	Lot 16, Block 7, Copper St.
1899	Alberta	Reneault & Gauvreau	Lot 4, Block 12, Silver St.
1899	Arlington	Cooper & Seymour	Lot 22, Block 7, Copper St.
1899	Armstrong	J.P. Armstrong	cnr. Government & Deadwood
1899	B.C.	Louis Forchner	Lots 15 & 16, Block 11
1899	Central	Posty & Villandre	Lot 10, Block 3, Government St.
1899	Leland	J.W. Powell	Lots 9, 10, 11 & 12, Block 4
1899	Log Cabin	J.J. Miller	near Elkhorn Brewery
1899	Miner's	Walter Waterland	Lots 3 & 4, Block 5, Copper St.
1899	Queens	David Manchester	Lot 5, Block 14, Copper St.
1899	Alhambra		Deadwood Street
1899	Temperance		
	National	Cascaden & Hornley	Lots 18 & 19, Block 7
	Norden	Andrew, Sater & Johns	Lot 6, Block 14
	Royal	Poupore & McVeigh	Lots 27 & 28, Block F, Fisher addition
	Victoria	Gilbert Gunderson	Lot 24, Block 12

The above list has been compiled from information obtained from the Boundary Creek *Times* and Greenwood *Miner* and is as accurate as possible, although there appears to be some contradictions. The Clarendon and International hotels, for example, were only separated by one lot according to the report of the fire which occurred in June, 1899. However, the information above places them in totally different blocks. This could explained if the Clarendon, when rebuilt, was not located on its original site. The history of Greenwood's numerous hotels could comprise a project in itself, so much more detailed work is necessary on this subject.

A general view of Greenwood's commercial centre c1900, with Boundary Creek on the left.

bed. Joe later testified that his father always carried between $1,100 and $1,200 in the pockets of his pants, but he found the pockets empty.

Chief McLaren, accompanied by Dr. Jakes, rushed to the scene, where the body of Samuel Feora, an Italian section hand, was examined. Jakes estimated that he man had been dead four or five hours. Dr. Foster, who later performed a post mortem, reported: "On examination I found a large lacerated wound on left side of head and in front of ear, wound about two inches in length, edges everted and ragged. On left side, behind the ear, I found another wound with edges inverted and depressed. Around these wounds was a great deal of charring." Further evidence revealed two bullet holes, with one of the slugs still inside the brain tissue.

After hearing all the evidence, the coroner's jury returned a verdict of "murder by some person or persons unknown." Both city and provincial policemen were assigned to the case, but there is no record of the murderer ever having been brought to justice.

Mining activity in the Boundary Country was depressed in 1900, part of the reason being, according to the *Times*, because of the Boer War. But there were other, more important factors. The Rothchilds and Rockerfellers had controlled world copper production for years. With the blowing-in of the B.C. Copper Company's smelter near Greenwood, and the record-setting pace at which copper was flowing from the Boundary Country, this upstart was fast becoming a threat to the American giants. So, in an attempt to curtail competition, they dumped hundreds of thousands of tons of ore on the international market. This immediately resulted in deflated copper prices and caused a temporary recession. Whatever the contributing factors, by the end of December, 1900, Greenwood's population had dropped to about 3,000, from a previous high of about 3,500.

During the spring of 1903, the coal mines in the Crows Nest Pass seemed to dominate the news. They supplied desperately needed coke for the furnaces, without which the smelters at Boundary Falls, Anaconda and Grand Forks could not operate. In January, the *Times* reported that the B.C. Copper Company's furnaces had to be blown out because of a lack of coke. On February 13, the paper reported that the coal miners were on strike at the Crow's Nest Pass Coal Company. With the coal mines and coke ovens closed, the mining and smelting operations of the Boundary ground to a halt. Two weeks later, with the strike no nearer to being resolved, the *Times* noted that an "exodus of mine and smelter employees, thrown out of work by the stoppage of fuel supplies from the Crow's Nest Pass coal mines, is taking place." Finally, on April 3, the newspaper was able to report that the strike had been resolved and a new two-year collective agreement had been reached.

Despite the desperate state of affairs that had resulted from the strike, Greenwood still managed to build some substantial structures in 1903. One was a new public school, built at a cost of $10,000. The other was a new, two-story, 44x62-foot provincial court house. The main floor contained offices and a jail, the top floor being used as the court room. Although built at a cost of $15,000, the *Times* was not very impressed with the final appearance of the building. Upon its completion in late September, 1903, the *Times* described

A general view of Greenwood c1900. The B.C. Copper Co.'s smelter can be seen in the distance, while the majestic Hotel Armstrong is visible in the lower right. The town of Anaconda existed just out of view to the top left, where Boundary Creek flows out of the photo.

it thus: "Viewed from the outside the building in colour and design resembles the barn of a well to do Ontario farmer, while its internal divisions are a marvel of inconvenience and architectural stupidity."

Another sour note, according to the *Times*, was supplying the building with used furniture from the Armstrong Hotel. "No man putteth new wine in old bottles, but in furnishing the court house the government agent has scorned this old maxim. The major portion of the furnishings that adorn the new building have done duty for years in one of the principal hotels of Greenwood, and not being worth moving to another locality were turned over to the B.C. Government for use in the new court house.

"They may have been purchased at a bargain. It may be business. It may be true economy in public service, but in our opinion the province is yet well able to properly furnish its public institutions without indulging in the second hand business."

By the end of November, Greenwood had rebounded from the economic slum caused by the lack of coke, and the *Times* reported that all the houses in the city were rented. The atmosphere of Greenwood had changed as well. Although the population of Greenwood was less than it was three years earlier, it was of a more permanent nature. As the *Times* noted: "Three years ago the hotels and blocks were filled by men who were here today and gone tomorrow; today the houses are filled with families whose breadwinners have decided to make Greenwood their home."

Although Greenwood continued to prosper, the heady days of 1899-1900 would never be seen again. Unfortunate-

ly, space limitations prevent me from continuing on with a detailed history of Greenwood. In fact, much more details could have been provided during the period already covered if this book was dedicated entirely to the city. Since this is not the case, and since Greenwood's heyday was now over, I will only briefly touch upon its more modern history.

On March 12, 1907, the Pacific Hotel was nearly destroyed by fire for a second time. The fire began around two o'clock in the morning while Howard Moore, the night cook, was frying several steaks. In seconds the range and entire kitchen were engulfed in flames. Fortunately, firemen were soon on the scene and prevented the fire from spreading to the adjoining Windsor Hotel. The lower floor was not badly damaged, except for the kitchen which, with the upper floor, was a total ruin. Gregg & Morrison's loss was about $10,000, half of which was insured.

Just over a month later, on April 15, Greenwood faced the fiery demon once again, this time with more disastrous results. The fire started about one o'clock in the morning in a small building opposite the Alberta Hotel on Silver Street. It was owned by the Stooke Bros. and was occupied by a Chinese laundry, the operators of which slept upstairs. The first eyewitnesses to the fire claimed that by the time the alarm was sounded, the entire front of the building was burning fiercely.

"The inmates of the building, numbering three, all slept upstairs," reported the *Times*, "and evidently made a rush to save their lives. Their bodies were all found at the foot of the stair, where they had evidently perished, rather from suffocation than fire, as the bodies were not burned beyond recognition." The three Chinese victims were "Quong Wong Hop, who ran the laundry, one Fool Keo, a domestic servant, for several years in the family of W.T. Hunter, and one 'Jim' a janitor about town.

The coroner's jury did not give any explanation as to the cause of the fire, although the *Times* suggested it appeared to have been deliberately set. As for the death of the three Chinese tenants, the *Times* felt that their living habits was a contributing factor, and warned that if the city did not exercise its authority over buildings of this type, a similar disaster might occur again. "Rudely constructed, densely tenanted, and with no adequate means of hurried escape, many of the Chinese tenants are a menace to the city and life."

Fires continued to plague Greenwood in 1908. On April 18, a fire totally destroyed the Elkhorn Brewery. By the time the fire was first detected, about 11 o'clock in the morning, it was blazing fiercely. Unfortunately, the brewery was located north of town, just outside the city limits. As a result, the hose from the wagon would not reach from the nearest fire hydrant. Although some of the stock was saved, the loss totalled $30,000, of which only $5,000 was insured. J.R. Docksteader had purchased the Elkhorn Brewery from Mr. Portman two years earlier, and since that time had been improving his plant and equipment.

During the same week, fire destroyed the slaughter house of Pat Burns & Co., at Anaconda. Of the 13 head of cattle that had been slaughtered during the day, half were destroyed in the fire. The total loss was $5,000, $2,000 of which was insured. The newspaper reported that construction of both the brewery and slaughter house was expected to begin immediately.

On September 19, a fire that had initially threatened the entire city, resulted in $10,000 damage. This fire originated in a building owned by Mrs. R.A. Bealey, and in which Mrs. Darling ran a "clothes-cleaning" establishment. Mrs. Darling apparently accidentally set fire to a can of gasoline, which exploded and set fire to the premises. Mrs. Darling, her clothing ablaze, ran into the street screaming. Passers-by acted quickly to extinguished the flames from her garments, but she was none-the-less severely burned about the arms and face.

Five minutes later the hose wagons were on the scene and six heavy hoses were spraying water on the flames. In 20 minutes firemen had the fire under control, although the fire had by that time spread out along a 100-foot street frontage. The Victoria Hotel and its contents was a total loss, as was Mrs. Darling's premises. The upper story of Holmes & Kennedy's building was gutted, and the stock and furniture suffered greatly from water damage. Jaynes' grocery enjoyed a little better fate. Practically all of their stock had been removed and the store reopened for business that same

Isaac Hallett and his son Jim, 1902. This photo was taken in front of his Greenwood home. Hallett was originally from Sussex, New Brunswick.

evening from a building across the street.

One of the more interesting projects associated with Greenwood was the scheme to construct a tunnel from Greenwood to Phoenix in order to tap the surface veins at depth. In February, 1908, Richard Armstrong, representing a number of Chicago capitalists, made such a proposal to Greenwood's city council. According to Armstrong, a 9-foot by 9-foot tunnel would be constructed from the base of Strathmore Mountain all the way to the Granby mines at Phoenix. In the first 3,000 feet, explained the tunnel's promoter, seven known veins would be cut, four on the Strathmore claim and four on the Defiance. Between the Defiance and the Crescent claims, about 3,000 feet further, it would cut across 11 more veins.

The *Times* reported that the project was given "an enthusiastic endorsation" by the largest meeting of the Board of Trade to assemble in Greenwood for a long time. However, a slight glitch appeared the following month when the B.C. government refused to amend the Municipal Clauses Act to enable Greenwood to give the promoters a subsidy. G.R. Naden, member of the legislature for Greenwood, tried to get the government to change its mind by informing them that the entire tunnel would be 15,000 to 20,000 feet long and cost over $1,000,000. Of this, Greenwood was only asked to provide a $50,000 grant.

Despite this setback, the Greenwood-Phoenix Tunnel Company Ltd., with a capitalization of $5,000,000, was established two months later. However, it was nearly a year later, in March, 1909, before Armstrong arrived in Greenwood to commence the project. A month later, on April 9, the taxpayers of Greenwood, in a "sweeping majority of 114," passed a bylaw that permitted the city to grant the $50,000 bonus.

With this final hurdle overcome, construction was finally started, and on May 15 the Phoenix *Pioneer* reported that the tunnel was 20 feet underground. A week later the 100-foot mark had been reached. This was relatively good time, but not, apparently, fast enough for Armstrong. He told the *Pioneer* that negotiations were underway to purchase a $60,000 Swiss-Chandler drilling machine that was capable of cutting an "eight foot bore at the rate of 50 feet a day."

By August 7, the tunnel had reached the 250-foot mark. Nothing further was heard of the project until February 25, 1910, when the *Times* reported that the tunnel, advancing "at the very respectable rate of 10 feet per day," was now 400 feet into the mountain. Obviously, since only 150 feet had been drilled during the past six months, there must have a prolonged work stoppage.

It would be over one year later, March 4, 1911, before progress of the tunnel was again reported. This time the *Pioneer* noted that the tunnel was in 1,460 feet and 24 men were

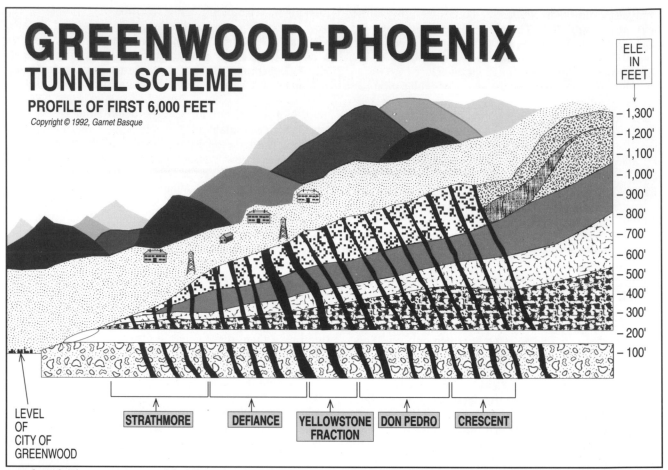

GREENWOOD-PHOENIX
TUNNEL SCHEME
PROFILE OF FIRST 6,000 FEET
Copyright © 1992, Garnet Basque

ELE. IN FEET

— 1,300'
— 1,200'
— 1,100'
— 1,000'
— 900'
— 800'
— 700'
— 600'
— 500'
— 400'
— 300'
— 200'
— 100'

LEVEL OF CITY OF GREENWOOD

STRATHMORE DEFIANCE YELLOWSTONE FRACTION DON PEDRO CRESCENT

employed. The newspaper added that "ore is not expected to be struck until about 2,300 feet." This seems rather odd, because in the original plans, it was expected to cut through 11 different veins by the time the 3,000-foot level had been reached. No explanation was given to explain why no veins had yet been struck. Perhaps they had merely been surface showings that did not continue to depth. In any event, ore was finally struck at the 1,800-foot level in mid-April, with the *Pioneer* claiming that it was "one of the most important strikes made in the Boundary Country for years." However, despite this optimistic note, nothing further is heard of the tunnel project until August 14, 1915, when the *Pioneer* reported: "The resumption of work on the Phoenix-Greenwood (sic) tunnel is to be considered at a meeting of the company in Chicago on September 1st." Results of that meeting were never publicized, but it appears the project was abandoned, probably a victim of high costs, almost non-existent returns, and a slumping copper market.

Twenty years later Greenwood, its population dwindled by the Great Depression, suffered its worst fire. According to T.W. Paterson's article "Historic Greenwood," the fire "erupted in the Imperial Garage, swept through the Ritz Cafe, Pincott and Pincott's law office, Charles King's insurance office, Gulley's undertaking parlor, a livery stable and the Greenwood Theatre, then jumped the street and threatened the government liquor store.." At this point the three-story Canadian Bank of Commerce was dynamited to create a firebreak. The strategy worked, continued Paterson, "although the force of the explosion shattered windows up to a block away. Damage was estimated at

$60,000. Less than three months later, a $20,000 blaze, which started during a blizzard consumed Trounsen's barber shop, Larsen's garage, Campbell's drugstore, Leask's drygoods store and the Mellor Block."

Greenwood's dwindling population received a big boost in 1942, although the 1,000 Japanese-Canadians who were interned in the city's vacant buildings were not there by choice. Prior to this Greenwood had only about 200 residents and the future did not look promising. Among the historic buildings renovated for living quarters were the Rendell Block, the Gulley Block, the Pacific Hotel and the Greenwood Club. The old Greenwood firehall was converted into a kindergarten for the Japanese children. A year after the war ended, about half of Greenwood's Japanese population had drifted away. Those who chose to remain told a Vancouver newspaper that they were happy in Greenwood.

Today, Greenwood's population is about 1,000. Visitors can still view quite a number of original business and residential buildings. In the last couple of years, assisted by B.C. government grants, the exterior of buildings on Copper Street have been repaired and painted, providing a typical frontier appearance. Greenwood has its own museum, located on Copper Street, where tourists can view old photographs and memorabilia of the city's past. As it was a century ago, Greenwood is centrally located to Deadwood and the Mother Lode, Anaconda, Phoenix and Eholt. With its modern motels, Greenwood can provide accommodation for visitors who may wish to explore these old townsites.

Deadwood/Mother Lode

Colin Scott McRae's cabin on the Deadwood Ranch. The cabin was built in October, 1894, and was destroyed by fire around 1935. This photo was taken c1907. (Left to right) Alex Bothwell, standing; Jack Luce, seated; Colin McRae, standing in doorway; Colin and Gordon McLaren, two boys; and Donald McLaren, far right. The man seated in doorway is unidentified.

IN the spring of 1891, two prospectors named William McCormick and Richard Thompson, intrigued by "a big copper-stained blowout" about three miles northwest of Greenwood, decided to investigate. On May 28, 1891, they located and staked the Mother Lode mineral claim. From that time until the summer of 1896, however, no work other than the assessment necessary to maintain their title to the claim was done. In June, 1896, Col. John Weir of New York, representing himself, F.L. Underwood and James F. Tichenor, purchased the property from the current owners, McCormick, McQuaig and Schofield, for $14,000. The Boundary Mines Company of New York was subsequently organized, and mining engineer Frederick Keffer of Anaconda was hired to develop the mine.

By the first week of September, a number of buildings had been erected, and on September 8 a cook arrived in camp. After a little surface exploration was done, a crosscut tunnel was started and run in 246 feet. A winze was sunk 152 feet from the mouth of the tunnel to the 100-foot level, where considerable undercutting was done. The owners

were soon pleased to learn that the "average values in the tunnel were much higher that the surface values, and the values on the 100-foot level were much higher than those in the tunnel." Put another way, the ore was richer the deeper they went.

In the spring of 1897, Keffer made a trip to New York, presumably to advise the investors firsthand on the mine's prospects. As a result, a new company called the British Columbia Copper Co., Ltd. was organized to develop the Mother Lode and to acquire adjoining properties. This new firm was capitalized for $1,000,000, divided into 200,000 shares worth $5 each.

"The company at once purchased a powerful plant from James Cooper & Co. of Montreal," reported the Boundary Creek *Times*, "representing the Ingersoll-Sergeant company. The machinery consists of one Ingersoll-Sergeant Class A air compressor, 18x24, for operating 10 drills; two 60-horse power horizontal tubular boilers with feed water heater and necessary pumps; one steel air receiver; air drills for compressor, 3¼ inches in diametre; all necessary mountings, hoses, etc.; one Northey-Cameron sinking pump, 10x5x13; one Ledgerwood reversible link hoisting engine, double cylinders, 8¼x10; drum, 30x26, and 600 feet wire rope; two steel ore cars, two ore and one water bucket, and over 2,500 feet of piping. There is also an electric light plant, consisting of an Ames Iron Works Lively engine and a 50 light Edison dynamo." By August, 1898, a large force of men were at work installing the plant under the supervision of Henry Johns.

Exactly one year later, on August 7, 1899, the Mother Lode claimed the first of its many victims. Dominic Matello, a 40-year-old Italian mucker, lost his life by falling to the bottom of a 215-foot shaft. According to the *Times*, the accident "was the result of carelessness on the part of Matello and the other men who were in the shaft with him." Upon reading the report, it does appear to have been a senseless tragedy that could easily have been avoided.

Signals had been devised to alert the man on the surface as to whether the bucket he was hoisting carried ore or men. The signal for hoisting ore was one bell, while hoisting men was 3-1. Continued the *Times*: "Matello and two other muckers got on the bucket, each thinking the other gave the proper signal to the engineer for hoisting men. But the engineer received only one ring — the signal for hoisting ore and the bucket came up at a much faster rate than is usual with men on. When it reached the top of the shaft the men became excited. The bucket went higher as is necessary to allow dumping the ore. Matello and one of his companions jumped, the other remained in the bucket. While his companion escaped clear of the shaft, poor Matello slipped and fell in, plunging to his death 215 feet below. He was frightfully mangled and death must have been instantaneous." His remains were buried in the Greenwood Cemetery.

By this time the Mother Lode, Sunset, Buckhorn, and other mines in the area were beginning to attract a great deal of attention. Although the nearest towns of Anaconda and Greenwood were only three miles away, Colin Scott McRae and Donald McLaren envisioned an opportunity for a new town-site. McRae was a prospector, trapper and taxidermist, and in his travels throughout the district, he came across a flat of land near the Mother Lode that would make an ideal ranch. McRae applied for a preemption, but as he was not a rancher, he did not want to go into the venture alone. McRae occasionally stayed at the Grande Prairie Hotel, in Carson, and during one of these visits in 1894, he convinced McLaren to go into a partnership with him. The exact date they preempted a 640-acre ranch is not reported, but back in October, 1894, the Midway *Advance* noted that

John East at his homestead on Ingram Mountain near Midway c1912. An early day prospector in the Boundary Country, East staked the Sunset mine at Deadwood.

McRae's new house was "completed and is reported to be the finest bachelor's hall in the country." McLaren, meanwhile, remained at his ranch at Carson.

In early December, 1899, McRae and McLaren decided to lay out a town-site on the northern portion of their ranch. As the "Deadwood" ranch was located in Deadwood Camp, it seemed only appropriate that the new town should be named Deadwood. There appears to be some uncertainty over the size of the original town-site. The Greenwood *Miner* claims it occupied a 40-acre site, while the *Times* said it was 80 acres. In any event, reported the *Miner*: "The lots will be 30 by 100 feet and streets 80 feet, with alleys 16 feet." Lots were expected to go on sale in 30 days.

On January 20, the *Times* described the new town-site, which was "traversed by the Deadwood spur of the Columbia & Western railway. It is an admirable location, on a series of gently sloping benches, covered with a light growth of timber and with abundance of clear spring water. But a beautiful location is not the only requisition for a prosperous town. Deadwood City is surrounded with developed mines and promising prospects.

"Immediately adjoining the town-site are the Ah There and Greyhound properties, both being developed. Nearby is the Sunset mine (staked by John East) that is now installing machinery and will shortly have a payroll of 40 or 50 men. Its next door neighbor, the famous Mother Lode, is ready to ship ore, and has made one shipment of 100 tons to the smelter, and the force is to be increased from 35 at present to 150 employees within the next 30 days.

"Yesterday a *Times* representative visited Deadwood City. The sound of the hammer was going merrily, for building has already commenced. W.T. Kaake, an enterprising hotel man from Phoenix, has finished his hotel (Columbia) and is doing business. (During the first week of March, 1900, Kaake sold the hotel to Robert Frey.) The Yale-Columbia Lumber Co. has a sawmill busy at work turning out lumber. The company has a dozen men at work on the townsite cutting timber, hauling and putting it through the mill. Foley Bros. and Walker & Posty, two Phoenix mercantile firms, are opening branches. H. Forbis of Nelson has secured lots and will build a hotel. J.P. Harlem is opening an assay office, and there are others whom the *Times* man was unable to obtain the names of who propose going into business in this, the latest townsite of the Boundary Creek district."

The town-site agent was James McNicol, the Midway general store merchant who had also established a branch at Anaconda.

On January 25, the *Times* reported: Deadwood "is a bustling little place just now. A large force is employed by the Yale-Columbia Lumber Co. in connection with their

(Above) Judge William Ward Spinks had enough faith in the future of Deadwood that he purchased several lots.
(Right)The Algoma Hotel, Deadwood c1934. For many years after the decline of the town, this hotel continued to serve trappers and prospectors in the area.

lumber mill at this point. The mill is being enlarged and considerable machinery added. Then too a force of men are working on the townsite erecting telephone poles. Others are clearing out timber and working on new buildings. The Columbia hotel is doing a good business and was crowded. A barber has opened up in the office of the hotel. Posty & Walker have about completed their building and today will have their stock of goods on the shelf. They are general merchants and the first ones to open up for business. What appears to be a flourishing business is the new laundry. Judge Spinks took a look at the townsite and was so satisfied that he made an investment in lots. A new hotel, livery barn, assay office and other buildings are shortly to be started."

By the first week of February, 45 town lots had been purchased at prices of $100 to $150, and the town was progressing rapidly. Foley Brothers, Phoenix general merchants, had established their store on the corner of Harlan and Third streets. W.J. Walker, also from Phoenix, had opened his grocery store on Harlan Street. Also on Harlan Street, near Fourth, was a restaurant conducted by Long & Elliott. Deadwood's second hotel, the Algoma, was erected between Third and Fourth streets. It was a substantial three-story building owned by former Nelson businessmen Hartman & Henderson. D.M. Wilkin's livery stable was located on Attwood Street. Wilson also conducted a twice-daily stage service between Deadwood and Greenwood.

Also on Attwood Street was an assay office owned by Mr. Harlan, after whom the principal street was named. Unfortunately, the only town-site plan that appears to have survived does not indicate the street names, so it is impossible to pinpoint the precise locations of these businesses.

On August 1, 1900, a post office was established in Deadwood with John Hambly as postmaster. During the fall of the same year, a one-room school was built on land donated by the town-site owners. Mildred Roylance, daughter of Donald McLaren, attended that school. In the Ninth edition of the *Boundary Historical Society* she wrote that the 23x28-foot school was built at a cost of $1,400.

Unfortunately, Deadwood, which in its first few months had held such promise, never really amounted to much of a town. It had been established to accommodate workers from nearby mines and, despite the fact that it was on the Columbia & Western railway spur to the Mother Lode, it's heyday had already passed. Of these mines, the

CPR trains loading ore at the Mother Lode mine c1903.

Mother Lode was by far the greatest producer. Entering production in 1900, 5,340 tons of ore was shipped during the year. In 1901, 120 to 150 men were employed by the mine, which shipped 99,034 tons of ore to its smelter at Anaconda. Building improvements made during the year included "a large general merchandise store, new blacksmith's shop, shaft houses," and new ore bins, which provided an additional capacity of 500 tons. In 1902, the Mother Lode shipped 141,326 tons of ore to the smelter, despite being shut down for a time because of coke shortages. During one week in October a record-setting 4,500 tons was shipped. By the end of the year, about 120 men were employed at the mine.

In March, 1903, the smelter was again forced to shut down because of a lack of coke. With no way of processing its ore, the work force at the Mother Lode was lowered to 25, only the married men being kept on the payroll. March was also a bad month for the nearby town of Deadwood. On the 29th, the Columbia Hotel, by then owned by Thomson & Hodgkinson, was completely destroyed by fire. According to the *Times:* "The fire was first noticed on the second floor above the kitchen stove. It soon spread, and in a short time the hotel, stables and outhouses were completely destroyed. The building was owned by J. Thompson and occupied by Bert Lay, who leased it a short time ago. There was $800 insurance on the building. Lay had no insurance and lost considerable liquors, furniture and supplies."

On April 10, coke shipments permitted the B.C. Copper Co.'s smelter to start up again, and the work force at the Mother Lode was promptly increased to 75 men. By mid-July the total had reached 100, with another 100 employed at the smelter. One of the mine workers, a machinist named A.L. Wilber, met his death on November 22.

Reported the Phoenix *Pioneer:* "An unusually heavy blast was being fired in the ore quarry, and the customary warnings were repeatedly given of the blast by the mine whistle, and Wilber, who was employed in the machine shop, had plenty of time to reach a place of safety. He preferred to take the risk of flying rocks, however, and a piece as large as a stove came through the roof of the building, taking off the top of his head, and killing him instantly, scattering his brains all over the room."

Despite the shutdown at the mine and smelter, production dropped only slightly to 138,079 tons in 1903, before setting a new record at 174,298 tons the following year. Production declined to 147,576 tons in 1905, and fell still further, to only 105,900 tons in 1906. In November, 1907, because of depressed copper prices, all mines in the Boundary were closed. "At the Mother Lode," reported the *Pioneer*, ". . .a force of (only) 16 men is now employed." By mid-December the newspaper reported that, except for the installation of some new machinery, nothing was being done at the Mother Lode. Despite being in production for only 10 months, the mine was still able to produce 208,321 tons during the year.

Deadwood, tied so closely to the fortunes of the Mother Lode, was also suffering. After the Columbia Hotel had been destroyed by fire, it had not been rebuilt or replaced. Thus the town's only hotel was the Algoma, now owned solely by James Henderson, who continued to renew the liquor license until at least 1907. There were two reasons why Deadwood did not develop to its full potential. First, of course, a work force of roughly 120 men at the nearby Mother Lode was hardly sufficient to maintain a town. Second, of this small force, some chose to live at the mine site, where the company had erected an excellent boarding house, a bunkhouse and a number of commodious buildings. And since Deadwood had little to offer the workers in their off duty hours, most travelled the short distance to

(Above) A general view of the B.C. Copper Co.'s Mother Lode mine site c1910. The building at far left was probably the large boarding house. Other buildings along bottom included bunkhouses and offices.

(Right) Ninety-four men pose for a photograph in front of the B.C. Copper Co.'s office and warehouse at the Mother Lode mine c1912.

Greenwood to partake of its numerous drinking and gambling establishments. It can well be imagined what a disastrous effect a work stoppage had on the small town.

On May 5, 1908, the B.C. Copper Co. announced that it would resume operations at both the Mother Lode and the smelter the following day. For nearly six months the combination of low copper prices and high operating costs had kept both closed. By the end of May, the *Pioneer* reported that the workforce at the Mother Lode was over 200. The following month the population was increased by the birth of three babies, and by July the *Pioneer* noted that 25 families were living at the Mother Lode. During the same week the paper announced that the mine had set a new weekly record by shipping 8,944 tons to the smelter.

With renewed activity at the mine, it was only a matter of time before tragedy struck again. This time the victims were Mrs. Dimmick and her three-year-old daughter. Rock was being blasted from a stope to a quarry when a flying piece went through the cottage occupied by James Dimmick and his family. "Mrs. Dimmick had both legs broken above the knees, and the little girl who had been on her mother's knee also had a leg broken and died shortly after the accident." A younger child, asleep in a baby carriage, miraculously escaped injury although the carriage was smashed.

On Wednesday, September 30, the mine claimed another victim. Hugh Stevens, 24 years of age, "was a skip tender," reported the *Pioneer*. "The skip was at the 60-foot level, and had been raised a few feet in order that he might adjust the chairs to allow the skip to be lowered, but before his work had been accomplished, the cage came down, killing him instantly."

Sports were important to frontier towns and mining camps, and the Mother Lode mine was no exception. Shown on the left is the Mother Lode soccer team in 1912. Note that the ball is sitting on 11 beer steins. These were either won in competition, or were used by the 11 team members to celebrate after a hard fought game. On the right, the Mother Lode hockey team poses with a trophy. This photo was probably taken at the outdoor ice rink at the Mother Lode mine. None of the players wear much protection, by today's standards, especially the goaltender, seen in the centre with the trophy.

Despite the tragic deaths, mine closures due to coke shortages, and living next to an operating mine, the Mother Lode almost took on town-site status in its own right. Mine workers even formed their own soccer team, which defeated Greenwood in a match played in October, 1908. The Mother Lode, like many other communities, also had its own hockey team. In fact, it even went one better, the *Times* announcing on December 10, 1909, that "A new skating rink, 50 feet by 100 feet is being constructed on the flat opposite the mine office." In March, 1910, the same paper announced that the Mother Lode even had its own baseball team. However, while the Mother Lode was a rich mine that produced a great quantity of ore for many years, it never amounted to much of a "town." Likewise, it neighbour Deadwood, apart from its initial spurt, did not develop either, although its school did not close until 1919. The Deadwood post office lasted even longer, closing on December 31, 1922.

In January, 1991, and February, 1992, I had the pleasure of interviewing Mrs. Mildred Roylance. Mildred, who lives in Greenwood, was born in Deadwood. Her father, Donald McLaren, one of the town-site owners, first preempted land near the Boundary line in 1888. He was joined there by his father and brother in 1894, and they promptly erected the Grande Prairie Hotel on a town-site they named Carson. In 1894, McLaren entered into a partnership with Colin McRae and they preempted a 640-acre ranch at Deadwood. However, while McRae immediately built a cabin, McLaren did not move there until 1901. Back in 1899, McLaren had made

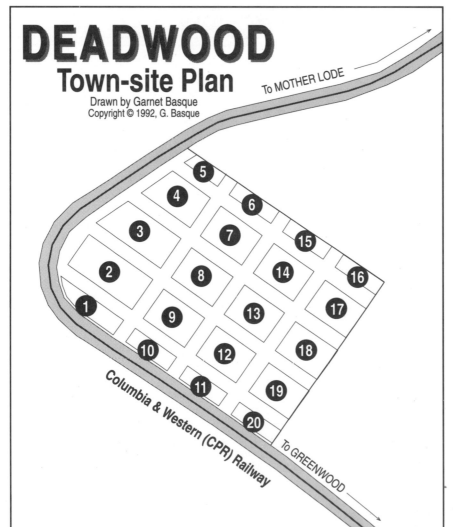

Students in front of the Deadwood School c1915. Mildred McLaren (Roylance) is second from right in first row. Mildred was born in Deadwood in 1908 and has lived all her life in the area. She currently lives in Greenwood. Note that all the boys were allowed to go barefooted after May 24 each year; the girls were not.

a trip back to Ontario, and while there, met his future bride, Mary Boswell. McLaren returned to Carson, but during the following year he corresponded frequently with Mary. In 1900 Donald returned to Ontario and the couple were married. They returned to Carson where they lived until 1901. By this time Carson was fading in importance, so McLaren decided to move to Deadwood where he built a home and raised a family.

Mildred was one of five children born in Deadwood: Alexander (1901); James (1902); Mildred (1908); Edward (1909) and Beatrice (1914). Two of the three brothers have since died. The remaining three children are among possible two dozen people still alive that once lived in Deadwood.

In 1904, the post office was operated from the McLaren home, with Mildred's mother being the postmaster until it closed permanently in 1922. Mildred remembers that a local stage operated on Monday, Wednesday and Friday between Greenwood, Deadwood and the Mother Lode. The mail was picked up at the Greenwood post office and delivered to their Deadwood home, where it was sorted. Similarly, the outgoing mail was delivered to the Greenwood post office.

The actual population of Deadwood probably never exceeded 100, while the population at the Mother Lode was considerably higher. Mildred recalls that there were as many as 100 families (roughly 300 people), plus about 100 single men living in the large boarding house and the two bunkhouses. In later years, there were only three businesses

in Deadwood: the hotel, a blacksmith and a shoe maker's shop. When the general store closed at the Mother Lode, some of the Greenwood merchants would take their wares up to the mine in wagons. A load of groceries might come one day, a load of meat on another. Of course, those residents who preferred not to wait, or who wanted a better selection, could always board the stage to Greenwood.

As for the two original town-site owners, Colin McRae continued to live in his cabin on the Deadwood Ranch until it was destroyed by fire about 1935. He then moved into the abandoned town-site office. When it was later also destroyed by fire, McRae moved into an old shack that had belonged to Theodore Whitey. There he spent the remainder of his life, dying at the age of 92. Prior to this, Donald McLaren had moved his family to Rossland, where he died in 1941.

Today, the old Deadwood town-site has been reclaimed by nature. When I last visited the area in June, 1991, two deer stood in the field watching as I took photos. As recently as 1984, there were still mine buildings standing at the Mother Lode. During my visit in 1991, however, they had been removed, and today, only some concrete foundations, an ugly scar in the mountainside and some scattered pieces or ore remain to indicate the site of what had once been a prominent mine. While it is enivitable that old mines and towns that have outlived their usefullness must fade into oblivion, hopefully there memory will never be forgotten. If this book contributes slightly towards that goal, I will be very satisfied. ✿

Phoenix

The glory hole of the Granby mines.

AFTER placer mining on Boundary Creek petered out in 1862, very little interest was taken by prospectors in the Boundary until 1891, and few claims were staked. In 1890, the discovery of gold-copper ore bodies at Rossland stimulated prospecting over extensive areas of southern British Columbia, and in 1891 the Mother Lode, Crown Silver and Sunset claims were staked in Deadwood Camp, not far from the future city of Greenwood. During the summer of that year, prospectors crossed to the future site of Phoenix. On July 15, Henry White, an old placer miner from Rock Creek, made the first discovery when he staked the Knob Hill claim. White's partner, Matthew Hotter, located Old Ironsides, which adjoined the Knob Hill, and named both claims, "the former after a gun boat which figured in the Civil War of the United States, and the latter after Nob Hill, a residential quarter of San Francisco."

During that first summer, most of the ground which later proved to contain valuable ore bodies was located. According to the Canadian Department of Mines' *Memoir No. 12*, published in 1912: "The Stemwinder was staked by James Attwood and James Schofield about July 25, and the fraction between it and Old Ironsides two days later, by Edmund Lefevre. It was known as the Silver King, and after being allowed to lapse was relocated by Robert Denzler as the Phoenix from which the city was named.

"The next discovery was made by Joseph Taylor and Stephen Mangott who located the Brooklyn on July 31. A few days later Robert Denzler and William Douglas located the North Star, and about the same time George Rumberger discovered the ground at present covered by the Snowshoe,

Rawhide and Monarch. He, with Taylor and Mangott, staked three claims on which considerable surface work was done, but the assessments were allowed to lapse. The War Eagle was located by Denzler and Douglas the latter part of August.

"In 1893, Thomas Humphrey and James Keightly located the Monarch; Robert Denzler, D. McInnes, and William Gibbs the Rawhide; Denzler and Gibbs the Snowshoe; and Joseph Hetu the Gold Drop.

"In 1894, the North Star was relocated by John Meyer and George Rumberger as the Idaho, and the Red Cloud was relocated as the Standard fraction by Thomas Johnston. The Victoria was staked on August 1 by John Stephens and the Ottawa on August 25 by George Rumberger."

Most of the mountaintop was now staked, and during the early years a considerable amount of surface work was done. However many prospectors, discouraged by low copper, silver and gold values, and cognoscente of the fact that a great deal of time and capital would be needed to develop the ore bodies, allowed their claims to lapse. But when the enormous size of the deposits became known, and the ores were discovered to be practically self fluxing, there was renewed activity in Greenwood Camp, as the collective mines became known, and most of the old claims were relocated by others.

In 1895 two Spokane businessmen, Jay P. Graves and A.L. White, formed a company to develop the mines of Greenwood Camp. However, they lacked the financial resources to see the project through, so they took in S.H.C. Miner, of Granby, Quebec, as a partner. In 1896, the Miner-

Graves Syndicate, as the association became known, commenced development work on the Old Ironsides-Knob Hill ore body.

By this time there was a growing number of men scattered over the mountain, but there was no commercial accommodation for them. This situation was alleviated somewhat when Fred Graff established the Gold Drop Boarding House. Very little is known about this establishment, although it was probably located on or near the Gold Drop mineral claim. The exact date it opened for business is also not recorded, but it was being advertised in the Midway *Advance* as early as April 27, 1896. As the first hotel in Greenwood Camp, it offered: "Good accommodation for travellers. First-class meals served. Good livery stable in connection."

As Greenwood Camp continued to grow and develop, Robert Wood, shrewd businessman that he was, decided to construct, at his own expense, a wagon road to connect the mines with his new town of Greenwood. By mid-September, the grade was completed. Unfortunately, the wagon road, which ended on the Stemwinder claim, left the Gold Drop Boarding House somewhat isolated, a situation Fred Graff moved quickly to resolve. What happened to his original establishment is not recorded, but by mid-November, the Boundary Creek *Times* reported that the enterprising

Graff was erecting a new two-story, 20x34-foot hotel on the Stemwinder claim. On December 19 the newspaper noted that the Brooklyn House, including stables and barn, had been completed and that Graff had received a liquor license. The hotel was apparently opened to the public for the first time on January 1, 1897, and on January 21, Graff celebrated his new venture by "giving a grand ball and supper."

For some time the Brooklyn Hotel remained Greenwood Camp's only commercial establishment. Meanwhile, throughout the summer of 1897, a large number of men were employed in Greenwood Camp, and on October 23, the *Times* prophesied that before too long a little town would likely spring up around Graff's hotel. "It is reported that Messrs. Hain & Co., of Midway, intend opening a branch store at this point, and that the Jackson Bros. will open a butcher shop."

Winter came early to Greenwood Camp, located at an elevation of 4,600 feet, and stayed until late spring. There was always lots of snow during the winter months, so it is not surprising that there was no new construction activity until the summer of 1898. However, by June, Wynkoop & Stephens had established the first general store. It was located on the Brooklyn claim. By late July, the homes of A. McIntosh, Thomas Roderick and Joseph Hedges were nearing completion. These homes were located west of the Brooklyn claim, probably on the Cimeron. This month also saw the construction of a large boarding house on the Stemwinder, and the establishment of J.E. Boss' assay office, near the Brooklyn Hotel.

In June, the residents had petitioned the government to

(Left) Getting supplies and equipment to the mines at Phoenix was no easy task in the early years, as this 1898 photograph illustrates.

(Below) This photograph of the first log cabin constructed in Phoenix was taken in 1895. George Rumberger is believed to be the man seated on the right in the doorway. The other pioneers are, unfortunately, unidentified.

establish a post office there under the name Brooklyn. However, when on July 30, the *Times* announced that a post office had been approved, it noted that it was to be called Greenwood Camp. The newspaper expressed concerns that this name would cause confusion with its neighbour, Greenwood. The residents of Greenwood Camp obviously agreed, for they requested that the name be changed to Knob Hill or Phoenix. On August 13 the *Times* reported that the new post office, which opened for the first time on October 1, would be named Phoenix.

Meanwhile, back on August 1, Graff had leased his Brooklyn Hotel to McDonald & McMillan. However, this arrangement was apparently not successful, for only two months later, the *Advance* reported that Graff had "again established himself at the old stand. Far and near the Brooklyn under Mr. Graf's (sic) management is noted for its excellent cuisine, and it will be admitted by all who have happened to be at some time guests at the hostelry, deservedly so."

Mining has always been a dangerous occupation which threatened life and limb, and the mines surrounding Phoenix were certainly no exception. There were numerous deaths by accident over the years, most of which were senseless tragedies which could have been avoided. While it is not my intention to provide a comprehensive history of these tragedies, the first three, which all occurred in 1898, are worth relating.

The first fatality occurred at the Snowshoe mine on July 21 when Hugh O'Thomas was struck by an ore bucket. "About four o'clock in the morning," reported the *Times*, "the bucket was sent up from the drift with about 40 pieces of steel. It had not travelled far when it became unhooked and plunged down the shaft where the deceased and John Pritchard were at work. O'Thomas was reaching for his candle at the time and was struck on the head by the bucket." His head was badly fractured and he died four hours later. Pritchard escaped unhurt.

Less than a month later, a young Welsh miner named Robert W. Roberts met his death in the Old Ironsides mine. "The deceased, M. Austin and W.J. Pierce went down the 200-foot shaft shortly after eleven shots had been fired. Roberts and Austin were overcome by the foul air. Roberts died shortly after being brought to the surface while Austin regained consciousness and is rapidly recovering."

The irony of this second accident, apart from its senseless nature, was the fact that Roberts was a close friend of Hugh O'Thomas, who had recently been killed in the Snowshoe. He and O'Thomas' sister were to be married at Christmas. The week prior to his death, Roberts had been making arrangements to take O'Thomas' body home to New Rockland, Quebec, and intended to leave for the east after his next payday.

As strange as it may seem, the next fatality, which also occurred at the Old Ironsides less than one week later, was also connected. Not only did John P. McCormick perish in the same manner as Roberts, descending into the mine before the foul air from a powder blast had cleared, but McCormick had only obtained his job at the mine through the vacancy caused by the death of Roberts. McCormick, who had several years experience in American mines, had only arrived in Phoenix three weeks earlier. He was survived by his wife and two small daughters.

On May 10, 1899, the *Times* told its readers that Phoenix had grown into "something more than a post office. Dwelling houses have been built, a large hotel (Phoenix) for Harry Nash is under course of erection, and a tonsorial artist (barber) has decorated a tree with the stripes to show that he is open for business."

In early June, John A. Coryell completed a survey of the Phoenix town-site. Although the newspaper is not specific, this was probably on the New York claim. The problem with being uncertain, is that what was commonly

Phoenix in 1899. At the upper end is the No. 1 terminal of the CPR, later merged with No. 2. Just below is the No. 2 shaft house, No. 1 shaft house, and No. 2 tunnel bins and crushing plant, on the CPR. These comprised the No. 2 terminal. Below is the Granby Company's bunkhouse and boarding house. The three log cabins far to the right are the original bunkhouse, cook camp and office. The group immediately to the right of centre are stores and rooming houses built on lots sold by the Granby Company. Beyond, to the right, is the Old Ironsides Hotel, the Granby offices, and beyond the superintendent's residence and the guest house.

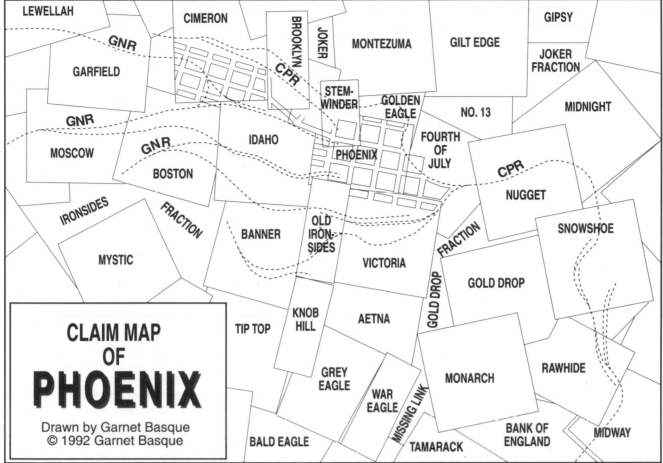

CLAIM MAP OF PHOENIX

Drawn by Garnet Basque
© 1992 Garnet Basque

referred to as the town of Phoenix, was taking form on three separate claims. Making the situation even more confusing was the fact that, as yet, no town-site had been registered, businessmen and residents, for the most part, merely erecting buildings along the Greenwood wagon road that cut across the claims. By the end of July, for example, 25 to 30 new buildings were being built, and the Greenwood *Miner* reported that they were "pretty evenly divided between the upper and lower and center parts of the town."

By late August, Phoenix was in the middle of a building boom. "Two months ago Phoenix was a geographical expression with a post office," reported the *Miner*. "Today it is a tripartite aggregation of business and building activity, with ambitions to become a city. Its growth is quite remarkable. There are three divisions to it. The first is Mr. Rumberger's site, upon which a large number of buildings are already located. The second is owned by the Knob Hill people, and it has a number of residences erected by the mining company, and several business places and a hotel. The third is located on the New York claim, and has already registered as a town-site, though the last in the field.

"Houses, hotels, building blocks are going up everywhere, both log and frame. The mill near Phoenix is kept busy beyond its ability to supply the demand. All along the gulch in among the trees shacks without number are springing up. There are applications for six more hotel licenses and as many buildings are going up to sell when the licenses are granted. Eight business houses in Greenwood are preparing to establish there.

"Wynkoop and J.M. Stephens and the Russel Hard-

ware Co. have been amalgamated and are being incorporated as a joint stock company, and will erect a large building on the Knob Hill property. Near them will be the Hunter-Kendrick store for which also a building is being erected.

"On the Rumberger townsite, H.A. King & Co., cigars, etc., Miller Bros. Jewellery, drugs, etc., and E. Weeks, hotel, all of Greenwood, are erecting suitable buildings, and will open up as soon as they are completed.

"Abbott & Traves are building a large three-story hotel; Mr. Gordon is going in gent's furnishings, etc; N. Burns in furniture; Chas. Thompson, formerly of the Gem restaurant, has opened up the Mint restaurant, and doing well; Burk and Postie are in the grocery business; Mr. Walmesly, of Cascade, is also opening up in groceries; Ira Black, of Cascade, is erecting a two-story hotel. The buildings for these are either completed or in the course of construction.

"On the New York site, Gus Jackson of Rossland, George Breckenridge, of the same place, and Mr. Dorsey of Gladstone are erecting hotels. There are other businesses contemplated, but all the particulars are not available. At the present rate of growth, which is sudden and somewhat unexpected, Phoenix will be a town of importance in a few months." (Strangely, although the New York claim was the first to register as a town-site, it apparently did not amount to much, and was not even listed on the Phoenix plan of 1912, included with this chapter. However, it was included in the Phoenix town-site plan produced in 1933.)

After the merger of Wynkoop, Stephens and Russel, the new firm, known as Wynkoop-Stephens, developed into one of the largest business establishments in Phoenix.

They owned two general stores, one on the Old Ironsides claim and the other at the corner of Dominion Avenue and Phoenix Street on the Cimeron claim. The main store, located on the Old Ironsides, "consists of a building 33x40, in which are the offices of the company and the dry goods, clothing and boot and shoe departments, and a building 28x82, two story, the ground floor of which is used for hardware and groceries and the upper floor as a warehouse. In the rear of these buildings, there is in course of construction a tin shop, 28x34 feet. The store on Dominion street is 16x24, but there is in course of construction a building 45x50. The Phoenix post office is kept in this building."

The firm was also responsible for managing the boarding house of the War Eagle mine, where they provided meals for 120 men, and the 40x60-foot Old Ironsides Hotel, owned by the Old Ironsides Mining Company. The latter hotel, however, was not a normal hostelry. The ground floor was divided into an office, wash room, two dining rooms and a 20x30-foot kitchen. Although the upper story did contain 14 rooms, these were essentially reserved for men employed at the mine. Another unique feature of this hotel was the fact that no intoxicants were sold on the premises.

By August of 1899, a stage line had been established, and residents were contributing funds to aid in the establishment of a school. By the end of September, "a comfortable, well built log structure with a single room, capable of accommodating about 50 pupils," had been completed. That month also saw the establishment of telephone and telegraph communication between Phoenix and Greenwood.

On October 14, the *Times* announced that Phoenix now had its own newspaper, "a healthy looking sheet" called the Phoenix *News*. It was published weekly by J.W. Grier, who had been associated with the *Times* for two years. Unfortunately, copies of the *News* itself were not available for research. However, some valuable information from its first issue was reprinted in the *Times*.

As mentioned, Phoenix was developing primarily on three claims. In the summer of 1899, the New York claim, owned by J.B. McArthur of Columbia, became the first to be platted into lots. Hotel owner George Breckenridge was the town-site agent. However, although the first to register as a town-site, this part of Phoenix apparently did not enjoy long-term success, for very little development appears to have been done in this area.

In September, 1899, George Rumberger platted the surface of the Cimeron claim and placed lots on the market. Two months later the Old Ironsides claim was also subdivided and placed on the market.

It was Rumberger's Cimeron claim, in general, and Dominion Avenue, in particular, that became the scene of greatest activity. By the end of September, 1899, three hotels were nearing completion on Dominion Avenue. The two-story Imperial Hotel was being erected by Weeks & Hogan, of Greenwood. Across the street, Abbott & McCreath, also of Greenwood, were erecting the two-story Butte Hotel. A three-story hotel was being constructed by Ira Black, formerly of Cascade. It contained 20 rooms, and at the time of construction it was the only three-story building on Dominion Avenue. (All three of these hotels were destroyed by fire on January 17, 1901.)

By the middle of October, a fourth hotel was being erected by Harry Nash, of Rossland, on the corner of Dominion Avenue and Phoenix Street. The Hotel Phoenix was a 48x50-foot, two-and-a-half story building with an 18x20-foot kitchen attached. The ground floor was divided into a dining room, office, club rooms and bar. The upper floor contained 18 bedrooms, all heated by hot air. A short time later Joseph Graham erected the Union Hotel on lower Dominion Avenue. Graham conducted the Union Hotel until the Vancouver, Victoria and Eastern (VV&E) extension of the Great Northern Railway (GNR) reached Phoenix. When the railway right-of-way was found to go directly through his property, Graham sold out to the GNR, who either demolished or removed the building.

Other businesses already established on Dominion Avenue included four general stores. The first general store to be established was owned by Posty & Walker, who advertised a splendid assortment of clothing, groceries and miner's supplies at "rock bottom prices." The firm of Wynkoop-Stevens operated one of their two Phoenix stores on this street. The post office was located in their building. The two other two general stores were operated by Bourke & Co., and Morrin & Thompson. Part of the 30x40-foot Bourke & Co. building was occupied by the Mint Restaurant, operated by Thompson & Harber. Similarly, a part of Morrin & Thompson's 24x40-foot, two-story building housed the real estate office of Hughes & Co.

Elsewhere on Dominion Avenue, Smith & McRae, of Greenwood, opened a 24x50-foot book and stationery store. There was also William Bennin's 20x30-foot blacksmith shop, Pat Burns & Co.'s 20x30-foot butcher shop, George Murphy's 24x40-foot livery barn, Paul Fischer's 34x40-foot bottling works, and G.F. Kuntze's barbershop.

On Phoenix Street, W.W. Greer had erected a 16x20-foot building and started a bakery, while Joseph Hedges operated a livery and feed barn. Elsewhere on the Rumberger town-site, A.P. McKenzie & Co., "druggists and stationers," were erecting a 16x30-foot building, while Miller Bros., "druggists and jewellers," had erected a 24x36-foot building with a basement.

According to the *News*, three unnamed hotels were being erected on the New York claim. The largest appears to have been the 30x72-foot, three-story hotel owner by town-site agent George Breckenridge. Gus Jackson, of Rossland, was busy building the second. However, the third, being constructed by John Dorsey, formerly of Gladstone, was not being erected on the New York claim. It was actually being built further to the northeast where the Canadian Pacific Railway (CPR) right-of-way branched off towards the Brandon and Golden Crown mines. A small settlement called Hartford Junction, or simply Hartford, sprang up at this junction.

The Old Ironsides town-site could also boast of its own hotels. The first of these to be established, in the spring of 1899, was the Old Ironsides Hotel,[1] owned by the Old Ironsides Mining Company. In October of the same year, Harry Bell, of Rossland, erected the 30x50-foot, two-story Bellevue Hotel on Knob Hill Avenue. Close on its heels came the Summit, erected on the corner of First Street and Knob Hill Avenue. The person who built this hotel went unrecorded, but shortly after being constructed, it was leased by David Oxley and John Hartman.

In addition to their general store in the Rumberger town-site, the firm of Wynkoop-Stevens operated their main store on Old Ironsides Avenue. Nearby, the Russel Hardware Company, of Greenwood, operated a hardware store in connection with Wynkoop-Stevens. Not far away, the firm of Hunter-Kendrick offered "a full line of dry goods, clothing, boots, and shoes, hardware and miner's supplies" from their new 30x60-foot building. They also had a 12x50-foot warehouse under construction. Adjoining the Hunter-Kendrick store, William Twist had erected a 24x40-foot, two-story building, from which he sold cigars, tobacco, confectionery, etc. The building even boasted a billiards parlour. Elsewhere on the Old Ironsides town-site, Vaughn & McInnes operated a butcher's shop from their 30x20-foot building. They offered "all kinds of beef, mutton and veal. Also poultry and oysters in season." In mid-January, 1900, they began excavations for a 28x70-foot, three-story cold storage warehouse on Knob Hill Avenue.

On November 12, 1899, the first wedding ever to be performed in Phoenix united William Twist and Florence Schubert. The ceremony, which was held in the parlour of the Old Ironsides Hotel, was performed by Rev. B.H. Balderson of Greenwood.

In late December, W.T. Kaake opened the Columbia Hotel on the corner of Dominion Avenue and Phoenix Street in the Rumberger town-site, thus bringing to at least 13 the number of Phoenix hotels by the close of 1899. The other was Fred Graff's Brooklyn, the first to have been built anywhere in Phoenix. By this time, Phoenix had a population of about 1,000 and business was brisk, the Wynkoop-Stevens company alone reporting an average business of $15,000 per month. By this time, also, Phoenix had a second newspaper called the *Pioneer*.

Although destined to be the leading voice of Phoenix for many years, the *Pioneer's* beginnings were anything but routine. The printing plant was freighted in from Bossburg, Washington, via Cascade and Grand Forks. In the words of the newspaper itself: "There were untold troubles trying to get the paper started on its feet, not the least of which was to secure a place in which to do business. After it was finally secured, the place was sans doors and windows for nearly a week, so great was the demand for mechanics and building materials of all kinds."

Phoenix continued to grow with such rapidity during 1900 that it quickly became difficulty to keep abreast of all the new construction that was taking place. Keeping track of the hotels, in particular, is extremely difficult, as new ones were built while old ones changed hands or were renamed. However, in January, 1900, at least two new hotels emerged on the scene. The Norden Hotel, owned by J.E. Ahlmstrom, was located on Dominion Avenue, while the Maple Leaf Hotel, on Old Ironsides Avenue, was being

conducted by Twist & Sanders.

By mid-January, Phoenix took another bold step forward with the completion of the framework for the 18x40-foot bank building. The building was being erected for the Eastern Townships Bank. First established in 1859, it was one of the oldest banking institutions in Canada, only the Bank of Montreal, Bank of Quebec and Bank of British North America being older. Until recently, the bank had confined itself to the Eastern Townships of Quebec. It now had 14 branches. However, the Phoenix branch, under the management of William Spear, did not officially open until June 15.

Also by mid-January, the Boundary Creek Telephone & Telegraph Co. had installed 35 telephones in Phoenix. A month later, a trial test of the Greenwood Electric Co. was rated "most satisfactory." From 4 o'clock on the afternoon of February 17 until late that evening, "those business houses and residences that had been connected were lit with electricity."

Probably of greater importance, to the hordes of thirsty miners, at least, was the production of "a fine quality Lager beer" in early March. The Phoenix Brewery, operated by Mueller Bros., was located at the corner of Standard Avenue and Banner Street in the Rumberger town-site.

In late April, the Metropolitan Hotel, owned by Russel & Russel, opened its doors to the public. This was followed in early May by the opening of the Victoria Hotel. Numerous other businesses were also being established.

On May 21, 1900, the residents of Phoenix had a special cause for celebration, as the CPR's spur line from Eholt was completed. In describing the event, the *Times* wrote: "Amid the striking steam whistles and the cheers of assembled miners and other citizens of Phoenix, and with the ore bunkers gaily decorated with flags, the last piece of steel was laid to the Old Ironsides ore bins at noon today. Immediately after the last spike was driven, the deep brasso profundo whistle of the Ironsides shaft house heralded the welcome news, quickly followed by the Knob Hill, and in turn taken up by the War Eagle, Gold Drop, Golden Crown and other mines. The terrible ear splitting din was not lessened by numerous explosions of dynamite and CPR locomotive whistles. The citizens of Phoenix sent 10 barrels of Phoenix beer to the workmen immediately after completion."

Despite the eager anticipation, however, the first shipment of ore was not made from Phoenix to the Granby smelter at Grand Forks until Wednesday, July 11. After what the *Pioneer* described as "the most vexatious delays, continually arising on the part of the CPR construction department," a five car train, carrying ore from the Old Ironsides and Knob Hill mines, left Phoenix at 1 o'clock. It was a joyous moment for Phoenix, but no less momentous for Grand Forks, where the ore shipment's arrival was greeted "with a brass band and all the jollification trimmings that could be thought of."

On October 11, 1900, Phoenix was incorporated as a city, and on November 2, the first elections took place. George Rumberger was elected mayor by acclamation. There were 167 voters registered to cast ballots, and of these, 147 exercised their rights in electing the six alderman: D. McInnes (118), James Punch (110), J.A. Morrin (108),

¹According to the January, 1905, "Special Holiday Number" of the *Pioneer*, the 14-room Knob Hill Hotel was the first to be erected in this part of Phoenix. However, the statement: "The house. . .was built in 1891 by Morrison & Anderson," must be considered incorrect. Since the first ore bodies were only discovered in the late summer of that year, and no real activity took place in the vicinity until 1894-95, it appears highly unlikely that a hotel would have been built in 1891. Furthermore, based on other research, it seems more likely that the Knob Hill Hotel was constructed in 1899 or 1900.

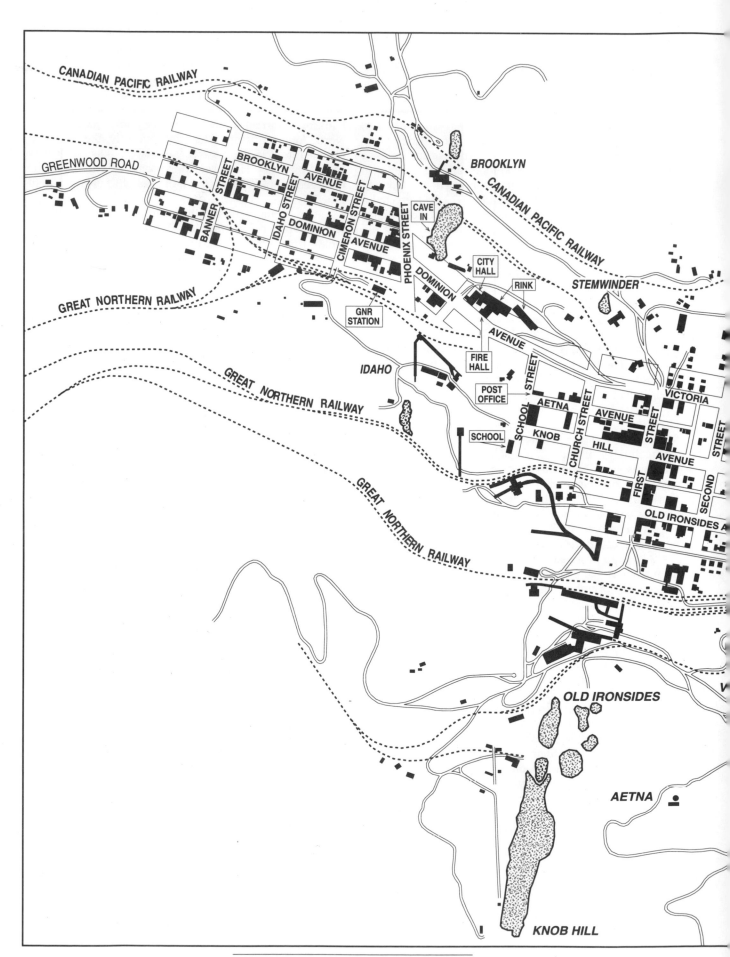

CANADIAN PACIFIC RAILWAY

GREENWOOD ROAD

BROOKLYN

BROOKLYN AVENUE

BANNER STREET

IDAHO STREET

DOMINION

CIMERON STREET

AVENUE

PHOENIX STREET

CAVE IN

CANADIAN PACIFIC RAILWAY

STEMWINDER

CITY HALL

RINK

DOMINION

GREAT NORTHERN RAILWAY

GNR STATION

AVENUE

FIRE HALL

IDAHO

POST OFFICE

GREAT NORTHERN RAILWAY

SCHOOL STREET

AETNA

SCHOOL

KNOB HILL

CHURCH STREET

AVENUE

FIRST STREET

VICTORIA

SECOND STREET

GREAT NORTHERN RAILWAY

OLD IRONSIDES A

OLD IRONSIDES

AETNA

KNOB HILL

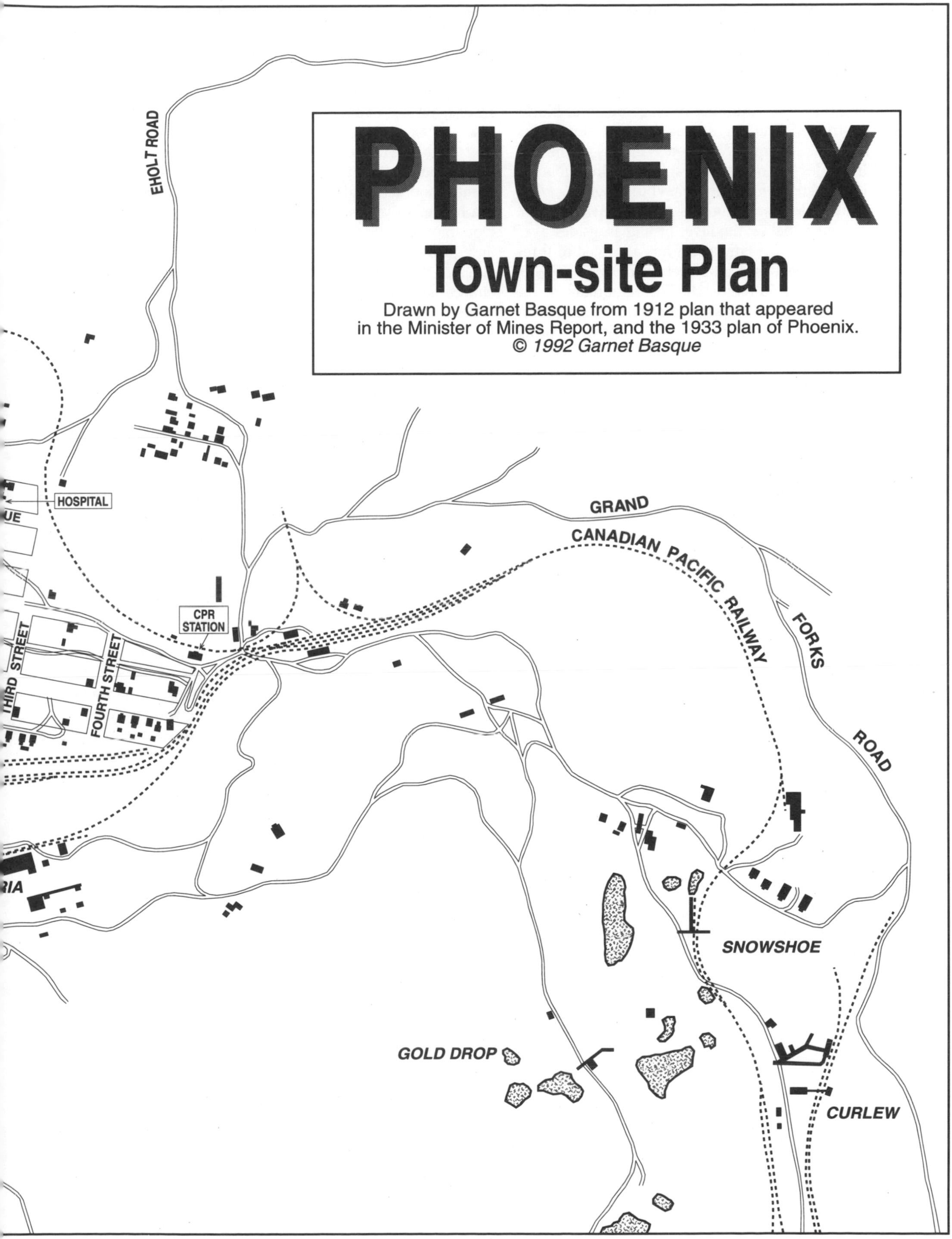

PHOENIX
Town-site Plan

Drawn by Garnet Basque from 1912 plan that appeared
in the Minister of Mines Report, and the 1933 plan of Phoenix.
© 1992 Garnet Basque

EHOLT ROAD

HOSPITAL

GRAND

CANADIAN PACIFIC RAILWAY

FORKS

ROAD

CPR
STATION

THIRD STREET

FOURTH STREET

RIA

SNOWSHOE

GOLD DROP

CURLEW

James Marshall (104), J.O. Clark (103) and M. McBean (99).

Phoenix had made substantial advancements in 1900, and as the year drew to a close, its population had increased by 50 percent, standing at about 1,500. In additional to the numerous business and residential buildings erected during the year, a number of large business blocks had been constructed. The largest was the three-story block owned by Jay P. Graves and W. Yolen Williams on the corner of Old Ironsides Avenue and First Street. On October 6, the *Pioneer* described the just completed building:

"It has three floors arranged as follows: the bottom floor or basement is below the level of Old Ironsides ave., but the steep grade down First street has admitted of three stores being faced east on that street. The dimensions of these are about 15 by 50 feet each. The remainder of the space here is divided between store room and a 20x20 barber shop, the latter being situated in the south-west corner and reached by a stairway down from Old Ironsides ave. The ground floor or first floor is divided into two commodious stores, each 25 by 65 feet with a portion of the front taken up by a stairway to the second or top floor. These fine stores are well lighted and each has two 38 inch by 80 inch and two 38 by 84 inch sheets of plate glass, with a double entrance door between each 76 inch show window. The difference in the length of the glass is rendered necessary by the grade of the street in front. The top floor is divided into eleven spacious offices, with stair landing and halls, the latter lighted by a skylight in the tin roof. There are bay windows at the north-east and south-east corners of the building on this floor and two others, one each on Old Ironsides ave. and First street.

"The building has a frontage on Old Ironsides avenue of 50 feet, and on First ave. of 65 feet, the latter being in depth. The total cost of the block is between $7,000 and $8,000."

On January 17, 1901, Phoenix suffered its first major setback when a serious fire threatened to engulf the entire lower town, as the Rumberger subdivision came to be known. The fire was first detected around 8:30 p.m. N.D. Palorcia, the shoemaker, had just entered the McBean & Co. store when he heard "a crackling noise." Palorcia and McBean rushed upstairs and found a room in the rear of the building, which was used as a kitchen, "one mass of flames."

With water scarce, and no fire brigade as yet established, it was impossible to stop the fire's progress in the normal manner. Unhindered, the flames spread westward and soon engulfed the Imperial Hotel and the Baldwin Block. In a desperate attempt to save the remainder of the town-site, "it was decided to use powder to stay if possible the march of the voracious flames," reported the *Miner*. "Accordingly, a charge was put into Henderson's small jewelry store, adjoining McBean's, to prevent the spread of fire to the east. This was effective to some degree. Then another charge was placed under the northeast end of McBean's store, as many buildings on the hill were threatened.

"It was impossible to stop the fire by ordinary means — the only plan was to destroy its path. McBean's and the Imperial hotel, as well as Baldwin's building, were doomed. Nothing could save these structures and contents. It was

only a question as to whether or not Black's hotel, Morrin & Thompson's and a row of two and three-story structures on the south side of the street could be saved. Hundreds of willing hands were using snow, with considerable success, to keep the buildings and roofs wet. Of water there was little or none, but of snow there was an almost unlimited supply.

"A third charge of powder was placed in the Baldwin block, and shattered that building to splinters, but still the flames mounted higher and higher, and men worked only the harder to protect the numerous buildings threatened. Dominion avenue was littered with merchandise, furniture and goods of all kinds, taken out of the buildings on both sides of the avenue. Unfortunately there was little or no chance whatever of saving buildings on either side of the street."

The losses included: McBean & Co., $13,000; Imperial Hotel, $10,000; William Hunter Co., $2,000; Baldwin Block, $2,000; Morrin & Thompson, $2,000; Butte Hotel, $600; Black's Hotel, $500; T.F. Hick's stock, $500; Electric Light Co., $300; Alex Henderson, $250; W.E. Mitchell's shop, $200; and numerous miscellaneous losses totalling $3,950. Despite the fact that there was only $13,300 in insurance, most owners were rebuilding within a month.

But Phoenix survived the fire, and by the summer of 1901 it was a rip-roaring, wide open town where poker, blackjack, roulette and other games of chance were played around the clock, seven days a week. For those gamblers who lost heavily at the gaming tables, they could find solace with female companionship in the red light district. According to the *Miner*, it was not the gamblers themselves that gave Phoenix a bad name, but rather "the toughs and thugs and boosters who congregate when gambling is carried on to any extent." The situation was so bad by late summer that the *Miner* claimed that 40 percent of the wages paid in Phoenix went to operators of the roulette wheel. "This can only result in injury to the business men there, besides attracting to the city hundreds of disreputable characters, who will resort to almost any means of obtaining money without working for it."

Oddly enough, the *Pioneer* did not comment on the gambling going on in the city, but on August 17, it did report an incident that occurred in the tenderloin district.

On Monday, August 12, a Swedish miner named Fred Johnson decided to visit a house of ill repute kept by Clara Wells. When he entered the establishment, Johnson had $1,800 in his possession. However, sometime after having enjoyed the feminine charms of one Bessie Burns, Johnson realized that his $1,800 was missing. Unfortunately, by the time police were informed about the situation, Bessie had a three hour head start for the U.S. border.

Meanwhile, Phoenix continued to grow and flourish. In late May, a fourth town-site was subdivided into 150 lots by John Coryell, P.L.S. This addition was on parts of the Idaho, Brooklyn and Stemwinder claims owned by the Dominion Copper Co. Located between the Rumberger and Old Ironsides additions, it effectively joined the two by extending Dominion Avenue from the Cimeron claim to School Street on the Phoenix claim.

On June 1, the *Pioneer* reported that a contract had been awarded for the construction of the first wing of the

Phoenix General Hospital. The site, on Victoria Avenue, consisting of five lots valued at $2,500, was donated by the Granby Company. The plans for the 32x112-foot structure were drawn-up by Victoria architect, F.M. Rattenbury.

The 1901 building record for Phoenix shows that $93,100 was spent in new business and residential construction, and a further $51,200 was spent in new additions and improvements. Today, $144,300 would not even purchase one comfortable home in the lower mainland, but in 1901 it was a considerable sum of money. Of the new buildings erected, 12 were business blocks, some of substantial size. The largest was the McMillan Block, erected at a cost of $8,000. On the lower end of the scale, the Kerr Block cost only $700. The other business blocks erected during the year included: Delahay, $3,500; Marah, $3,500; Hardy-McKenzie, $3,000; Aetna, $2,500; Baldwin, $2,000; Boyle, $2,000; Topp, $1,300; McRae, $1,100; Biner, $1,000 and Pioneer, $800. Three churches had also been erected during the year. The Presbyterian cost $2,500, the Congregated, $2,400 and the Anglican $2,000.

The largest expenditure made for improvements was the $25,000 spent by the Phoenix Water Supply Co. The City of Phoenix came next with $13,000, most of which was spend on grading and improving the streets. Of the remaining $13,200, half was spent on improvements or additions made to eight hotels.

With the economy of Phoenix surging ahead, it is hardly surprising that in early November a fifth addition, on the Golden Eagle, was platted into lots. Located adjacent to the Stemwinder and between the Montezuma and Phoenix claims, the Golden Eagle, owned by Judge W.R. Williams, was not a full-size claim. As a result it was only possible to subdivide 35 lots, which were offered for sale at $200 each. However, there appears to have been little activity in this particular area.

On November 13, Phoenix suffered its second major fire in less than a year. Once again it occurred in the Rumberger subdivision. The fire was first detected in the Phoenix Laundry, in the basement of the Miller Block on Dominion Avenue, about 11 p.m. Before the fire could be extinguished it had completely gutted the basement and practically destroyed the Union clothing store, which was overhead. Fortunately, this time a water system was in place, and everyone was unanimous in praising its effectiveness in preventing the entire side of Dominion Avenue, which was closely built, from being destroyed.

Although Phoenix was essentially a copper mining town, its citizens never lacked for social functions and sports. Ping pong, baseball, tennis, skating, curling and hockey were the early favourites. In 1911, a ski club was formed, and over the years, Phoenix came to be associated with hockey and skiing.

Back in November, 1900, William Drever announced plans to construct a skating rink in Phoenix. "The building," noted the Pioneer, "will be 70x170-feet in size and will have an ice surface of 50x150-feet." A month later the newspaper announced that the rink was nearing completion and that plans were "underway to organize a hockey team." On December 25, the skating rink was opened to the public for the first time. By this time, the hockey club had been organized, and on January 12, 1901, the Pioneer noted that the

squad were holding practices four nights a week in preparation for an upcoming match against Greenwood. The first hockey game ever to be held in Phoenix was played on January 23, 1901, before "an enthusiastic crowd of 250." Greenwood silenced the crowd early by scoring its first goal only 30 seconds into the game. But the Phoenix team rallied, and won the game 8-4.

In March, 1902, a sort of grudge match was played between the "Granby Hungry Seven" and the "Knob Hill Coons." After the game, won by the Hungry Seven, the Coons challenged them to a rematch. "It is understood the Coons have an idea that they know how to play hockey," wrote the Pioneer, "and are willing to back up their belief with hard coin of the realm. Of course, the Hungry Seven are only two willing to accommodate them to almost any amount, and a game, the like of which has never been seen in the country, will be the result. All kinds of money is being wagered on the outcome."

The following week the Pioneer published the results of the game, which ended "in an ignominious defeat for the Hungry Seven, who were taken down the line in one, two, three order by the coloured gentlemen. . . . The Hungry Seven fought manfully, and the battle for the puck raged hard and fierce, but the Knob Hill Coons were too much for their opponents, and the score resulted in a total of 10 to 1." The newspaper added that there were a number of "casualties" during the game, but "none of them resulted seriously or required the attention of the club's surgeon."

Phoenix's greatest moment of glory, as far as hockey and skiing were concerned, occurred at the 1911 Rossland Winter Carnival, where both teams made "a clean sweep" of the trophies. The hockey team won the Boundary Hockey Championship Cup, the Giant Powder Shield, emblematic of the hockey championship of B.C., and the International Cup, emblematic of the hockey championship of B.C. and Washington.

For its part, the ski club won the Jeldness Cup, emblematic of the ski-jumping championship of Canada, and the Sullivan-Seagram Shield, emblematic of the record ski jump of Canada. The gold medal in both events went to Engwald Engen. The ski club also won first and second place in the Seven Mile Race, the One-and-a-Half Mile Race and the Ladies' Ski Jump.

Coming off its impressive victories, the Phoenix Hockey Club sent a wire to Ottawa asking for an opportunity to challenge for the Stanley Cup. A short time later they received word that, because three challenges were in before them, it would not be possible to arrange dates in 1911. However, William Foran offered to arrange a series of matches at the opening of the next hockey season. It is not known if Phoenix accepted this alternative.

Meanwhile, back in the fall of 1902 Phoenix, and other mining and smelting towns of the Boundary Country experienced the first of many frustrating work stoppages. The smelters at Grand Forks, Greenwood and Boundary Falls all relied on coke from the Crow's Nest Pass Coal Company to fire their furnaces. Without coke, the smelters could not process ore from the numerous mines, and the entire operation ground to a halt. Unfortunately, shipments of this valuable fuel was frequently suspended because of work stoppages. By mid-August, the strike had been resolved and

(Above) In the early days of mining in Phoenix, horses and mules were used underground to pull the ore carts. In November, 1903, the Granby Company became the first to switch to steam locomotives. This photo was probably taken at one of the Granby mines. (Left) A GNR section crew with handcar at Phoenix in 1913.

coke shipments began to flow into the Boundary once again.

However, the peace in the coal mines was short-lived. On February 11, 1903, the employees of three collieries, at Michel, Mossissey and Coal Creek, struck over wages, working conditions and the employment of Chinese workers. As the strike dragged on into March, the *Pioneer* estimated that some 20,000 people were either directly or indirectly affected. Some 750 workers were affected in the Phoenix mines, 1,000 in the Rossland mines and 1,200 in the East Kootenay coal mines. Added to this total were 450 men in the Boundary smelters, 800 in the Trail smelter, and 500 in other smelters. Even some 300 railway workers were affected. The families of these men added about 10,000 to the total directly affected, and an additional 5,000 businessmen and their families were indirectly affected.

On April 4, the *Pioneer* reported that the strike was finally over.

Prosperity soon returned to Phoenix, and by the summer of 1904, at least 500 men were employed in the mines and an equal number were employed by Burns & Jordon, railway contractors for the Great Northern. With the payroll from this body of workers alone totalling $57,000 per month, Phoenix was enjoying an economic boom. Yet the year will probably be best remembered as one of crime, and political scandal.

Most of the furore revolved around the actions of the Chief of Police, Charles H. Flood. It all started on the evening of March 1, 1904, when Flood went down to the tenderloin district to serve a summons on Alice Chase, a lady of the evening. After serving the summons, Flood assaulted Chase by throwing her to the ground, partially strangling her, and drawing his revolver in a threatening manner.

Chase filed charges, and on March 3 the Phoenix board of police commissioners, headed by Judge W.R. Williams, convened to hear the case. They heard Dr. Boucher describe the woman's injuries, and listened to testimony from three witnesses, Georgia St. Clair, Annie Johnson and Nattie Hampden. For his part, Flood did not deny the charge, but claimed he acted in self defense. During the trial, R.B. Kerr, the prosecuting attorney, objected strongly on several matters and insisted his objections be noted for the record. In the end, however, the board completely exonerated Chief Flood. To make matters worse, Judge Williams then "gave the women a strong warning lecture, saying that there had been many complaints from that house, and that another complaint would result in closing it for good, and the inmates being sent to Nelson."

When the decision of Judge Williams became known on March 4, several of the city aldermen and many of the citizens of Phoenix strongly objected to the outcome. Mayor Rumberger was asked to call a special meeting of city council, which convened on March 5. At that meeting a resolution was put forth calling for the resignation of Chief Flood and Judge Williams. If this was not done, all six aldermen threatened to resign.

The regular meeting of city council, held on March 9, was another four hour heated discussion of the Flood incident. Finally, Judge Williams agreed to resign as a police commissioner, and Mayor Rumberger announced that Chief Flood would be suspended as soon as a provincial constable could be obtained to relieve him. For the moment, it appeared the problem had been resolved.

However, the peace was short-lived. At the regular council meeting held on April 6, the aldermen charged Mayor Rumberger with failing to keep his promise to discharge the chief of police and appoint a new police commissioner. Acting as a unit, they berated the mayor for the delay and stated categorically that his refusal to remove Flood smacked "strongly of partisan politics," and warned that "the scandal was becoming a widespread disgrace to the city of Phoenix." Before the meeting broke up, two resolutions were put forth calling for the removal of Chief Flood and Police Magistrate Williams, both of whom were "unfit to hold office." The five aldermen present then tendered their resignations.

Faced with the resignations of his aldermen, Rumberger finally agreed to suspend Chief Flood. Unfortunately, however, the mayor was only one member of the board of police commissioners. Judge Williams, holding office by virtue of provincial authority, still insisted on retaining Flood. Thus, the beleaguered chief of police remained in office.

The situation grew a little nastier in early May when Donald J. Matheson, the city clerk, refused to pay Flood his full wages for April. Instead, Matheson offered to pay him up to the time he had been suspended by Rumberger. Flood insisted on his full pay, but Matheson flatly refused. Mayor Rumberger tried to intervene on Flood's behalf by telling Matheson that he would assume all responsibility in the matter. Matheson responded to that suggestion by stating that he was only responsible to the city council for his actions, not the mayor, and he refused to budge.

On May 31, a commission headed by Dep. Att.-Gen. Hugh Archibald McLean was convened at Phoenix to inquire into the entire situation. R.B. Kerr represented the aldermen, while Judge W.R. Williams represented Chief Flood. During the trial, the entire messy situation, going back to the assault on Alice Chase was presented. According to the *Pioneer*, a "sensation" was created when Matheson, under oath, testified that Chief Flood has once told him that he was a partner in two roulette wheels.

Annie Johnson and Alice Chase, now living at Moyie, presented some sensational testimony of their own. After repeating the evidence given at the original trial, Johnson went on to accuse Flood of robbing "Robert Barr of $100 in her house." Barr testified that he had indeed been robbed,

but he was unable to say who did it.

Frank Golden, a bartender, and Lisa Noakes testified on behalf of Flood, and their testimony tended to discredit that of Annie Johnson. Flood himself was then called upon to testify, and he spent several hours on the stand, denying the theft from Barr and a number of other charges. However, despite the investigation into the whole affair, there appears to have been no decision rendered one way or the other; at least none was reported in the local press.

One week later, on June 1, an election was held to fill the vacancies left by the six resigning aldermen. Four of the aldermen who had resigned decided to run again, claiming that their re-election would be proof that the citizens of Phoenix endorsed their position. All four were re-elected.

Their first order of business, one week later, was to vote that Flood be paid $80 for April. Flood, however, continued to refuse this amount and demanded full payment, failing which, he threatened to sue. The council probably grinned as they read his ultimatum, then choose to ignore it. Flood then accepted his cheque for $80.

The new council lost little time in opening old wounds. At their June 22 meeting, they unanimously passed a resolution asking the Lieutenant-Governor to remove both Judge Williams and Chief Flood from office. This the Lieutenant-Governor apparently choose not to do, so relationships between city council and Chief Flood and Judge Williams continued to be strained.

Mayor George Rumberger, left, and Chief of Police Charles Flood, right, were the main focus of a political scandal in Phoenix that was believed to be the main reason the mayor was defeated twice.

In mid-August an incident occurred which, for a time, deflected attention away from Chief Flood. About 2 o'clock on the afternoon of August 12, a black prostitute named Annie Allen was murdered in the red light district. The murderer was a black boxer named Joshua Bell, who had arrived in Phoenix with a group of other boxers only a few days earlier.

It would later be learned that Allen and Bell were married and had lived together in Spokane. However, after Bell stabbed his wife, she fled to Phoenix. Bell went to Northport for a time, where he "administered a frightful beating" to another black man. To avoid the consequences of this act, Bell fled to Rossland, where he achieved a reputation for having an ugly temper.

How Bell learned of his wife's location is not revealed, but on the day of the murder he lay in hiding on Banner Street, where Allen lived with Annie Swan. When Allen finally appeared, Bell "stabbed her in the breast with a knife, and then kicked her in the teeth." When Annie Swan heard the commotion and went out to investigate, Bell chased her around the house and would surely have mur-

This undated general view of Phoenix was photographed from approximately the same position as the photograph on page 84. Compare the two photographs for an indication of Phoenix's growth.

dered her too had not Hank Allen, who was sawing wood nearby, started shouting for the police. Bell at once gave up the pursuit of Swan and took to the woods in the direction of the United States border.

Bell's escape from justice was short-lived, however. Chief Flood figured that the murderer would try to make his way to the U.S. by an unused trail and headed for the hills towards the War Eagle mine to intercept him. After encountering Bell's tracks some two miles west, Flood took a shortcut that put him ahead of the murderer. When Bell walked casually past the deserted shack where Flood lay in hiding, he was surprised and placed in irons before he knew what had happened.

On August 14 a coroner's jury determined that Annie Allen had met her death "by a knife wound inflicted by Joshua Bell." Bell was subsequently tried in the Supreme Court in Greenwood in late October, found guilty and sentenced to hang. At 9:30 a.m. on January 13, 1905, the sentence was carried out at the Kamloops jail.

Under different circumstances, the capture of this murderer by Flood would have endeared him to the citizens of Phoenix. But the bad feelings remained until, on June 14, 1905, Flood finally resigned and went to work in the mines.

In January, 1906, George Rumberger was elected mayor of Phoenix for the seventh straight time. Three weeks later, at the newly-appointed board of city police commissioners, Flood was reappointed chief of police despite numerous objections. A year later, Donald Matheson, the city clerk who had taken such a strong stand against Flood, defeated Rumberger and became the new mayor of Phoenix. According to the *Pioneer*, it was "a clean sweep for Matheson and his supporters, the entire ticket being elected.

"The chief issue was the conduct of the police department, growing out of the trouble of a couple of years ago caused by Chief of Police Flood. Mr. Rumberger won out that time, and Mr. Flood, after a vacation, retained as chief until the present. The majority of citizens wished a change and so expressed themselves at the polls."

Meanwhile, while the Flood scandal seemed to preoccupy the citizens of Phoenix, other important events were unfolding in the history of the city. At 10 o'clock on the morning of February 14, 1905, for instance, mine whistles once again gave the dreaded alarm of fire in the city. This was the third major fire in Phoenix, and like the other two, it occurred in the Rumberger addition.

It is thought that the fire originated in the second floor of the Brooklyn Hotel and was caused from a heating stove. Within minutes the Brooklyn Hotel was ablaze and the flames had spread to the adjoining Phoenix Hotel. The inferno spread so rapidly that a dozen men, who had just come off night shift at the mines, barely escaped with their lives. Some had to jump from second-story windows, while another was rescued from a third-story window by a ladder.

"Smoke and flames rolled up to the heavens as the fire gained headway," reported the *Pioneer*, "and not a spectator would have given a dollar for all the buildings on that side of the street. When the imminent danger of the extensive conflagration was appreciated, many willing hands began to remove furniture and valuables from the Mine, Butte and Norden hotels and other buildings. As is always the case, much of this was ruined in moving.

"Both volunteer hose companies responded quickly to the alarm, and while there was a little delay in getting the water turned on, owing to a defective hydrant, splendid work was done by the fire boys when water did begin to flow. At first the streams were playing on the postoffice block, which would undoubtedly have gone from the intense heat, as it was smoking, but for the water. It was so hot that while one gang held the nozzle, another threw blankets over them and then heaped the blankets with snow — and then the first gang would be relieved. But the postoffice block was saved, as was also the Mint Hotel, right in the path of the fire. No one, for a time, thought there was the barest possibility of saving the Mint, but it was done by the most strenuous and dangerous of work on the part of the fire fighters, although the side of the building was partially ruined and the flames got through into the lower floor at one time."

The biggest lost was suffered by seven-time alderman James Marshall and his partner E.P. Shea, owners of the Brooklyn Hotel. The hotel was known as the Columbia when it was first erected by W.T. Kaake in December of 1899. At some point a subsequent owner changed the name to Brooklyn. In the summer of 1904, Marshall & Shea purchased the building from F.J. Finucane, and since that time they had spend a considerable amount in repairing the three-story, 35x65-foot hotel. It was considered one of Phoenix's finest hotels, and now it lay in ashes. The building, furniture and stock was valued at $8,000, but there was only $2,600 in insurance.

The Phoenix Hotel, currently owned by George Rumberger, had been erected by Harry Nash in October, 1899. The building and furniture was valued at $5,000, half of which was insured. J.H. Graham's Mint Hotel had suffered $1,000 in damage, and there was an additional damage of $1,750 to other businesses.

On June 3, the *Pioneer* announced that Marshall and Rumberger were planning to erect a substantial hotel to replace the two lost in the fire. Costing $20,000, the three-story hotel, plus basement, was 60x65-feet in size and sat on the corner of Dominion Avenue and Phoenix Street, not far from the GNR station. In addition to a 14x14-foot office, a 23x60-foot bar and a 16x40-foot dining room, the hotel had 40 bedrooms. It was opened to the public for the first time on November 9.

1905 was another banner year for the copper mining city of Phoenix. In March, the first passenger train of the VV&E extension of the GNR, which was completed to Phoenix in 1904, began running regularly. In mid-June, R.H. Karatofsky opened a regulation-size bowling alley using the "latest and best Brunswick-Balke-Collender" equipment. In mid-November, the mayor and city council met for the first time in the new Phoenix City Hall. The lower floor of the 44x50-foot, two-story building contained an 18x50-foot hose reel house, an 18x20-foot city clerk's office, a 9x18-foot office for the chief of police, and a 14x17-foot prisoner's chamber containing three 7x9-foot cells. The second floor contained three large rooms. Above the second floor was a 7x9-foot tower. The building, erected at a cost of $4,345, was located on the northeast corner of Montezuma Street and Dominion Avenue in the Dominion Copper Co.'s addition. In December, the Phoenix Miners' Union completed its new opera house and meeting hall. During the year, 980,000 tons of ore had been shipped from the mines around Phoenix, and the city's population had grown to about 2,000.

Beneath Phoenix, 50 miles of tunnels were interconnected in a giant maze that employed about 800 men. As production continued to soar during 1906, the very foundation of the city was threatened. Finally, it happened. In the early morning hours of Tuesday, October 2, 1906, a heavy blast that had been set off in a stope rising from the 250-foot level, broke through the surface. The drift ran directly under Dominion Avenue, below the city hall, to a connection with the Idaho mine. Part of Dominion Avenue began to slide into the hole, and in four days it had expanded to a chasm 50-feet wide and 50-feet deep.

Built on a honeycomb of mine tunnels, Phoenix was the scene of several cave-ins over the years. The one shown above occurred in April, 1919.

On August 10, 1907, a much more serious cave-in occurred. This time the collapse occurred "under the ore bins and two CPR tracks running past the bunkers sank, the hole covering a space of 75 to 100 feet in width by perhaps 400 to 500 feet in length. . . ."

Although, once again, no one was hurt or injured, one man had a narrow escape. John Picthal was in the engineer's room when a "carman" rushed in and said something was wrong. Picthal went to the ore bunkers to investigate, and while there the structure began to quiver. Sensing the danger, Picthal ran for his life and had barely reached safety when two-thirds of the bunkers collapsed into the chasm with a crash.

"One CPR track was carried down by the massive timbers of the orebunkers," reported the *Pioneer*, "the other still remains suspended in mid-air, held only by the fishplates and the spikes in the ties. And yet, across this abyss, taking his life in his hand, one man — perhaps more — had the temerity to go, and that without the need for doing so whatsoever, except to say that he thus dared death."

In April, 1907, the collieries at Bellevue, Frank, Hillcrest, Lille, Lundbreck, Michel, Coleman, Bankhead, Fernie and Canmore were closed because of another coal miner's strike. Because of a lack of coke, the Phoenix mines were soon forced to suspend operations, and on May 4, the *Pioneer* reported: "For the first time in years, hardly a wheel is turning today at any of the large mines of Phoenix Camp, and practically all the copper mines in this camp are closed tight, in most cases only the engineers, pump men and the like being on duty at the several large properties, which combined usually ship upwards of 4,000 tons of ore each 24 hours." A week later, however, the newspaper was able to announce that the strike had been settled and that normal shipments of coke would be renewed shortly.

In November, the mines of the Boundary Country were shut down yet again. This time, however, it was not due to a coke shortage, but something far more sombre. The low price of copper, combined with high operating costs, had forced mines throughout the west to close without any warning.

"Last Monday evening (November 11) orders came from headquarters of the several mining companies, and the hundreds of men employed were immediately notified and preparations made to definitely close," reported the *Pioneer*.

"At the Granby mines every miner, mucker, blaster and machinist, tram man, crusher man, electrician, carpenter, etc., was let go, only the heads of departments being retained to put things in shape for idleness. All drilling machines were taken out and stored, together with other tools, the pumps were connected up by steam, so that the big compressor can be idle. Practically the same thing took place at the Mother Lode, Snowshoe and Emma mines, and hereafter scarcely any but watchman will be seen around either mines or smelters.

"While figures are not given out, it is known that over $100,000 was paid out in wages alone to the men, to which should be added say $30,000 more from savings accounts (from men who decided to leave Phoenix). Consequently, the force of the (Eastern Township) bank was working night and day, and currency was shipped in from Winnipeg and Vancouver by the thousands of dollars, as fast as express could bring it, to meet the temporary drain."

After cashing their cheques and closing their savings accounts, men began to leave Phoenix in droves.

"As could be expected," continued the *Pioneer*, "the outgoing trains since Tuesday have been heavily loaded, on both the Canadian Pacific and Great Northern, the latter getting by far the largest traffic, as Spokane seemed to be the immediate goal of many." Tickets were also purchased to almost every part of the United States and Canada, while others returned home to England, Ireland, Scotland, and Wales.

Phoenix, which had survived three major fires, two coal miner's strikes and political scandal, now faced its darkest hour. Of the men who had not abandoned the Boundary Country, some obtained work at logging camps at Grand Forks, others cut ties for the railroad, while many others simply went fishing or hunting. All hoped for an early resolution to the problem.

When the Rossland Miners' Union voted to accept lower wages in order to ensure that operations there would continue, it offered Phoenix a glimmer of hope. On December 1, Gen. Mgr. Jay P. Graves announced that the Granby Company would resume operations on December 4, partly because of reduced operating expenses, but also because Phoenix miners had agreed to accept a lower wage scale, like Rossland, Butte and elsewhere.

However, the Phoenix Miners' Union wrote a letter on December 4 claiming that "the Granby Co. had agreed not to make any alterations in the wage scale until they had communicated with the Miner's Union." A special meeting of the union membership was then held to discuss the proposal. The members of the Phoenix Miners' Union voted 177 to 129 in favour of accepting the wage reduction. However, the Grand Forks Smeltermen's Union voted 135 to 35 to reject the offer. Thus workers at both the smelter and the mines refused to return to work.

The stalemate continued for over two weeks, until, on December 24, the proposal was put to another vote at Grand Forks. This time there were only 30 opposed, and the day after Christmas, the mines resumed production.

Amazingly, despite the problems of 1907, the Phoenix mines were still able to produce 868,000 tons of ore. For the first quarter of 1908, ore shipments from the Granby mines alone totalled 264,581 tons. The output for March was not only the largest in the company's history, but also the largest for any copper mine in the whole of Canada. When all Phoenix mines were included, 1908 turned out to be a fantastic year, with a record 1,083,353 tons, all but 16,564 tons from mines belonging to the Granby Co. 1909 turned out to be another record year. Although the Dominion Copper Co. mines did not ship a single ton, the Granby Company mines produced 1,238,343 tons.

Phoenix, meanwhile was maturing. It was no longer the wide-open, free-wheeling, rough and ready gambling city of the past. Each year saw new bylaws passed to improve the quality of life. On July 5, 1909, Rev. S. Lundie, of the Presbyterian Church, and Rev. R.W. Hibbert, of the Methodist Church, appeared before the board of license commissioners with a petition signed by 248 residents asking that the number of liquor licenses in Phoenix be reduced.

Whether as a result of their petition or not, the commissioners voted to renew the liquor licenses for only seven hotels: Brooklyn, Dominion, Alexander, Knob Hill, Central, Butte and Bellevue. That meant that the liquor licenses of seven other hotels, Summit, Stemwinder, Cottage, Mint, Norden, Maple Leaf and Golden, had been turned down. Two other hotels had not bothered to apply. Thus, of the 16 hotels that held liquor licenses prior to the meeting, nine were now prohibited from selling intoxicants.

City council was outraged by the decision of the commissioners. The cancelling of seven liquor licenses meant a loss of $10,500 in revenue to the city during the first six months, and the aldermen were certain that the city's finances would not survive the shock. At a heated meeting held on July 14, aldermen Rogers and McKenzie introduced a motion to empower the city clerk to issue license renewals to all license holders, upon the proper fee being paid. Mayor Rumberger, who had been reelected in 1909 after losses in 1907 and 1908, ruled the motion out of order because it was illegal. An adjournment was then made so that the city clerk could obtain legal advice.

The meeting resumed on July 15, at which time the city clerk advised the mayor and council members that the city's solicitor stated that council "would be taking grave responsibility in passing such a motion." Despite this warning, the motion was again presented, but once again, the mayor ruled it out of order. Accordingly, aldermen Rogers, McKenzie and Deane informed the mayor that they would not sit at future council meetings. Thus, civic affairs were temporarily placed on hold, since a quorum could not be reached until aldermen Cook and Marshall returned.

The following December, city council, having apparently been unsuccessful in overturning the decision of the commissioners, decided to recover at least part of the lost revenue by increasing the license fee to the remaining

(Top left) Some buildings were still standing at the Mother Lode in August, 1984, when this photo was taken.
(Top right) All that remains today are some concrete foundations.
(Left) The pit of the Mother Lode mine in June, 1991.
(Bottom left) A view of the Deadwood town-site in June, 1991, looking southwest from the road leading to the Mother Lode mine.
(Below) Buckhorn Creek skirts the western edge of the Deadwood town-site.

(Left) The Sanctus Bell from the Roman Catholic Church at Phoenix.

(Above) A roulette wheel from a Phoenix gambling establishment. The plate is from the Brooklyn Hotel in Phoenix.

(Top right) This ugly scar is all that remains of the once bustling city of Phoenix.

(Opposite page, inset) A coloured postcard depicting an underground mining scene at the Rawhide mine in Phoenix.

(Right) This sculpture of the mythical Phoenix, which once stood watch over the copper mining city of the same name, now spreads its wings beside the Greenwood City Hall.

Raw Hyde Mine, Pheonix, B.C.

(Far left) The Phoenix memorial to the men who died in the First World War.

(Above) These rock ruins are located a couple of miles beyond the town-site of Phoenix.

(Left) The final resting place of Baby Dawson in the Phoenix cemetery.

(Below) These concrete ruins are all that remain on the site of Phoenix today.

(Left) The Championship Cup won by the Phoenix Hockey Team.
(Above) A beer label from the Phoenix Brewing Company.
(Top right) A key to room 31 of the Brooklyn Hotel in Phoenix.
(Right) A Phoenix firemen's helmet. Note the lion perched on the top. These four items, as well as the roulette wheel, plate and Santus Bell on page 98 are on display at the Grand Forks Museum, Grand Forks, B.C.
(Below) A colorized photograph of the ruins of the Phoenix City Hall. The road is Dominion Avenue, leading to the Rumberger addition, on the Cimeron claim, in the distance.

This painting by artist Bill Maximick was one of three original paintings commissioned especially for this book. It shows the Canadian Pacific Railway yards in the foreground, and the main business section of Eholt during the winter of 1906. Based on actual photographs of Eholt, this painting is historically accurate.

(Above) The old Eholt town-site is now rolling farmland. This photograph was taken from the CPR right-of-way in June of 1991.
(Top left) Only a few ties remain to indicate where the CPR spur line veered of towards the copper mining city of Phoenix.
(Above right) The location of the CPR yards at Eholt. The Eholt station and water tower stood about where the small pile of debris is visible in centre of photo. The opening directly over the pile of rails in the foreground was where the spur turned towards Eholt.
(Opposite page, top inset) Lilac bushes grow at the edge of a CPR building foundation at Eholt.
(Opposite page, centre inset) The author's 4x4 driving down the old CPR right-of-way from Greenwood to Eholt.
(Opposite page, bottom inset) A view of the CPR yards at Eholt when the town was at its peak.

(Above) The remains of Paulson, a CPR railway station of more recent vintage, along the right-of-way to Gladstone.
(Left) The Paulson CPR station.
(Below) The CPR right-of-way at Paulson, looking west toward Gladstone. Like elsewhere throughout the Boundary, the rails were removed in the spring of 1991.

(Above) Today, all that remains of Gladstone is this widening of the CPR right-of-way where the siding was located.
(Top inset) An old railway wheel.
(Left inset) Old window pane from a building that has long since disappeared.
(Below) Foundation of what was probably the CPR water tower at Gladstone siding.

This full-colour painting, by artist Bill Maximick, is one of three especially commissioned for this book. It depicts freight teams from Bossburg, Washington, passing through Cascade's First Street in 1898. Based on historical photographs and research, the painting is historically accurate.

(Opposite page, main) Cascade Gorge, viewed from the bridge near the powerhouse. The Cascade dam was further up the river.
(Opposite page, inset) This penstock once carried water from the dam to the Cascade powerhouse, and is located at the powerhouse.
(Above) Although this home has been re-roofed and a carport has been added, the basic building is an original Cascade building.
(Right) One of several foundations near the corner of Main Street and 2nd Avenue in Cascade, the area which once housed Cascade's main business section.
(Below) Cascade's brick powerhouse in June, 1991.

(Above) The name Niagara lives on in this modern street sign.
(Right) Fisherman Creek at Niagara in in the summer of 1991.
(Below) The Niagara town-site today has about a dozen modern homes.

hotels to $650 a year. In February, 1910, the city continued its crackdown on gambling and drinking by abolishing slot machines and forcing bars to remain closed on Sundays.

On Friday, August 12, 1910, Phoenix suffered its fourth and most destructive fire. Although only an hour elapsed from the time the fire originated until it had spent itself, it left only a trail of ruins where substantial buildings had once stood.

Because the office of the *Pioneer* was also destroyed in the fire, the newspaper did not publish from August 6 to September 10. Fortunately, on that date, the paper gave a brief account of the conflagration.

"The fire started at 4 p.m. in the oil house at the mouth of No. 3 tunnel of the Granby mine. Fanned by the draft from the tunnel the blaze shot down the long tram shed to the No. 3 crusher and ore bins with lightening rapidity, spreading at the same time to the Granby's new machine shops, the power generator station, the company's officials' cottage and Superintendent Smith's residence. These buildings were all a mass of flames in a very few minutes, the occupants of the houses having barely time to escape, while a brisk breeze carried the flames and sparks to buildings on the lower streets, the school, the Methodist church and *Pioneer* printing office apparently taking fire simultaneously. All the buildings being frame they were eaten up like matchwood by the fire and the heat was terrific. When the fire was burning fiercest near the crusher a compressed air pipe burst and acted as a bellows to a fiery furnace, forcing large burning embers great distances and starting fires in various parts of the city as far as the Catholic church and the general hospital.

"That the entire city was not wiped out is regarded as a miracle; certain it is that such a prospect appeared inevitable at times and every householder in the city was making preparations to vacate as much personal effects as possible. But the credit for saving the city was widespread; hundreds of fire fighters worked heroically, but not least among them were the property owners who climbed on the roof with buckets of water and protected his own. The strenuous fights of the fire departments were successful in saving the old Ironsides hotel and Black's jewelry store; had either of these buildings got a start the city would have been doomed, while an equally brilliant fight accounts for the Miner's Union Hall escaping with a slight scorching. The fire fighters worked under the disadvantage of poor water pressure, which resulted from practically every tap in the city being open. One thing favourable to preventing the spread of the fire was the fact that one shift of miners was just going to work and another shift was coming off at the same time, and a force of a couple of hundred men were on the scene with Granby's special lines of hose in but a few minutes from the time the fire was discovered.

"The fire occasioned a property loss of $115,000, the Granby Company losing about $90,000 on which they carried $70,000 insurance. Other losses amounted to $25,000, upon which there is $12,000 insurance."

But, as they had in the past, most Phoenix businessmen and residents began to rebuild almost immediately. Nor did the frequency of fires appear to discourage new enterprises, for in December Cosgrove & McAstocker opened a "moving picture theatre" in the basement of the Royal Bil-

(Above) The Phoenix General Hospital.
(Below) The Phoenix Hockey team in 1915, photographed with trophies. The trophy in the centre is now on display at the Grand Forks Museum.

liard Parlour. On January 14, 1911, the *Pioneer* wrote: "The Picture Theatorium is growing in popularity; some excellent pictures are shown and the admission is two bits."

In two separate fires in 1911, on January 15 and December 11, the Queen's Hotel (formerly the Summit), and the Alexander Hotel were destroyed. Quick action from fire fighters in both instances prevented the fires from spreading.

By this time the population of Phoenix was nearing 4,000, and, although the mines were still productive, there were ominous clouds on the horizon. Since 1910 the Granby Company's engineers had been warning that the ore values were diminishing. Subsequently, the company began to search for new ore bodies. In late January, 1911, the company secured options of 50 claims northeast of Chesaw, Washington. But its best prospects lay at Hidden Creek, on the northern coast of B.C. about 50 miles from Prince Rupert. On November 15, 1910, the Granby Company had optioned 70 percent of the property, and between then and January, 1911, some 5,000 feet of diamond drill cores were taken out.

During the first quarter of 1911, the Phoenix mines shipped over 500,000 tons of ore, a new record. Then, on April 1, the coal miners went on strike again, affecting 16 collieries and 7,000 men. The Grand Forks smelter, which

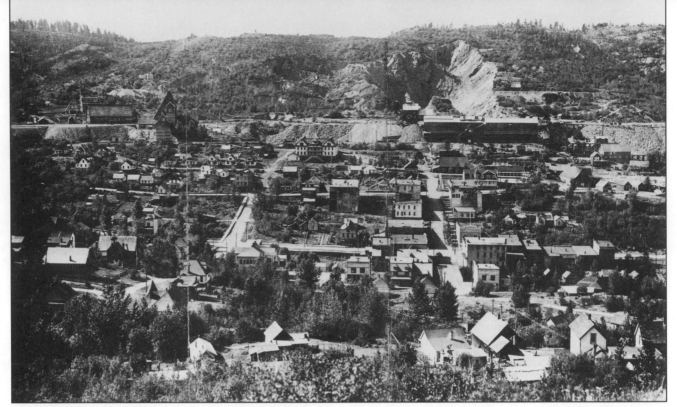

The mountaintop city of Phoenix at its prime. Unlike its namesake, it did not rise from the ashes after the mines played out and its residents moved away. Compare this view with the colour photograph on pages 92-93. Part of the skyline are all that remain the same.

had enough coke to sustain its furnaces for about seven weeks, used up its reserves by late May, after which operations at the mines and smelter ground to a halt. Only three weeks later, however, the Granby Company announced plans to resume full operations on June 12. Fed up with being at the mercy of the Crow's Nest Pass Coal Company, Granby officials had decided to buy coke from Pennsylvania. Unfortunately, this coke proved to be of poor quality, and on August 12 the Granby Company shut down its mines and smelter and began paying off its employees.

Meanwhile, the Hidden Creek mine was proving to be far richer and larger than first expected, and on June 14 the Granby Company increased its holdings to 80 percent. The minority shareholder was M.K. Rogers, who sold his stock to the company a week later.

By October 300 men were employed at Hidden Creek, developing and improving the property. Bunkhouses had been erected, together with a sawmill and storehouse, and work was continuing on the dam that would provide water power for electricity.

This same month the coal miners' strike was finally settled. As coke shipments were resumed, the Granby Company reopened its mines, and on December 20, the first shipment was sent to the Grand Forks smelter. By March, 1912, the daily average shipments were exceeding 4,000 tons, well in line with the projected daily goal of 5,000 tons. From 1912-14, The Granby Company poured its profits from the Phoenix mines into its new property at Hidden Creek, where millions were spent in construction and development.

During this period, Phoenix continued to prosper. In June, 1912, the Morrin-Thompson Company established the first auto dealership in Phoenix when it purchased four automobiles from the Overland Company of Toledo, Ohio. On January 1, 1913, Phoenix celebrated the opening of a new $10,000 skating and curling rink. But these were isolated highlights. Overall, Phoenix was in its twilight and it was beginning to show.

More and more frequently the *Pioneer* printed little announcements of well known Phoenix residents leaving the city. James Marshall, who had been an alderman in Phoenix for the first seven years of its existence, moved to Nelson in the fall of 1913. Even George Rumberger, the father of Phoenix and the city's mayor for so many years, the first seven consecutively, had moved to Regina.

On August 14, 1914, a fire destroyed the Maple Leaf Hotel. Eight days later the Union hall was also destroyed by fire. Although the Union building was subsequently rebuilt, there was little new construction in the mile-high city. With the mines closed because of high operating costs and low metal values, the future of Phoenix did not look good. On August 15, the *Pioneer* reported: "The Canadian Pacific Railway and Great Northern Railway depots are the scenes of no little animation these days, scores of people leaving for points in Canada and the United States. Among the passengers departing are a number who have booked through to England."

At Hidden Creek, meanwhile, the town of Anyox had sprung into existence and the work force had been substantially increased. With little work available in Phoenix, many families packed up their belongings and moved there. When George Rumberger visited Anyox in August, he saw quite a number of "old-time residents of Phoenix," all of whom appeared to be doing well.

In December, 1914, the Granby Company agreed to reopen the Phoenix mines after workers agreed to a 25 percent reduction in wages. By April, 1915, the mines employed 400 men, but by this time the population of Phoenix had dropped to under 1,500. The First World War made copper a vital commodity, and it soon increased in price from 11¢ to 13¢ a pound. This increase, combined with the lower wages, allowed the Granby Company to resume mining of its lower grade ore at Phoenix. The price of copper continued to rise until, in 1918, it stood at 28¢. Following the war, however, prices plummeted back to 14¢, and the Granby Company closed its Phoenix mines and concentrated on the richer ores at Anyox.

As the months passed, and the mines did not reopen, many of the unemployed workers packed up and moved away. Many believed the situation would improve, so they simply left their homes and businesses intact. But when copper prices continued to fall, the Granby Company decided not to reopen the Phoenix mines. This was devastating news for the city, and the end was rapid and ruthless.

"In a race against winter," wrote T.W. Paterson, "salvage crews began to tear up railway tracks, as residents packed up what belongings they could take with them and the city council. . .concluded the work of wrapping up the town's affairs by selling the skating rink to a Vancouver company for $1,200. The money received was invested in the erection of a cenotaph which, despite the fact that Phoenix was no more, would continue to honour those of its citizens who had died for their country during the First World War.

"A portion of the $1,200 was given to the Royal Canadian Legion in Grand Forks to insure that the monument would be cared for, and a further sum was used to create a fund to pay a town watchman for a year, by which time all Phoenix residents would have moved away. This post went to an old resident, Adolph Cirque, better known as 'Forepaw' because of the crude iron hook and braces he wore after losing most of an arm.

"Carrying a billy club and wearing a home-made star cut from a tomato tin, Forepaw moved into the steepled city hall and proclaimed himself mayor and chief constable of Phoenix. Two others also remained: carpenter W.H. Bambury and Robert Denzler, the miner who had coined the name Phoenix for his claim and for which the town was later christened."

When, in October, 1927, an American newspaper reporter visited Phoenix, there was still a lot to see. Although some 200 buildings had been torn down or moved away since the mines had closed, many still remained, and they were "an impressive sight, boarded, ghostly and silent in the canyon." The three-story Brooklyn still stood and was in good shape, but the old Morrin-Thompson hardware store across the street had crumbled to pieces. "Higher up the hill, looking spick and span, is the hospital, although the insides is in ruin.

"In the main part of the city and flanking the hills are scores of beautiful residences, boarded and ghostly, while in the lower end of town is the remains of an old brewery. As one stands on a knoll at the upper end of the canyon, across and high up on the hillside rears the mammoth building of the Granby Company, which alone at one time employed a thousand men. . . ."

Over the years, scavengers from neighbouring communities continued to tear down the buildings for their lumber and bricks. Those that remained eventually collapsed, and once busy streets were reclaimed by nature until only piles of lumber or foundations gave testimony to the once mighty city. Before long, only the cenotaph, cemetery and old shaft houses remained.

In August, 1956, the Granby Company, encouraged by high copper prices, decided to resume mining at Phoenix once again. This time, however, the operation consisted of an open pit mine. For 20 years production continued, during which time 140,000,000 pounds of copper, 1,400,000 ounces of gold and 200,000 ounces of silver, valued at $80,000,000, was mined.

Unfortunately, the gouging away of the mountain top removed any traces of Phoenix that had remained. Today, these enormous open pits give mute testimony to the effectiveness of the latest effort, and, except for a few crumbling ruins in the woods, a building made of rock, the cenotaph and the cemetery, not a trace of old Phoenix has survived. It is a sad finish for a city that began with a single cabin and climbed to such lofty heights. ❧

Although this photograph of Lower Town is dated 1909, the deserted streets would suggest it may have been taken during the 1907 coal miner's strike, when many miners and their families deserted Phoenix.

Eholt

Eholt's main business section. At its prime, the town boasted five or six hotels and a variety of other businesses.

LOCATED on the divide between Grand Forks and Greenwood, Eholt was named after Luxembourg native Louis Eholt, who operated a cattle ranch alongside a small creek that would also bear his name, in 1890. In 1895, Thomas Corkill and A. Hamilton located the Great Laxey and Twin claims on the south side of Eholt Creek, about seven miles from Greenwood. However, these and other nearby claims did not generate a great deal of interest until the spring of 1898 when a large ore body of quartz, carrying copper, gold and silver, was discovered on the Great Laxey. Development work on the Twin revealed the same encouraging results, and soon the mountains were alive with prospectors. Later the same year, when the Canadian Pacific Railway (CPR) designated Eholt as a railroad divisional point along its Columbia & Western Railway right-of-way, its future as a town-site was assured. H.T. Wilgress, the CPR's land development representative, was appointed to oversee its early progress.

It is not surprising that Pat Burns & Co., which supplied meat for the construction crews and had branches at other locations along the railway's construction line, also was the first to establish at Eholt. The first mention of Eholt in the local papers appeared on December 3, 1898, when the

Boundary Creek *Times* reported that a hotel was to be erected there. Unfortunately, the paper failed to mention the hotel's name or its builder. However, other research suggests that this first "hotel" was actually a boarding house operated by Sam McOrmond, formerly of Cascade and Gladstone.

On May 6, 1899, the Cascade *Record* noted that the town-site of Eholt was being cleared and "will soon be surveyed and platted and lots placed on the market." In its June 3 issue, the *Record* described Eholt as "a hotel (boarding house), two barber shops and a restaurant," although no lots had yet been sold. Later that month McOrmond, who had been conducting the boarding house, began construction of a 30x50-foot three-story hotel called the Merchant's Exchange. This was Eholt's first real hotel.

Finally, on June 29, surveyor Wollaston began laying out the town-site. By July 8 the town had been subdivided into lots, but because the plans had to be filed with the Department of Lands and Works, lots could not be placed on the market until August 29. Three days later the Greenwood *Miner* reported on the sales: "The townsite of Eholt was thrown open to purchasers on Tuesday. The sale was very successful, about all the lots on both sides of the main street having been taken. Some half dozen business buildings are going up, and a number of residences. Applications have been made for four or five hotel licenses. Property is moving freely."

One of Eholt's first businessmen was George Rendell, who, you may recall, established the Boundary Country's first general store at Boundary Falls in 1894. Rendell established the Eholt Trading Co., and on September 1 a post office was opened in his store. Already Eholt was booming. Only two weeks after the first lots went on the market, the *Miner* reported that "over a hundred lots have been sold and some 30 buildings are in course of construction. The prospects of the town are the brightest in the Boundary. Among the prominent buyers of lots is the Hudson's Bay Co. This is the only town in the district in which this Co. has lots, and it looks well for Eholt. The CPR mainline runs through the place and from this point branches for Phoenix and Long Lake camps. Surrounding the town are many promising mines; the most prominent of these are the B.C., Emma and Oro Denoro. Sam McOrmond is building a 3-story hotel on which work is being rushed. Mr. Munro and Mr. Kaiser are also putting up hotels.

"Knox and Delaney are building on Barclay Ave. and will put in a stock of jewelry. A.B. Ripley, druggist, will occupy a part of the building.

"Thompson & McKenzie's building on Barclay Ave. is fast nearing completion, and they will put in a stock of dry goods as soon as completed.

"Otto Leidiger will put in a barber shop in a couple of weeks.

"Mr. Telo, the hotel man, is erecting cold storage near the CPR depot. The building will be 25x115 feet."

The next day the *Times* reported that Fred Munns was opening a hotel, and on September 29, the *Miner* reported that the CPR track layers were expected at Eholt the following morning. "The company is building a siding 1,500 feet long, and the orders have been given to rush it with all possible speed."

On October 27, the *Miner* printed another update:

"Now that the railway is in Eholt is a rather lively place. A large quantity of freight has been delivered — hay, coal, machinery, etc. Work of laying steel on the spurs has been delayed on account of the lack of steel. Grading is completed to the B.C. mine. P. Welch & Co., are putting in their camp here to carry on the work from this point. The CPR is building a tank and a section house for the present. Three tracks have been laid the whole length of the station ground, with double tracks for 2,000 feet and 1,700 feet of siding."

Eholt's business community included a livery stable operated by McKeller & Tighe, who were also operating a stage line between Eholt and Greenwood. J.L. Chase had opened the Eholt Butcher Shop in competition with Pat Burns. Rendell's Eholt Trading Co. was doing a large business in groceries and mining supplies. Others included: Alexander McKenzie, news and fruit stand; Angus B. Ripley, drug and stationery store; Knox & Delaney, jewellers; McKinnon Bros., clothing and dry goods, and T. Denton, building and contracting. There were also three restaurants, a barber and a blacksmith shop. A building had also been completed for J.J. Caulfield, of Caulfield & Lamont, Greenwood, who planned on opening up a hardware store. However, when the Eholt Trading Company decided to deal in hardware in addition to their other lines of merchandise, Caulfield & Lamont decided not to proceed. Their building was then taken over by the McKinnon Bros.

As Eholt continued to attract residents, railway workers, miners and businessmen, Barclay Avenue, the town's main street, was graded, and sidewalks were constructed. There were reports that Rev. D.A. Stuart, a Presbyterian minister, had purchased a lot and planned to erect a church as soon as arrangements could be made. A school was soon being talked about, and the *Miner* even claimed that some Greenwood businessmen had formed a company "for the purpose of erecting and operating a $20,000 brewery at Eholt."

By late November Eholt had five hotels in operation, although only three, Northern, Eholt and Kaiser, had been

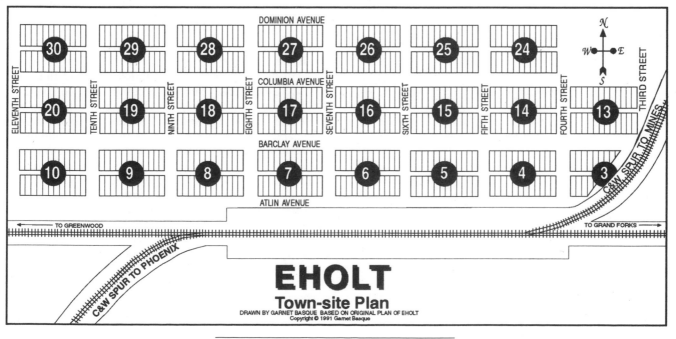

EHOLT
Town-site Plan
DRAWN BY GARNET BASQUE BASED ON ORIGINAL PLAN OF EHOLT
Copyright © 1991 Garnet Basque

The Emma mine near Eholt.

granted liquor licenses. Sam McOrmond's Merchant Exchange was the first to open on September 16. Fred Munns' two-story Hotel Northern appears to have been the second to open. Complete with bathrooms and hot air heating, it was operating by the first week of October. J.A. McMaster and Julius Black's Columbia Hotel, on Barclay Avenue, was third, opening about two weeks after the Northern. Norman Luce came next with the Summit Hotel. The name was later changed to the Eholt Hotel, then back to the Summit. Fred Kaiser's Hotel Kaiser, a three-story building, was open to the public on November 22.

By the end of November, roads had been completed between the Jewel and B.C. mines, and a wagon road to Phoenix was being discussed. "There are now five wagon roads and three railroads leading to Eholt," reported the *Miner*, "all tapping some of the most valuable mineral wealth of the Boundary Country."

On December 1, the *Miner* noted that Dr. Kingston, who had been appointed physician for all the principal mines surrounding Eholt, had decided to locate there and planned to erect a small hospital. As a thriving new town, Eholt was twice blessed. It enjoyed the obvious benefits of being a CPR work yard, and it was fast becoming a mining centre. North of the town lay the Jewel and Old Rambler mines; east, the Strawberry; southeast, the Main and Rathmullen; south, the B.C. and Mountain View; and west, the Oro Denoro, Emma and a host of others. All of these mines, except the Jewel, were within a two-mile radius of the town.

In its December 22 edition, the *Times* reported that Fred Kaiser was "excavating for another building, adjoining the large building he has already built." This building was also to be a hotel, according to the March 28, 1900, issue of the *Times:* "The new Kaiser hotel at Eholt will be opened to the public on Friday with a dance and supper." A month later, the *Miner* described the establishment: "The Commercial

Hotel is undoubtedly one of the best in the Boundary district. It is completely furnished from roof to cellar. The dining room is large and commodious, and Mrs. Kaiser looks after the welfare of between 30 and 40 guests at each meal. The bar is well appointed and the smoking room is very cosy. There are two large parlors upstairs with a fine piano in each. . . The walls are all plastered and the floors boast of rich carpeting."

Since there is no evidence to indicate that Eholt now had six hotels, it must be assumed that Kaiser closed down the Kaiser Hotel when his new hotel was completed. To what use the old building was put is not recorded.

During the spring of 1900, Eholt continued to be active. The Hotel Northern had become "the headquarters for the commercial fraternity," but all hotels were doing a brisk trade. By the end of April, carpenters were busy building a freight depot at Eholt, and a week later construction crews arrived to complete the spur line between Eholt and Phoenix. About this time, the Hotel Northern changed hands, having been purchased by H.M. Flint, of Phoenix. On May 19, the Phoenix *Pioneer* noted that a schoolhouse was being erected at Eholt, "by the people of the town. It will be what is known as an assisted school. That is, the government allows $50 annually besides paying the teacher's salary."

Following Eholt's rapid early growth, the town stabilized, and the only noteworthy item to be publicized in local papers for the balance of 1900 occurred on May 19 when a burglar broke into the Eholt Trading Company store and stole $17 or $18 from the till.

During the first eight months of 1901, except for a small fire that was quickly extinguished at the Hotel Northern in January, most of the activities reported at Eholt concerned the CPR. In January, the *Pioneer* noted that its "two-stall roundhouse" had been completed. Six months later the paper reported that the CPR was "putting in three new side tracks, with a capacity of 60 cars each. Six stalls are to be

The CPR work yards at Eholt gave the town an economic boost. The above photo, looking west, shows the station and water tower, the roundhouse and the ill-fated shay locomotive that was destroyed when it went over a steep grade en route to Phoenix. (Below) A group of passengers waiting for the train.

added to the roundhouse, and a weigh scale will also be added."

Then, on September 9, 1901, Eholt gained notoriety when three masked men committed a daring robbery at the Commercial Hotel. The incident occurred at 9:45 p.m. on September 5. Several men had just completed a card game and had gone into the bar for a drink. Suddenly three armed men burst in from the street and ordered the men to "throw up their hands." Two railway men, who were in the dining room having supper, were also brought into the bar and lined up with the others. At first the eight victims thought it was just a joke. But when one of the men did not raise his hands fast enough, and was pistol-whipped on the side of the head, the other victims realized the robbers meant business.

After ordering Kaiser to open his safe, the thieves grabbed currency and jewellery, tossing aside cheques and documents. The cash register was also emptied, as was the pockets of the eight men.

"Altogether about $400 in cash, three gold watches, a diamond breastpin, a valuable diamond ring, and other trinkets were taken," reported the Midway *Advance*. "The robbers then took four bottles of champagne, two of whisky, and two of beer, and warning their victims that anyone showing himself whilst they were within range would be fired at, left the bar."

A railway engineer who was being transferred to another area, had a lucky escape. He was headed for the hotel while the robbery was in progress. A short distance from the hotel he stopped to light a cigar, which, because of the wind, required several matches. During this brief delay, "he noticed a man walking up and down the sidewalk in front of the hotel, and then three others came out, and the four hurried away. When he entered the bar just afterwards he learned the story of the robbery. He was wearing a valuable gold watch and had about $400 in currency in his pocket, having just closed up his affairs in the town in readiness to leave on the next day's train."

By the time news of the robbery reached Constable McMynn at Greenwood, all telephone and telegraph offices in the district were closed for the night, so communications with other stations was not possible. McMynn then sent out men along the most likely escape route, but they returned without spotting the felons. With no clue as to the robbers' identities, and without even knowing in which direction they had fled, the manhunt was doomed to failure. Despite a $250 reward, offered for evidence that would lead to the arrest and conviction of the robbers, no one was ever captured.

On April 26, 1902, the criminal element struck again. This time two men broke into W.S. Torney's general store and stole seven pairs of pants. Word of the break-in was telephoned to Greenwood and two men, Michael Hays and Thomas Stewart, were promptly arrested when they tried to sell the stolen goods in Greenwood.

A week later a more serious altercation occurred at Eholt when two men named Buckworth and Coultas, who had been drinking heavily, attacked Mr. Choate, the telegraph operator, "for some fancied grievance." Not only did Choate hold them off until help arrived, but in the meantime he gave his two attackers "a good drubbing." The men were subsequently arrested, tried in Nelson and sentenced to six weeks.

By this time, Eholt was beginning to show signs of decline. The first to feel the financial pinch was druggist A.B. Ripley. At the end of March, his stock of merchandise was sold to satisfy creditors. Smith & McRae, of Greenwood, and J.B. Boyle, of Phoenix, were the purchasers.

Although Eholt was no longer a thriving community, an unnamed Eholt correspondent to the *Times* tried to reassure readers of that paper that it was far from dead. "While we have not been making much of a splurge of late, our town has not been standing still by any means. Quite recently Mr. Kaiser the proprietor of the Commercial Hotel, completed two fine buildings on Barclay ave. and is at present erecting a very nice residence on Columbia avenue, to be occupied by W. Woodhouse, who has lately come from Trail, to take charge of the CPR shops.

"Messrs. Paulson & Bilton, also in the employ of the CPR are building residences for themselves. In fact this place is rapidly becoming a railway town, whereas this time last year it was purely a mining town, so that when the mines in this vicinity, such as the B.C., Rathmullen, Oro Denoro, Emma, & etc., start working again we shall be in a very enviable position, being both a railway and mining center."

The correspondent then went on to voice his anger at Greenwood officials who had allowed Hays and Stewart to escape from the Greenwood jail.

"The people of Eholt are very much disappointed and disgusted at the escape of the prisoners from the Greenwood jail, last Monday night. Mr. Torney and Judge Rendell spent considerable time and money in securing the arrest of these men, and then for them to simply walk out of prison, and across the line is very annoying. The negligence which has been displayed somewhere should be certainly remembered.

"On Sunday morning last another robbery was committed here, but the robber made his escape before he could be arrested. The want of a provincial policeman is greatly felt, and we cannot but think that if Mr. Darraugh was stationed at Eholt, instead of Phoenix it would be a much more satisfactory arrangement than at present."

In another section of the *Times*, under the heading of

JAIL DELIVERY, the newspaper echoed Eholt's disgust regarding the escape, and provided further details.

"On Saturday last Court Stenographer Brydges reached here and Constable Young brought over two prisoners from Nelson to stand their trial at the court on Monday. They were Hayes (sic) and Stewart charged with burglarizing Torney's store at Eholt. The learned Judge was delayed and notice was sent to registrar McMynn to adjourn the court until Friday of this week which was done.

"Now the two prisoners should have been kept in close confinement in the cells of the Provincial Police jail, but there is a rather congested state of affairs down there. The building is small and there are no less than four officials with offices there. There is William Grahame McMynn, who has offices too numerous to mention; F.M. Elkins, sheriff, James S. Birnie, clerk and Geo. Cunningham, deputy mining recorder and police constable.

"None of these gentlemen are too greatly blessed with avoirdupois, in fact outside of Mr. Cunningham who is fast getting fat and good natured, the bunch hover round the ragged edge of tenuity. But even thin men take up space and when four officials and their desks are placed in the building there is little space left, save the cells. But there are thousands of official documents to be kept there. When every nook and corner was filled, the cells had to be used and they have been converted into rather unsatisfactory vaults for the preservation of state papers. A larger and more suitable government building is of course needed but that is another subject.

"When constable Young arrived with his prisoners, the Province had no place to keep them and the City lock up was placed at the disposal of the Provincial officers.

"The City cells are evidently not built to keep prison-

A general view of Eholt showing the layout of the CPR work yards in the foreground and the town-site in the background. Although the photo is dated 1910, there appears to be too much activity for that year, and it is more likely 1905 or earlier. The white building just above and to the right of the water tower is the Union Hotel.

ers. Greenwood being certainly an extremely law abiding town, it was doubtless considered that any kind of cell would do in the City or long before this the government would have built a strong jail to keep the bad men that came from Eholt, and other uncivilized places. The City cells have a unique record, and any prisoner who remained there for more than 24 hours was considered a very dull fellow, while he who staid confined until committed to a common jail was looked upon as a veritable chump.

"But Hayes and Stewart were placed in the city cells on Saturday afternoon because there was no other place to put them. The bars were placed in position, doors were securely locked and Provincial and city police solemnly resolved that no more prisoners would escape from the city cells.

"Alex Currie city driver and special policeman was deputized to feed the prisoners. He did so on Sunday and Monday and early Tuesday morning he walked in with the cheery 'well boys here's your breakfast.' He unlocked the door, let down bars, and marched boldly into the cells, but no boys were there. He minutely examined the various corners of the cells but could find no one, and coming to the conclusion that they must have escaped through the key hole, he gave the alarm. All the Provincial officers in the various towns were notified and the sheriffs on the other side, but Hayes and Stewart are still breathing the air of liberty. How they got out can only be surmised. As there is no jailer or night watchman at the city hall, an accomplice secured keys that would fit the lock, and thus liberated the prisoners, taking the precaution to relock the doors after them."

There is some confusion concerning Eholt's hotels in the summer of 1902. On May 23, the *Times* published a list of five hotels and their owners. On June 21, the *Pioneer* did likewise, but the names do not match. Each newspaper agreed on four of the hotels: Columbia, C.E. Roberts; Northern, G.A. Rendell; Summit, Norman Luce; and Commercial, Fred Kaiser. According to the *Times*, the fifth hotel was the Miner's Exchange, owned by Sam McOrmond. But the *Pioneer* listed the Union Hotel, with J.A. McMaster as owner, as the fifth hotel. McOrmond, you may recall, had established the "Merchant's" Exchange as Eholt's first hotel. McMaster had once owned the Columbia, which was now owned by Roberts. The confusion might be explained by a December 20 notice in the *Pioneer* which stated that five liquor licenses had been renewed at Eholt, and one new one issued. If this is accurate, Eholt now had six hotels. Unfortunately, with the frequency with which hotels were bought, sold or renamed in frontier towns, it is often difficult to accurately track their activities.

On September 29, the *Advance* reported a "decided improvement in general business at Eholt" during the month. "The resumption of work at the B.C. mine, situate about 1½ miles from the town is chiefly responsible for this gratifying change for the better. About 70 men are now employed at the B.C. mine which is shipping an average of 130 to 140 tons of ore a day to the Boundary Falls smelter."

On January 22, 1903, the CPR recorded its first accidental fatality at Eholt when A.J. Greer, a CPR brakeman, was crushed to death. While coupling a passenger coach to a locomotive, Greer slipped and fell between the two. Horribly mangled, he was rushed to Greenwood Hospital by a special train, but died before he arrived there. Greer, a native of New York, was an experienced railway man and was brakeman on the passenger train from Eholt to Phoenix.

On a more pleasant note, contractors Bunting & Dempsey, of Greenwood, began erecting a new one-room schoolhouse at Eholt a few days later. Although this was not a major project, for some reason it was March 7 before the *Pioneer* was able to announce that finishing touches had been completed. Two days later Miss Norton, the teacher, occupied the premises with her students. When the Superintendent of Schools visited Eholt on March 18, 19 pupils were enroled. When the school was inspected a year later, the enrolment had dropped to 17.

As a CPR divisional point, Eholt continued on an even keel throughout 1904, neither booming nor declining. In June, five hotels had their liquor licenses renewed. They were: Northern, G.A. Rendell; Union, J.A. McMaster; Summit, Norman Luce; Commercial, Fred Kaiser and Columbia, Julius Black. In January, 1905, at the next license renewal, there were only four, Kaiser's Commercial Hotel having apparently closed down by this time. Six months later, the number dropped to three when Julius Black closed his Columbia Hotel and moved to Midway. Of the three remaining Eholt Hotels, only the Union had a restaurant. In September, 1906, Norman Luce leased his Summit Hotel to George Bloor and moved to the coast.

If hotels could be considered a symbol of a frontier town's vitality, Eholt's fortunes were steadily declining. The entire business community was suffering and, to make matters worse, on September 12, 1906, thieves broke into the Union Hotel and stole $685 from the safe.

Thanks to the CPR, Eholt was able to cling desperately to life. Now, however, even that stability was threatened. As early as March 16, 1907, the *Pioneer* warned: "There are again rumours from Grand Forks that the CPR is contemplating the removal of its shops to that point from Eholt. As yet, however, the people of Eholt are not worrying about it."

If the possibility of losing the CPR work-yards to Grand Forks was not a pressing concern to Eholt residents, other economic factors must certainly have been worrisome. That November the *Pioneer* reported that, outside of the Phoenix crew, "the CPR is operating but one train crew out of Eholt nowadays."

Then, on August 5, 1908, the CPR machinist at Eholt went out on strike. Reporting on the walkout, the *Times* wrote: "The men at the Eholt shops of the CPR walked out on Wednesday morning at 10 o'clock along with the other mechanical employees from St. John to Vancouver. At Eholt about 20 men are affected, these being carmen, blacksmiths, machinist and helpers. One man, a carman at Greenwood, is also out.

"As yet there are no local signs of the company's fighting the strike. It is understood that the company is making preparations however, to fight the issue and that preparations are being made at Eholt to use one of the company's houses there as a boarding house."

On August 22, the *Pioneer* reported an altercation between the striking machinist and replacement workers. "Trouble with CPR striking machinist at Eholt has been brewing all week. Early in the week a bunch of strike-breakers arrived on the scene and were not given a very cordial reception. Const. Docksteader was summoned late Monday evening and went down to quiet things. In a fracas during the early part of the evening several shots were fired. The citizens of Eholt held a meeting on Tuesday evening and have been endeavouring to pacify the strikers."

But as the strike dragged on, bad feelings intensified. Finally, on September 21, there was another confrontation, although there appears to be some question as to whether it was labour oriented.

"There was trouble at Camp Eholt, the Boundary Railway headquarters, on Saturday night," reported the *Pioneer* the following Wednesday. "In a melee of some kind, the facts of which cannot be obtained, C.H. Roberts, a special constable, and J. Konalki, a foreigner, who was car inspector, were seriously injured. Dr. Kingston, CPR physician, was wired for, and arrived by special train from Grand Forks at 5 a.m. Sunday.

"Roberts was badly cut about the face and arms, one cut on his head requiring several stitches. He is progressing favourably, but is still under medical attendance. The car inspector is able to be around again.

"Trouble has been brewing at Eholt more or less ever since the CPR merchants' strike commenced, but residents there claim the strikers have not been the cause. The town is again in quietness."

On October 24, the *Pioneer* reported that most of the striking machinist had returned to work. This bit of good news was apparently sufficient for the owners of the Northern Hotel to renovate their establishment. Others, however, had had enough, the *Pioneer* noting one week later that Mrs. Kaiser had sold her hotel and six cottages to Sam McOrmond.

The exodus continued throughout 1909. In early May, M.J. Merrihew left Eholt to take a position as Greenwood's chief of police. He was followed in July by the resignation of Mrs. Lyons, "chief of the Union Hotel's culinary department." In mid-August, Harry Shrapnell moved his family to Greenwood, and a week later long-time Eholt businessman and resident W.S. Torney, left for the coast. By December, he was a sales representative for an eastern cigar firm.

Others, however, held on to the slimmest hopes that business would improve. On November 23, 1909, the *Pioneer* announced that long-time businessman, J.A. McMaster, proprietor of the Union Hotel, had been elected mayor of Eholt. But it would be almost another year before Eholt would seen any signs of encouragement. On September 24 the *Pioneer* reported that John McKeller had been granted a liquor license and planned to reopen the Union Hotel, which had been closed for some weeks. Two week later the *Pioneer* announced that D.R. McElmon was opening a cigar store.

But these were minor glitches in an otherwise steady decline. In January, 1911, the *Pioneer* reported that one-time mayor, John McMaster had left Eholt for Vancouver, where he had purchased a hotel. The paper followed that information a week later with the announcement that E. Bailey & Co. had suspended business.

Still, Eholt clung tenaciously to life, refusing to give up.

Then, on August 25, 1912, the end came suddenly. Under the heading "FIRE AT EHOLT," the *Pioneer* wrote:

"Eholt about saw it finish early on Sunday morning, when a fire broke out in one of its buildings and quickly spread to adjoining structures. To fight the fire a locomotive was called into service and fair supply of water was secured in that way. This with a bucket brigade was all that could be done to keep the fire within bounds. The damage done was considerable, six buildings being totally destroyed, besides the Summit and Northern hotels. The premises destroyed include the drug store and post office. Insurance to the extent of $4,100 was carried on the two hotels and the origin of the outbreak is up to the present unknown."

Elsewhere in the same issue, the newspaper described the looting of Eholt:

"An urgent wire from Eholt on Monday notified Geo. Stanfield of the provincial police that looters were at work in the burned area in that burg. Accordingly that officer left immediately for the scene to investigate. The result of his watchfulness was the arrest of a couple of Austrian section men, Mike and John Papey, father and son, who were observed packing and caching a sack under suspicious circumstances. On the sack being opened it was found that the culprits had anticipated Labor and Christmas Day jags by taking in a large supply of headache powders; there was also a pair of rubbers to account for. The accused received a preliminary hearing before Justice of the Peace Woods, of Greenwood, who remanded them until the following day, when they appeared before Messrs. Woods and McCutcheon. The old man was discharged, but his hopeful offspring was ordered to the Nelson pen for thirty days. He offered no defence, other than the remark that our alert police official had 'worked fine trick on me'."

This disastrous fire was followed by further bad news when the CPR finally decided to move its roundhouses and shops to Grand Forks later the same year. During its prime, Eholt had boasted a population of about 300. After the collapse of the world copper market following the First World War, it population was estimated at 100. Two decades later it was less than 50, and when the post office was officially closed on November 15, 1949, only 17 hardy souls resided there. Of these, the last permanent residents were Mr. and Mrs. Enoch Moore. A dairy farmer, Moore had arrived in Eholt in 1907. When he passed away in 1960, Mrs. Moore moved to Beaverdell.

Before long, the railroad and mining centre had completely vanished. Today, not a single building from the town or the CPR operations remain. Where the CPR workyards had been, there is still a couple of foundations and some lilac bushes, but very little else. Three farms now occupy the meadow where the town itself once stood.

During the summer of 1991, the last tangible evidence of Eholt's early history was removed when the CPR pulled up its tracks throughout the Boundary Country. It is now possible to drive a car over the original Columbia & Western roadbed that once carried millions of dollars worth of rich ore to smelters at Greenwood and Grand Forks. The old branch line from Eholt to Phoenix is still visible, although overgrown, but it too is rapidly disappearing. At Eholt, even the ghosts have gone. �֎

Brooklyn

Three stern-wheelers, the Kootenai, Columbia *and* Lytton *(from front to back) at Robson Landing c1894.*

ALTHOUGH Brooklyn, at the foot of Lower Arrow Lake, is actually located in British Columbia's West Kootenay region, it can legitimately be included in a book covering ghost towns of the Boundary Country. That is because the town, like a number of towns in the Boundary Country, owed its brief existence to the Canadian Pacific Railway (CPR), or more specifically, the Columbia & Western (C&W) branch of that railway. In the spring of 1898, when the CPR decided to built the C&W from Robson to Midway, the route took them through what was soon to become the town-site of Brooklyn.

William Parker, a prospector, had ventured into this primeval wilderness several years earlier and staked some mining claims, which soon proved worthless. In 1896, Parker noticed some fine clay on the lake shore opposite Deer Park. A town-site was probably the farthest thing from Parker's mind when he preempted the land that year and built a log cabin. As luck would have it, when CPR officials arrived in the spring of 1898, they found Parker's preemption to be an ideal location for their headquarters. The CPR viewed the site as a convenient point from which to start a tote road along its railway right-of-way. The lake was two

miles wide at this point, and easily accessible to steamers, upon which men, equipment, animals and supplies could be brought in.

It was not long before the CPR contracting firm of Mann, Foley Bros. & Larson started landing equipment and supplies, and by June the shoreline was dotted with tents. Parker quickly realized he was sitting on a bonanza, and had the town-site, which he named Brooklyn, subdivided into lots.

As hundreds of railway workers moved in, businessmen were quick to seize the opportunity. Most came from nearby Trail, and in the vanguard were Messrs Blackmer and Esling. In most frontier towns, newspapers were only established after the town had grown to a certain size and gave indications it was there to stay. But Brooklyn was different. Blackmer and Esling arrived while the surveyors were cutting trees and before the first house had even been built. They established the weekly Brooklyn *News*, the first issue of which was published on June 19, 1898. Unfortunately for posterity, no copies of the first three issues appear to have survived.

A host of other Trail businessmen arrived at virtually

the same time and promptly began to establish businesses. J.S. Peterson and his brother established Brooklyn's first hotel, the two-story Crown Point, which opened around June 21. In a short time they had raked in $3,000 from thirsty railway workers. "Everyone wanted to drink," noted Robert Lowery in the New Denver *Ledge*, "and they lined up to the bar as thick as editors in Paradise."

Brooklyn's first month of existence displayed unprecedented growth. When the fourth issue of the *News* appeared on July 9, it chronicled its rapid rise, already declaring Brooklyn as "the banner town of the Arrow Lakes." During these first 30 days, huge loads of merchandise of all description arrived by steamer to be distributed among the various railway construction camps. Carloads of powder, condensed milk, canned fruit and meats arrived continually for the CPR's stores. Horses were brought in to pull wagons and to be used as pack animals.

About 1,000 men were already employed in construction, and the smoke from the clearing of the right-of-way sometimes darkened the sky with its intensity. A belt of white rock was already visible where the mountain side had been cleared in preparation for those who would follow with drills and picks. Sometime, when the wind was favourable, faint sounds of blasting could be heard from the lower end of the line. Men were deployed to camps along the line as rapidly as they apply for work and sub-contractors were pushing the work as rapidly as possible.

Many of Brooklyn's early businessmen came from Trail. The Peterson brothers, owners of the Crown Point Hotel in Trail, seen above, were one of the first to arrive. In June, 1898, they opened Brooklyn's first hotel, a two-storey building also called the Crown Point.

To accommodate all the freight, two wharves were under construction, one by the CPR and another, at the foot of Stewart Street, by the town itself. At the CPR wharf, Parker, displaying the racial bigotry evident throughout the West Kootenay at the time, had erected a large sign which read: "No Chinamen need land." This might have been a direct reference to the Chinese cook employed by the CPR carpenters.

But even two wharves could not cope with the tremendous amount of freight that was passing through mushrooming Brooklyn, as the July 23 issue of the *News* indicated: "The new wharf is one of the many new improvements, yet it is found to be too small to accommodate the vast cargo of goods daily unloaded, and steamships must seek the beach for a part of the shipload. The structure is 50x100 feet and is reached by a 260-foot runway, but the ideas of man were built too small for the bounding, booming trade of Brooklyn. Yards and yards of snowy canvas cover tons and tons of merchandise, through necessity unloaded on the beach these rainy mornings, while teams, drays, carts, pack trains and anxious seekers of boxes and bundles soon diminish the pile, much to the satisfaction of the CP freight agent. It may seem odd that immense loads of potatoes,

flour, milk, wagons, carts, horses, and dozens of other things, are unloaded here daily, but when the fact is considered that Brooklyn is the headquarters for 105 miles of railroad through the heaviest mountain rock in the northwest, employing fully 5,000 men along the line, it is not wonderful in the least. This point is the supply station, the headquarters and general offices for construction work of this line."

To this point, at least three immense rafts of lumber had been unloaded, providing the army of carpenters with some 750,000 feet of lumber. "For a town only a month old," boasted the *News*, "72 buildings are not too bad a showing. Many of these are large frame structures, fairly well built, considering the rush in which carpenters are under at all times. Many of these are hotel buildings, restaurants and lodging houses to accommodate the heavy travel. A number of well stocked stores are now doing business, where one can find almost everything needed in a new town."

The Hotel Anderson, Brooklyn's second hotel, opened around July 7, with proprietor H.Y. Anderson offering "good airy rooms" with clean beds, lit by acetylene gas lamps, for $1.50 to $2.00 per day. The dining room was "supplied with the best the market affords," and its first-class bar" offered St. Louis, Pabst and Schlitz brands of beer. At least three other hotels were also nearing completion by the end of the first month: Columbia, Brooklyn and Varnamo.

Some of the other businesses established or nearing completion at the end of 30 days included: Mitchell Bros., general merchants, who offered tailoring and gents furnishing; Thomas Wilson, another general merchant, sold groceries, provisions, clothing, boots, shoes and campers outfits; A.H. Bigney, operated the Brooklyn Boot and Shoe Shop; the City Drug Store, operated by Fred Pollock, and the Brooklyn Drug Store, operated by J.M. Perdue, both dispensed drugs and sold patent medicines, stationery, fishing tackle, books, fine cigars and tobacco; S. Oliver, an agent for the Kootenay Lumber Company, provided lumber for the burgeoning town; town-site owner William Parker operated the Brooklyn Novelty Store from his log cabin, offering fancy groceries, tobaccos, cigars, stationery, fresh fruit and nuts. He also carried newspapers from Brooklyn, Spokane, Seattle, Portland, Trail and Rossland. E.O. Nelson had opened a fruit, cigar and tobacco store; S.M. Barry, a restaurant and bakery. Shaw & Shaw sold hay, feed, produce and vegetables; F.C. Boles offered hardware, stoves and tinware; S.H. Brown offered his services as a contractor and builder, and A.J. Lapworth was a sign writer.

Pat Burns, who had a contract to supply meat to railroad construction crews, established a slaughterhouse and corral at the edge of town and had already processed several loads of cattle. C.W. McMillan, manager of the Calgary Brewing Company, was erecting a 20x30-foot warehouse and 20x24-foot cold storage cellar. George Willard was establishing a wholesale liquor warehouse. This must have been welcomed news, for Robert Lowery commented in the *Ledge:* "Brooklyn is a hot town, and only a few of the inhabitants drink water."

For those who preferred water, the infant town could even boast of its own water system. The Brooklyn Light & Water Company, headed by B.M. Smith of Revelstoke, intended "to lay a six-inch main from Stewart avenue up First street to Brooklyn avenue, thence up the alley to lot 14 and into the creek; thence up the creek 3,000 feet to the reservoir, where a head of 200 feet is obtained. This will give a pressure of 100 pounds to the square inch. The reservoir will be 12x6 feet, 24 feet long, and will furnish storage capacity for fire use and can be drawn for an indefinite period as the natural supply in the creek would be quite ample for two large fire hoses.

"The pipe has been ordered and work on the construction of the dam has begun. The people need feel no alarm as to the water supply, as every effort will be made to push the work and bring in water at the earliest possible moment.

"In addition an electric light plant will be installed as quickly as it can be arranged. The poles are being taken from the timber at present and will be erected just as soon as that part of the work can be reached. The plant will be of the latest type and be efficient in every respect."

On the hill at the rear of the town, overlooking the lake front, the 24x50-foot Brooklyn Hospital was nearing completion. The building was divided into three rooms, and patients were under the care of Dr. Ewing.

One service that Brooklyn still lacked, however, was an efficient post office. "The town needs a postoffice," said Lowery in the *Ledge.* "Mail is now brought in a gunny sack from Robson and dumped into boxes in front of Parker's cabin, where every man sorts the mail and picks out what belongs to him." The situation improved a short time later, when the *News* announced that Parker had a contract to deliver mail to the various construction camps.

Brooklyn's reason for existence, as noted earlier, was construction of the C&W. By mid-July 1,000 men had been employed. During the first week of August another 500 workers were hired, but the demand for labourers was still so great that agents were sent to eastern Canada on recruitment drives. Woodman, the paymaster for Mann, Foley Bros. & Larson, estimated there was enough work for 4,000 men.

Although Mann, Foley Bros. & Larson were the largest contractor, and employed the most men, there were many others. McPherson Bros. and J.W. Stout were awarded a large timber contract to cut 5,000,000 feet of trees to be processed into 175,000 ties, several million feet of bridge timber and lumber. This operation employed 65 men. At Winter, Parsons & Boomer's camp, 10 miles from Brooklyn, a force of 75 men were employed and another 100 needed. McLean Bros. had 65 men at work on the preliminaries of their 3,100-foot tunnel contract, but also needed 100 more.

On July 13, Patrick Fitzgerald stabbed Matthew Hays

in the Brooklyn Exchange Hotel. Since Brooklyn did not have a policeman at the time, G.H. Owen escorted the prisoner to Nelson where he was tried, found guilty, and sentenced to 12 months at hard labour. Probably as a result of this incident, a short time later a B.C. provincial police constable, Alan Forrester, was assigned to Brooklyn to maintain law and order. He also had to ensure that the laws governing the hotels were strictly enforced. This must have been no easy task, for Brooklyn already had 10 hotels in operation, with five more under construction. Forrester also had to concern himself with the businesswomen who had taken up roots in the town, the *Ledge* noting that "about a half dozen dwelling houses have red curtains." If workers were not drinking or being entertained by the soiled doves, gambling was another favourite way of passing their off-work hours. Noted the *Ledge:* "Schools of black jack and horse poker have been established and sleep is scarce in the town."

By the first week of August, Forrester had secured a "location for a jail for the temporary accommodation of offenders against the majesty of the law." The one-story, 12½x36-foot building was located behind the Hotel Anderson. The front of the building contained a large courtroom used by Judge Cooper, behind which was the accommodations for the officers, and then two prison cells.

Notwithstanding the many nationalities represented in Brooklyn, the town was quite law-abiding. However, an incident that occurred on August 8 illustrates how swift and effective Constable Forrester and Judge Cooper were in punishing the criminal element when it did appear.

According to the August 13 issue of the *News*, a stranger from Chicago named Paul had spent the previous Monday night being entertained "at the red-curtained house of Lizzie Oleson, in the east end of town. When he awoke in the morning he was minus $75 or $80. He had a bad cut on the side of his head and blood was found on the bed clothes and on his shirt. The woman claimed he had left the house about one o'clock and returned about four and had received the cut and been robbed meanwhile, but Mr. Paul denied this flatly.

"Information being laid, Lizzie Oleson and Sadie Woods, an inmate, were arrested by officer Forrester and brought before justice of the peace Cooper. After hearing the evidence on both sides, the judge read the law and fined Miss Oleson $50 for keeping a house with red curtains, $200 for the price of a liquor license and $50 for selling without a license, together with $5 costs. Miss Woods was fined $20 and costs for being an inmate. The total amounted to $330. In as much as the statutes read that $250 or six months at hard labor may be exacted for selling liquor without a license Miss Oleson got off pretty light, considering all the circumstances of the case."

As Brooklyn continued to grow and prosper during the month of August, a number of new businesses were established. James Gill & Co. sold "clothing, gent's furnishings, boots, shoes, blankets, etc." A. Sanderson advertised "fresh and salt meats," D.M. Crowley opened the Brooklyn Furniture Store, George Motosawa operated the Mikado Laundry, and two restaurants, the Queen and the Owl offered meals 24 hours a day. Brooklyn even boasted a bank of sorts, when W.H. Cooper & Co. advertised their services as "bankers, brokers, financial agents, etc." In addition to these new establishments, several of the hotels on First Street were sporting new verandahs which, noted the *News*, "greatly improve their appearance."

However, Brooklyn's greatest achievement for the month of August was none of the above. On August 13, the *News* proudly announced: "Among the notable institutions of which this progressive, young and vigourous town will soon be able to boast, will be an opera house and summer garden." Located on the lake front near the International Hotel, the Opera House was the brainchild of D.M. Crowley and Tom Reid. With a spacious, well appointed stage and a seating capacity of 250, the 62x32-foot Opera House truly gave the ramshackle town cosmopolitan airs. "There will be no intoxicating liquors of any kind sold on the premises," promised the proprietors, "but patrons may be accommodated with soft drinks if they so desire."

Brooklyn's greatest period of growth, without question, was June, July and August of 1898. Business-wise, September was also a strong month, but there was no notable growth during that month. As the centre of railway construction, Brooklyn was connected by steamer to Robson four times daily. The CPR steamers used on this route were the *Rossland*, *Kootenai*, *Lytton* and *Illicilliwaet*. Other vessels making daily runs between Robson and Brooklyn were the steam launch *Oriole* and the steam yacht *Myrtle B*.

By mid-September, Brooklyn had 16 hotels catering to the needs of workers, and none cried for lack of patronage. At least six of these hotels were located on Front Street: Windsor, E.A. Dillis, proprietor; International, Graham & McManus; Park, Frederick & Peterson; Columbia, McNeil & Hector; Hoffman House, Couglan & McDonald, and Cosmopolitan, Linderman & Anderson. At least six others were located on First Street: Anderson, H.Y. Anderson, proprietor; Brooklyn, McDonald & Bolen; Stockholm, Johnson & Lockhart; Alliance, Nelson & Johnson; Central, Blomberg & Dahl, and Palace, William Walmsley. The Crown Point Hotel, operated by the Peterson Bros., was probably located on Front Street. The location of two other hotels, Varnamo (Gus Jackson, proprietor), and Brooklyn Exchange (Aune & Hoven, proprietor), is not recorded, although the latter might also have been located on Front Street. The name and location of Brooklyn's sixteenth hotel is not recorded in local papers.

By this time, the tote road had been completed for a distance of 20 miles beyond Brooklyn, and workers were strung out along the line and at the different camps of the subcontractors. This created a demand for services and facilities at various points of the route, and as these became established, more and more workers made use of them. By the end of August, there were nine good stopping places on the tote road between Brooklyn and Christina Lake.

After leaving Brooklyn, the tote road ascended a six-mile hill. Teamsters were glad to rest their tired horses after the up-hill climb. Foot travellers also found the small flat a convenient spot to rest, and in early August H.W. Cotton decided to open a restaurant there. At first Cotton did business under canvas, but by the end of August his patronage had increased so dramatically that he erected a commodious 18x24-foot roadhouse with eight rooms and a kitchen. First known as Cotton's Hotel, the name was changed to the Workingman's Home after being purchased by John McMillan in early October.

About three miles further, J.H. Bolen and James Ennis had erected a 20x36-foot log building which they named the Porcupine Hotel. Also known as 10 Mile House, construction had started in early August and business was being conducted by mid-month. In addition to their popular hotel, the partners erected a barn that could accommodate 16 teams of horses. The site proved to be a popular stopping place, for by October, "the little settlement of Porcupine Creek," could boast a second hotel. Named the Hotel Kootenay, it was built by Norman Luce, who went on to establish a hotel at Eholt.

About 14 miles from Brooklyn, Tom King and Israel McInnis erected a 30x25-foot roadhouse they named, appropriately enough, 14 Mile House. This hotel included an adjoining bunkhouse and a 72-foot-long barn. When the hotel first opened for business in early September, the partners did not have a liquor license. On November 5, when a reporter for the *News* passed through, he indicated that the establishment was now called the Mountain House and McInnis was the sole proprietor.

A mile beyond Mountain House, close to the Heinze Pass, proprietors Graham and Sparks operated the Divide Hotel. "The hotel building is 25x33 feet in size, and two stories high," reported the *News* on August 20. "Barns and stables will be added at once, making the establishment one of the most desirable to put up at between Brooklyn and Christina Lake."

The next stopping place, located 17 miles from Brooklyn, was the Summit House. According to the August 13 issue of the *News*, the hotel was established by A.J. Jackson and A.P. Cummings, both of whom were "old hands in the business." Jackson apparently had sold out his interest by the time the *News* reporter visited on November 5, for he wrote: "Andy (Cummings) has a host of friends on the road, and he is prepared to take care of man and beast, internally or externally, in good shape. This point also has the distinction of having a branch of Pat Burns' slaughter house located here, whence the beef can be distributed either way to the railway camps, with a down hill pull."

Three or four miles further, J.T. Donaldson, who had previously operated a hotel at Goat River Landing, erected a 54x20-foot, two-story hotel in partnership with "Scotty" Campbell. Located roughly halfway between Brooklyn and Cascade, it was naturally named Half-Way House. Although completed in early September, the hotel owners did not receive their liquor license until early November, by which time they had made extensive improvements that included a large stable.

"From this point," wrote the *News* reporter on November 5, "the sandy and rocky road winds down the long hill to where McPherson Bros. & Stout's saw mill was located up to a few days ago. This swampy place is beginning to look like a deserted village. Thence the road is built over long, strong hills for several miles until the bustling little berg of Gladstone is reached." Gladstone, of course, developed into a town in its own right. At McRae's Landing, the Christina Lake terminus of the tote road, Mr. McRae had built a log store.

With sub-contractors, railway crews and roadhouses

already stretched out from Brooklyn to Cascade, one did not have to be a superior intellect to realize that Brooklyn's days were numbered. Brooklyn businessmen who realized the demise of their town was imminent, did not wait long to react. As early as August 20, the *News* reported that Brooklyn's Park Hotel owners Frederick and Peterson had leased a hotel in Cascade.

The Boundary Creek *Times* probably put the situation in proper perspective in its September 10 issue when it stated: "Brooklyn is the liveliest, the flimsiest built and the least substantial looking town in British Columbia. It sprang up in a day and is not there to stay. It is simply a collection of cheaply built hotels, a few stores and the contractor's offices and warehouses. It sprang into existence because it was a convenient point from which to start a tote road along the line of railway. When the railroad is completed from Robson to the summit about four miles above Brooklyn, the contractors will move their offices there; then Brooklyn will disappear. Today it is a busy place. Several steamers call there daily. Men are coming in to work on the road; the dozen hotels are doing a rushing business and everyone is making money. But the most enthusiastic Brooklynite does not think the town will last. 'If we get two months more of this we will be satisfied' is the common expression with the Brooklyn business man."

Two of the earliest Brooklyn businessmen to become aware of the town's early demise may have been Blackmer and Esling, publishers of the *News*, who sold the newspaper to W.B. Wilcox after only seven weeks. Wilcox, who would later establish the Cascade *Record*, appears to have ignored, at least initially, the obvious signs of decline that was appearing in his own newspaper. On September 10 the *News* reported that Capt. C. Benjifield, owner of the *Myrtle B*, had sold the yacht to "Messrs. Beattie and Matheson, who have already started on the job of transferring her to Christina Lake. The *Oriole*, belonging to Rumball & Bullen, will also be taken to the lake, probably early next week, and put on that sheet of water." The newspaper also noted that the *Marion*, a small stern-wheeler, which had operated on the Kootenay River, was to be put on Christina Lake before long.

These activities, and the increasing popularity of distant roadhouses, and advancement of railway construction crews further and further from Brooklyn, were clear indications that the centre of activity was rapidly changing to Cascade, near Christina Lake. But Wilcox and others could be partially forgiven for being optimistic about Brooklyn's future, for the news was not all bad. Back on August 20, the *News* reported that there were over 25 children of school age in Brooklyn. Since the legal requirement for a school was 20, a petition, signed by 50 citizens, was forwarded to Victoria requesting that a school be established. On Septem-

This is the only known photograph of Brooklyn. Because the town is virtually deserted, it appears likely that this picture was taken in the summer of 1899, after most businessmen simply left their establishments intact and moved on to more promising ventures.

ber 17, the *News* announced that the petition had achieved the desired result, and on October 15, the paper was able to inform its readers: "Brooklyn's first public school will start up Monday morning at nine o'clock. Miss Elizabeth Fletcher, the new teacher, arrived on Thursday, and for the last two days carpenters have been arranging the home made desks to the best advantage." However, although between 30 and 40 "scholars" could be accommodated in the school room, the school opened with only 16 students.

Brooklyn was obtaining other institutions during the same time. In mid-September a new courthouse was erected for Judge Cooper. Describing the building, the *News* wrote: "It is a neat structure, conveniently located on First street, near the townsite office, and is surmounted by a flag pole flying the Union Jack. It is quite an addition to the architecture of the city."

Another institution which Brooklyn had previously lacked was a post office, but on September 24 the *News* advised its readers that L.M. Livingston had been appointed the town's postmaster. Livingston had been instructed by Inspector Fletcher to be ready for business by October 1. "In accordance, therewith, Mr. Livingston has neatly fitted up a corner of his store with letter boxes and everything is conveniently arranged for the speedy transaction of business." In its October 1 issue, the *News* added: "Postmaster Livingston opened up the postoffice, as ordered by the Government, in his store today. Call boxes have been conveniently arranged and can be secured at the rate of $1 per month. There will be no lock boxes for the present."

Normally, the establishment of a school, courthouse and postoffice would indicate growth and stability in any frontier town. In this instance, although misdirected, it certainly gave the *News* reason to be optimistic. In an editorial published on October 8, the paper said: "Anyone who thinks that building operations have ceased in busy Brooklyn should take a stroll through the town any of these frosty mornings. He would be agreeably surprised at the evidences apparent that the place is not yet large enough to accommodate the incoming multitudes with which every boat touching here is crowded.

"Among the new structures of the building line, one of the most useful will be a good sized addition to the Anderson House. This will occupy the open space to the north of the present building, and will be 22x40 feet in size. It will increase the sleeping accommodations of the hotel by about

(Above) The remains of what was once the post office and general store in Brooklyn, c1950.
(Below) The site of Brooklyn, looking across lake to Deer Park, in 1949.

50. Lumber has been ordered, and the work will be pushed with all possible expedition as soon as it arrives. When completed the hotel will be able to take care of 115 people each night.

"Manager Shanks, of the Windsor hotel, is putting on a 14x50 addition on the south side of the building, now nearly completed. He has also put a lunch counter in the front of the building.

"E. Parris & Co. have put on a 14x14 addition to their store, necessitated by the increase in their business.

"Mann, Foley Bros. and Larson have this week put up sleeping quarters for the men employed in their various stores and warehouses, and also put up another large barn on the hill.

"D.A. Munro, the blacksmith, has put up a commodious house, 12x20, for a residence for the winter.

"Shaw and Shaw have built an addition to their warehouse, and a number of other improvements are being made."

But the newspaper, businessmen and residents of Brooklyn were only deceiving themselves it they truly believed that Brooklyn had a future. That became painfully clear on October 29 when the *News* excerpted a brief news item that had appeared in the Winnipeg *Free Press*: "Mr. L.A. Hamilton, CPR land commissioner, returned to Winnipeg last week and informed a *Free Press* reporter that he had decided upon the location of the principal townsites along the road. They will be Gladstone, Cascade, Grand Forks and Greenwood and arrangements have been completed whereby the company becomes interested in the development of the towns."

That should have ended all doubt about Brooklyn's future as a railroad town, but in another column in the same issue, the paper advised its readers: "An erroneous impression seems to prevail that one of these fine mornings the office of the contractors, Mann, Foley Bros. & Larson, will be moved, bag and baggage to Cascade City. When questioned by a *News* man, Paymaster Woodman stated that no preparations were made or likely to be made for some time to move the office. To the contrary, everything has been arranged for spending the winter in busy Brooklyn."

However, the exodus had already begun, and on November 12 a small ad appeared in the *News* that might best symbolize the situation: "Pool table in good condition and complete in every respect. Will be sold cheap for cash. Apply at International Hotel, Brooklyn." November 12 was also the last time the *News* appeared. Wilcox had finally realized the futility of Brooklyn's fading economy and, like others, took the stage to Cascade where, on the same date, he published the first issue of the *Record*.

On December 3, the *Times* advised its readers that Brooklyn had run its course and its "merchants are fast leaving the town." On December 17, the *Record* carried several items relating to the exodus: A.J. Lapworth had sold his laundry and bath house and moved to Vancouver; the Crown Point Hotel had again changed hands and Thomas & Greiger had closed up their wholesale liquor establishment and returned to Rossland.

As the year drew to a close, Brooklyn businessmen virtually abandoned the town. Some established new businesses in up-and-coming towns like Gladstone, Cascade, Eholt and Niagara, where, ironically, the same fate would once again befall them. A few lingered painfully on, hoping to survive on the transients that passed through the dying town.

As though the businessmen who clung on did not have enough problems, on January 8, 1899, fire destroyed two buildings. Reporting on the fire in its January 14 issue, the *Record* said: "Last Sunday night about 2 o'clock the frame hotel on the lakefront at Brooklyn, known as the Brooklyn Exchange, was burned to the ground. Shaw & Shaw's feed store adjoining, was also totally destroyed. Fortunately the breeze was off shore and as the buildings were isolated no further damage was done. The origin of the fire is not known, and the loss is almost total, as little could be saved. Shaw & Shaw probably lost $500 and the two-story hotel building was probably worth $800. There was no insurance and no means of fighting the flames. Fortunately no lives were lost."

Two months later, on March 11, the *Record* printed a brief interview with John Magney, who had just come from Brooklyn. Magney said that "Brooklyn is daily looking more like a deserted village. Two or three hotels are still running; a few stores are open. Its chief support in the future will be the business from the men employed on the long tunnel, under contract to McLean Bros., four miles from Brooklyn."

Two weeks later the *Record* noted that the "Stockholm Hotel at Brooklyn has been closed by the police. That town now has five hotels. At one point there were 16 of them."

At the end of March, Rev. John Munor, "formerly of the Presbyterian Church at Brooklyn," was reassigned to Golden. Two weeks later, the *Record* announced that, "owing to completion of work in their immediate vicinity, the Mountain House, Summit House, Half Way House and Peterson's Hotel, between Brooklyn and Cascade, have all closed up."

In early May the railroad contractors began moving their storehouses from Brooklyn to West Robson. By early June, the once thriving town had sunk to such lows that, according to a reliable observer, residents of Brooklyn, "when oppressed with ennui, amuse themselves by throwing stones through the windows in the many vacant buildings in that town."

On July 22, the *Record* noted that the International Hotel was the only one still operating. "Mr. Dahl, of the Central wants to move his hotel to the tunnel, four miles from Brooklyn." By early September, Brooklyn consisted "solely of one hotel and one store, in which the post office is located." Later that month a fire destroyed much of Brooklyn's remaining buildings. "A fire broke out at Brooklyn a few days ago and did considerable damage before it spent itself," reported the *Record* on September 30. The flames started in DesBrisay's store where the post office was located, and the entire contents were destroyed. The fire burned down several of the unoccupied buildings adjoining."

The last reference to Brooklyn in local papers appeared on October 28, when the *Record* noted: "The only liquor license granted was to the Hillside Hotel, prop. Frank Corte, which was located near Brooklyn." Brooklyn's life had come full cycle. ❊

Gladstone

LIKE Brooklyn, 24 miles to the east, Gladstone was a product of the Columbia & Western Railway (C&W). Construction of the C&W began at Robson in the spring of 1898. In June of that year, contractors selected a location on the western shore of Lower Arrow Lake as their centre of operations, and Brooklyn burst upon the scene. Within two months railway surveyors, work crews, subcontractors and roadhouses were spread out from Brooklyn to Cascade. Established as one of the stopping places along the right-of-way, Gladstone quickly developed into a town.

However, the history of the area predates the C&W. In the fall of 1896, Charles Wilson staked the Mystery group of mining claims about a mile from the future town-site in a region that came to be known as the Burnt Basin. In the spring of 1897, the Edson group was staked by Hunter and Henderson of Rossland, and then the Bryan group was located by the same parties. The Solid Gold group, originally located by Fred Fredericks, was sold for $50. In 1898 the new owner, Richard Cooper of Rossland, turned down an offer of $4,000 for it.

These discoveries and others soon attracted a large number of prospectors to the Burnt Basin. Although specific details are lacking, we know that two of the prospectors to stake claims were William Forrest and Angus Cameron. They were undoubtedly aware of the route the C&W would follow when they decided to lay-out a 640-acre town-site on a level flat lying between the hills. This probably occurred in late July or early August of 1898, for on August 27, the Boundary Creek *Times* reported that a number of hotels and stores were being built there. "There is a general store at Gladstone. Lots are selling and men are getting ready to start business there."

On September 3 the Brooklyn *News* claimed: "There are at present seven or eight hotels in operation and all of them appear to be doing a good business." However, this was a gross exaggeration, for during its brief history, Gladstone never boasted more than four hotels. In fact, the *News* corrected its own error two weeks later when it noted: "Messrs Dorsey and Wisner have the only hotel at Gladstone, and are catering most successfully to the constantly increasing traveling and freighting trade."

The Hotel Gladstone was 30x40 feet, two-and-a-half-stories high and entirely built of hewn logs. It was well fitted and furnished for its use as a hotel.

By mid-September the original town-site owners, Forrest and Cameron, had taken in two new partners named Good and Dixon, and they were busy constructing a good trail to the Burnt Basin. Unlike Brooklyn, which owed its existence entirely to the railroad, Gladstone was also a mining centre. In Fact, the Burnt Basin was believed to be so rich that the Peterson Brothers, owners of the Crown Point Hotel in Brooklyn, were "building a road house at Basin City, six miles beyond Gladstone, where they have also applied for permission to purchase a townsite. The location is where the trail strikes off into the Burnt Basin, and ought to be a good one."

Although Basin City never rated another mention in local papers, Gladstone continued to grow and thrive. Town lots were "selling readily at $50 and $75 each," and businessmen, quickly sizing up its potential as a railway and mining town, began erecting businesses. As already noted, John Dorsey and J.S. Wisner had established the Hotel Gladstone, the town's first. Grant Brothers soon followed with a 24x30-foot general store stocked with $2,000 in merchandise. By mid-September, James McMunn had opened his barbershop; Pat Burns had established a slaughterhouse under the charge of Joe Davis, and Sam McOrmond was erecting a 24x30-foot general store. On September 24, the *News* announced that McOrmond would "soon open a restaurant and bakery in connection with his other business." Another store had been established by G.J. Hall, although what he sold went unrecorded.

Although Gladstone could boast a hotel, two general stores, a barbershop and a couple of other businesses, at this stage of its existence it was really little more that a rough and tumble railway construction camp. In early frontier towns of this sort, before law and order was established, workers usually settled disputes with their fists, or whatever else was handy. On October 22 a particular ugly incident occurred at one of J.G. McLean's camps, near Gladstone. The confrontation "nearly cost one son of sunny Italy his life," reported the *News*. "He was, in fact, close to the happy hunting grounds, and but for the interference of several other workmen, his troubles for this life would be over.

"Two Italians got into a fight over some trivial matter, when one man began to enforce his arguments with a sharp axe. So well did he succeed that his victim, Sebastian Deneiro, received a severe cut on the head, a deep gash on the shoulder, and he was also bitten on the arm, as if to complete the job.

"At this point in the fracas brother workmen realized that the place was becoming a slaughter house and interfered. The Italians secured the assailant, and with cocked revolvers marched him to Gladstone, where he was delivered into the custody of Mr. Forrest, J.P., who took him to Grand Forks for safe keeping.

"There being no surgeon at hand, G. Sturgis, the cook, undertook the job of sewing and patching up Deneiro, the victim, and at last accounts he was doing as well as expected."

On November 12, following the trial, the Cascade *Record* provided additional details about the incident and its aftermath: "Last week an Italian named Bramouse Tomass was sentenced at Grand Forks to six months at hard labor in the Kamloops jail for attempting to chop up a former friend, Sebastian Denny (sic).

"The trouble took place the previous week near Gladstone, both men being railway laborers employed by John

Maglio, who had a sub-contract for several stations from J.G. McLean & Co. They had decided to dissolve partnership in 'batching' and had a dispute as to the ownership of some pots and pans. One word led to another, and finally Tomass used an axe to enforce his arguments. Denny was badly cut up when rescued by his companions, and as no surgeon was at hand, the cook put several stitches in his scalp. He was then brought to the hospital in Cascade for treatment.

"Tomass was taken to Grand Forks and sentenced on Tuesday of last week. Constable Elkins took Denny, who was sufficiently recovered, to testify against Tomass."

Meanwhile, Gladstone continued to move forward. McPherson Bros. & Stouts sawmill, which had been located four miles east of Gladstone, was moved to the town on October 22, "where it will probably be located all winter," stated the *News*. "It is now expected to be run night and day to cut 60,000 feet every 24 hours, there being a fine belt of large timber at the present location.

On November 5 the *News* printed a small article on the status of new town: "Gladstone is a thriving little place on the new railway line, and being located in the neighborhood of half way between Brooklyn and Cascade, gets the benefit of a great deal of traffic from both directions.

"John Dorsey, who has bought out his partner's interest in the Hotel Gladstone, is putting up a 30x16 foot addition, to be used as a bar room.

"Two new hotels are now talked of for this place. One of these is to be opened in the near future by McDonald & Miller, while J.S. Wisner, formerly of the Hotel Gladstone, is contemplating building the other. (Wisner, however, did not rebuilt in Gladstone. Instead he purchased a hotel in Niagara.)

"A livery barn will soon be in operation here, a branch of that of C.W. May, of Cascade City. Another new enterprise is a blacksmith shop. Both of these concerns will doubtless do well. All three of the stores here, R.D. Hawks, Sam McOrmond and Grant Bros., carry good general stocks, and are preparing to do the trade of this section for the winter."

A week later the *Record* noted that McOrmond was en route to Grand Forks to secure a liquor license. Business was so good during Gladstone's early days, that McOrmond, who already owned a general store and restaurant, had decided to open a hotel as well. On November 26, the *Record* noted that McOrmond's new hotel, the Victoria, was "enclosed and will soon be ready for business." Built in partnership with a man named Miller, it was "favourably located on the main street."

By the end of November, Thomas Flynn, formerly of Ymir, B.C., had come to Gladstone seeking business opportunities. Meanwhile, James Ennis, who previously operated the Porcupine Hotel about 14 miles east of Gladstone, had apparently sold out his interest to his partner, J.H. Bolen. Ennis and Flynn then formed a new partnership and decided to erect a new hotel at Gladstone. Named the Burnt Basin Hotel, it was "20x30 with an addition, and the barn is 30x50 feet in size."

Although Gladstone could never hope to achieve the spectacular growth of Brooklyn and Cascade, it was nevertheless a busy little community with its three hotels cater-

ing to the needs of its patrons. With its proximity to the Burnt Basin properties, and with the announcement by the Canadian Pacific Railway that Gladstone would be a main station on its line, the town's future seemed assured. So much so, that on December 24, the *Record* announced that the "promising townsite of Gladstone" had been sold to an English syndicate.

William Forrest, one of the original town-site owners, who was now Gladstone's Justice of the Peace, told the *Record* that "the property will shortly change hands, the price being $30,000. Of this amount $1,000 is to be cash, and the balance is to be paid over by July of next year, or within six months. As soon as the title from the government can be perfected by the vendors, probably by February 1st. unless something happens to prevent, the deal will be made. The CPR are owners of one-quarter of the townsite, and in the pending sale the townsite people will reserve one lot in every block."

While this syndicate may have had faith in Gladstone's future, Angus Cameron, one of the original town-site owners apparently did not. Back in October he left Gladstone to take an appointment as Cascade's postmaster.

January, 1899, proved to be another busy month in Gladstone. A new 30x50-foot dance hall had been completed and furnished, and the C&W sidetrack was nearing completion. About 400 men were employed in the vicinity, providing a monthly payroll of about $8,000, and there was even talk of constructing a narrow-gauge railway over Norway Mountain to connect Gladstone to Rossland.

But Gladstone, like Brooklyn, was not designed for longevity. Its peak had already passed, and when the mines of Burnt Basin proved to be little but surface showings, its days were numbered. Evidence of the decline began to appear later that spring. In early March, James Ennis sold his interest in the Burnt Basin Hotel to his partner and left for Idaho. A month later, McOrmond sold his stock of general merchandise to Grant Brothers. Although McOrmond retained his interest in the Victoria Hotel, it was probably being run by his partner, because by June, McOrmond had started construction on a three-story hotel at Eholt. Nevertheless, by mid-June, there were still three licensed hotels still operating at Gladstone: Victoria, McRae and Burnt Basin.

On June 17, the *Record* noted that the C&W was nearing Gladstone. "The putting down of steel on the new railway is proceeding steadily, and early in the week it was understood that the track would reach Gladstone by tonight. On account of some small slides, however, this has not been quite accomplished. The gang with the track laying machine, including surfacers, varies from 60 to 100 men, but of late, men have been scarce. At the summit, near the Divide hotel, a side track has been put in, and a telegraph office established. This side track will be a great convenience for the several locomotives employed in bringing rails and other construction material to the front. There are some large sandbanks here also, which are being drawn on for surfacing.

"A side track is to be built at Gladstone, and then the steel gang — with the exception of some bridges and trestles, work on which is now well in hand — will have a straight course, as it were, to Cascade. If the weather has finally cleared up for good, the probability of being bothered by further slides is small, and in the course of three or four weeks we will hear the whistle of the iron horse as it comes snorting down the long Christina lake grade."

The appearance of the track-layers added a brief spark to Gladstone, the *Record* noting on July 1 that "this town is a lively place at present, owing to the presence of the track-laying and surfacing gangs. The rails are now a few miles below town, but the numerous bridges to be built will keep the force near for a time yet."

Earlier in the same issue, the paper noted that the Hotel Gladstone had changed hands, Albert Belgrove, having taken a year's lease on the property. When, on October 28, the *Record* announced that the Hotel Gladstone was the only one to be granted a liquor license, it was then owned by William Forrest. In mid-November the paper reported that there "is talk of changing the name of the town of Gladstone, on account of there being another place of the same name in Manitoba." On January 8, 1900, the Midway *Advance*, referring to the town-site as a "station," said its name had been changed to Coryell.

In fact, the town was little else but a station on the C&W by this time, although the Hotel Gladstone continued to operate, under different owners, for some time. Although "considerable improvements" were made to this hotel in November, the old Burnt Basin Hotel did not fare as well. In December, Mr. McMunn moved his barbershop into the building. "He will have snug quarters for the winter," noted the *Record*, "and will serve his customers as formerly to a neat haircut, clean shave and a nice bath."

In February, 1901, Martin Johnson had acquired the Hotel Gladstone, renamed it the Hotel Coryell, and applied for a liquor license. As late as June, 1902, the hotel was still operating, now under the ownership of James McMunn. But Gladstone had run its course long before this.

Today, nothing remains to indicate the town ever existed. During the summer of 1991, the CPR decided to pull out the rails throughout the Boundary Country. Since the only access to the Gladstone town-site was by rails, this proved to be a blessing in disguise. I was now able to drive down the old right-of-way to the town-site.

Turning left off the main highway just before the Paulson bridge, I followed a gravel road several miles east. Eventually this road turns and crosses the old railway right-of-way. At this point, I turned west, driving on the old roadbed itself. It was not long before the remains of Paulson appeared. But finding the old Gladstone town-site was far more difficult.

After passing under the Paulson highway bridge and through a short railway tunnel, I eventually reached the only area where Gladstone could have existed. With railway foundations and clear evidence that this was where the C&W had their sidetrack, it was undoubtedly the site of the town. Today, just below the railway, the town-site is completely overgrown. A trail that slopes to the northeast through the trees might be the remains of the old tote road, or it might be the remnants of old logging operations, there is really no way of knowing. But of the town itself, there is nothing. Not even the sign Coryell, that still stood at the railway sidetrack until recent years, was evident. With Gladstone vanished from the face of the earth, it is particularly sad that not even a single photo has survived to verify that it once existed.   ❧

No photos of Gladstone have apparently survived.

Cascade

OF all the towns which sprang up in the Boundary Country during the 1890s, Cascade, "The Gateway City," could be considered unique. Although, like most of its contemporaries, Cascade was founded as a commercial centre because of its strategic location, for many years it owed its existence to water power. The booming mines of the Boundary district needed electricity; and it was the availability of a hydro-electric power supply that sustained the hopes of this community for so many years. However, its birth must be credited to the Columbia & Western Railway (C&W).

According to the November 19, 1898, issue of the Cascade *Record*, Aaron Chandler first saw the flatland upon which Cascade would later develop around 1888. Chandler was so impressed by what he saw that he immediately proceeded to get title to the property. For years, however, the land lay undeveloped.

One of the first to realize the importance of establishing a town-site beside the Kettle River was Fritz Augustus Heinze, a 26-year-old mining millionaire from Butte, Montana. By the fall of 1894, Heinze had organized the C&W and hired John Coryell, provincial land surveyor, to prepare a town-site survey. It is unclear if Heinze had obtained an option from Chandler, of if his proposed town-site was on adjacent property. In any event, Coryell completed his survey on October 24, 1894, and deposited the plans in the Kamloops Land Registry office on January 10, 1895. The town-site was named Cascade because of the cascading waterfalls nearby.

Heinze proposed to construct the C&W as a standard gauge from Robson to Midway, and in 1896 he was granted a provincial charter and land grant. However, it was probably the mining activity in the region that inspired C.H. Thomas, of Rossland, to establish the Hotel Cascade. Construction on the 20-room hotel, the first anywhere in the area, was started around the end of February, 1896.

Unfortunately, there were few local papers to record Cascade's earliest history, which, in any event, was slow in developing. We do know, however, that George Stocker, a former Spokane businessman who had made and lost a fortune in banking and real estate, with two partners, built the town's second building and a sawmill.

On November 10, 1896, a group of Englishmen, quick to note the potential powers of the falls, filed an application for incorporation of the Cascade Water, Power & Light Co., Ltd. According to the application, which was published in the December 19, 1896, issue of the Boundary Creek *Times*, the company wanted the right to "appropriate and use 150,000 miner's inches of water from Kettle river, near Cascade City, for the purpose of generating electricity for the supply of light, heat and power to the inhabitants, cities, towns, mines, smelters and tramways within a radius of 40 miles from the said townsite of Grand Forks, and to construct, erect and maintain all necessary works, buildings, dams, race-ways, flumes, poles and erections, lay pipes and stretch wires for generating and supplying electricity as aforesaid, and to enter upon and expropriate land for the purposes of the company, and also to construct, maintain and operate tramway and telephone systems within the said radius of 40 miles, and to do all other things necessary or conductive to the attainment of the above objects or any of them."

By this time, increasing traffic and supplies were coming north from Spokane, Washington, through Marcus and Bossburg, the latter town springing into existence just south of the International Boundary. As it rapidly became the main point of entry, Cascade began to take on an air of permanency. Despite its increasing importance, it was October 15, 1897, before the town was mentioned again in local papers, the *Times* reporting that "a post office, with Mr. Campbell in charge," had been opened there. A week later the *Times* reported two new appointments: Angus Cameron, one of the original town-site owners of Gladstone, was the new postmaster, and George C. Ross the customs officer and Justice of the Peace.

Meanwhile, Heinze, who had obtained the C&W charter in 1896, had

Fritz Augustus Heinze

also applied for a federal subsidy. But there was opposition to Heinze's project, and in the summer of 1897, the Parliament's Railway Committee rejected his application. Financial difficulties then forced Heinze to sell his C&W charter to the CPR in February, 1898. The CPR, anxious to forestall American railway builders from the potentially lucrative Boundary market, began construction immediately. By June, 1898, Brooklyn, on the western shore of Lower Arrow Lake, had burst upon the scene. Then, as thousands of construction workers arrived and spread out farther and farther along the right-of-way, dozens of new roadhouses and settlements popped up virtually overnight.

Cascade, with its strategic location as a mining, freighting and hydro-electric centre, was now also about to enjoy the tremendous benefits of being a railway centre. By July, 1898, the *Times* noted that Cascade real estate had rapidly escalated in price. "Half a lot opposite Rochesen's store sold lately for $300 cash. A hotel will be erected on this lot." The newspaper also reported that the CPR had made arrangements with the town-site owners regarding lots and station grounds. The prospects of the railway had an immediate impact, and within a week several new businesses and resi-

dences were being erected throughout the city.

By late August the tote road had been completed between Brooklyn and Cascade, allowing people, freight and supplies, most of which was destined for Cascade, to move more freely.

"Cascade City has been picking up wonderfully since the assurance of a new railway line," said the Brooklyn *News* on August 13. "A new hotel has just been opened up, and several stores have come in. In order to accommodate the building operations the local saw mill is running overtime. Business is good in all lines, and the indications are that the place will be one of some little importance in a short time."

Two weeks later a correspondent for the *News* visited Cascade and wrote that "there are now two hotels running, with five more building. Several general stores and a good dry goods store are among the other businesses represented. While business generally is none too brisk, there is a good deal of freighting going on. Two stage lines run through there and twenty-four horse teams pass the city daily. Lots on Main street are selling from $800 up, and on side streets they bring $300 and $400. Lots can be rented for $10 to $20 per month. Appearances indicate that Cascade City will be overdone.

"The railway contractors (Mann, Foley Bros. & Larson) have let a contract for a warehouse, although the main supply depot will continue to be at Brooklyn. They have also ordered the construction of a hospital. Freighting from Bossburg costs $15 per ton. Donald McLeod, purchasing agent for the contractors, started Wednesday evening for Cascade City, where he will arrange matters for the reception of stores."

On September 10, the *Times*, in a brief article, echoed those sentiments: "Cascade is booming. Men are rushing in there; large substantial buildings are being constructed and lots are selling freely. Cascade also is going to be a city of hotels seven or eight being in the course of construction."

The boom would even have been more intense if not for the scarcity of lumber. Although the Cascade Sawmill Co., owned by Lynch and Earle, was able to supply 25,000 feet of lumber daily, it was unable to keep up with the demand. Sensing an obvious need, Holt & Brown decided to establish a second sawmill across the river by late September. Even with both sawmills producing to capacity, however, they barely kept up with the demand.

On September 17, the *News* announced that L.A. Hamilton, the CPR's land agent, had made a deal to purchase one third of all the unsold lots in Cascade. Two weeks later a reporter for the *News* again visited the infant town and filed this report: "This city is growing steadily. Strangers are daily coming in and notwithstanding the increase in number of hotels, it is often difficult to secure a bed in the evening. Besides the several hotels, there are two general stores, two chop houses, two restaurants, two bar-

(Above) A freight team arriving at Cascade from Bossburg, Washington. Prior to the establishment of the CPR to Cascade, all freight came in by this route. (Right) The public school, Cascade with teacher Mr. Whiting. Photo was taken before 1917.

ber shops, two livery stables, two fruit and news stands, etc. All are doing a good business. The business at the post office has doubled in a short time, there now being two full sacks of mail matter received and dispatched daily."

By this time the Cascade Hospital had been completed, although there are conflicting reports on the number of patients it was designed to accommodate; one paper stating 60, another 100. In any event, it was constructed for the use of CPR employees, and during the first week of October the *Times* reported that it had only four patients. However, as Cascade suffered through a typhoid fever epidemic later that month, the situation got dramatically worse. On October 22, the *Times* reported that there had been one death and there were 32 patients in the hospital, including the doctor in charge. These numbers, however, apparently referred only to CPR employees. Residents of the town who became ill were not admitted, for when Constable Elkins arrived on October 21, he had to ask for permission to rent a building where they could be cared for. By the beginning of November, the typhoid epidemic appears to have run its course, for there is no further mention of it.

Meanwhile, the establishment of new businesses continued apace. Williams & Elkins, who operated the Boundary Creek Stage & Express Co., and offered daily service between Cascade and Grand Forks, were erecting a stable near the Customs House. A passenger stage service had also been established by George Cormack and Ernest Livermore between Cascade and Brooklyn. These would later

receive competition from Bell & Davidson's Rapid Stage Line. Based in Bossburg, it provided service between there and all points in the Boundary.

D.M. Crowley, the Brooklyn furniture store owner, had decided to open a branch in Cascade. Wallace & Miller had opened a clothing store; Gagner & Roy, a wholesale liquor house and W.M. Wolverton, a warehouse.

The most significant enterprise, however, at least as far as posterity is concerned, was the establishment of the town newspaper. During the first week of November, P.J. O'Reilly, formerly of the Nelson *Economist* and Walter Wilcox, current publisher of the Brooklyn *News*, arrived in Cascade. It is unclear if each had plans to start their own newspapers, but after getting together, they decided to form a partnership. Contractor D.D. Ferguson was hired, and in 24 hours he and his crew had erected a commodious 20x30-foot two-story structure on Third Avenue, near the corner of Main Street. Wilcox, meanwhile, had returned to Brooklyn, where, on November 12, he published the last issue of the *News*. On that same date, O'Reilly published the first issue of the *Record*.

For a brief period, Cascade was to have not one, but two weekly newspapers. Published by Nisbet & Sanders, formerly of Kaslo, the *Maple Leaf* appeared for the first time on November 17. However, while the *Record* routinely mentioned all new businesses being established in Cascade, there was nary a hint of a competing newspaper in its pages until December 10. Then, under the heading MAPLE LEAF IS DEAD, the *Record*, in apparent glee, announced: "The little paper called the *Maple Leaf*, a few issues of which have appeared in this city, has at last turned up its toes, and now occupies a choice spot in the journalistic graveyard. Evidently the chilling frosts were too much for it. Appearing first on Thursday, the next week it came out on Friday, and this week it failed to issue at all. In the language of the poet:

"Whatever was I begun for
"If I was to be so soon done for."

Meanwhile, back on November 12, the first 8-page issue of the *Record* was virtually crammed with information about Cascade. Already the town could boast of 13 hotels: Cascade, C.H. Thomas; Cosmopolitan, F.W. Branson; Metropolitan, McDonald & Flood; Scandia, Oscar Stenstrom; Montana, Nelson & Co.; International, Seyler & Crahan; Railroad Headquarters, Eckstrom & Simpson; Britannia; Olson & Bergman; Commercial, Frederick & Peterson; Club, Quinlivan & Ross; Black's, Ira & Julius Black; Columbia, John McMaster and the Grand Central, also owned by McDonald & Flood. At least seven were located on First Avenue.

(Above) *An undated general view of Cascade City.*
(Below) *This photo of Cascade was taken either in 1898 or 1899. The building on the right is the Cascade Livery & Feed Stable. In the centre of the photograph are a number of freight teams from Bossburg.*

As freight continued to pour through Cascade from Brooklyn and Bossburg, the rates were increased from 75¢ per 100 pounds to an even dollar. Yet, despite the fact that there were approximately 100 teams operating over the Brooklyn-Cascade route alone, merchants were continually complaining about delays in receiving merchandise. D. McLeod, purchasing agent for Mann, Foley Bros. & Larson, informed the *Record* that there were now 246 horses employed in freighting his firm's merchandise from Bossburg to the storehouse in Cascade.

An indication of the tremendous freight destined to or through Cascade at this time can be gathered by the following example. According to the *Record,* on Monday, November 14, "some 40 four-horse teams were assembled in a phalanx, four and five deep, the driver of each waiting more or less patiently to get clearance papers for his particular load of merchandise." Passenger traffic was also dramatically on the increase.

Although Cascade's current boom was due to railroad construction, the potential of its hydro-electric power was also noted in the *Record:* "Of all the significant development now taking place in this rapidly growing centre, none is more fraught with greater possibilities for the future than the magnificent water power at our very doors."

William Anderson, the engineer who superintended the great hydro-electric plant at Bonnington Falls, near Nelson, had been sent to take charge of the Cascade plant. After a month of making extensive preparations, he furnished the following information to the *Record:* "About half a mile above the bridge, at the Cascades, work has already been started on a dam, to be 35 feet high and 400 feet long. A flume will convey the water to the power house, to be located on this side of the river, near the bridge. To build this flume 1,300 feet of rock will have to be blasted out. The power house will be a substantial pattern, built of stone and brick, and will be constructed so that at least 5,000 h.p. can be developed.

"At the site of the dam, where the work has been start-

(Above) First Street, Cascade, in 1898. In this scene, the street is overcrowded with freight wagons from Bossburg. This is one of the photographs used in research for the full colour painting of Cascade on pages 108-109.

(Right) The R.G. Ritchie General Store in foreground, with the B.C. Hotel the centre building on opposite side of street.

ed, a blacksmith shop and tool house have been built, and just now the men are putting up a storehouse and office on the flat, of sufficient capacity for all needs."

Anderson had also been instructed to look at the feasibility of supplying the residents of the city with a water system, and "has made a favourable report along this line. This will probably be done in the near future."

By the middle of November, First Avenue had been graded and grading was about to commence on Main Street. A schoolhouse had been built, which doubled as a church when Rev. G.K. Bradshaw, of Grand Forks, came to hold service.

With the two sawmills producing their daily combined capacity of 50,000 feet of lumber, they were barely keeping up with the demand. By this time, in addition to its 13 hotels, Cascade could boast a wide variety of other businesses.

W.M. Wolverton's Pioneer Store, the first general store to establish in Cascade, offered groceries, clothing, boots, shoes, hardware, etc. It soon had competition from the B.C. Mercantile and Mining Syndicate, which opened the English Store on July 2. It advertised: "The largest and most complete stock of hardware, dry goods, clothing, groceries, drugs, miners' supplies, etc., in the Boundary Creek country. Enlarged premised, increased staff and double stocks ensure for patrons the utmost satisfaction at the lowest possible costs. An assay office and laboratory, under the supervision of a thoroughly competent and reliable expert, is attached; also a public telephone office." This firm also operated a branch store at McRae Landing. On November 28, the Dominion Supply Company joined the competition with "an immense stock of general merchandise, all new goods, bought in car-load lots, at lowest possible prices."

Francis & Milne sold all kinds of produce in addition to confectionery, stationery, cigars and tobacco. V. Monnier & Co. were wholesalers for liquors, wines and tobacco and sole agents for Pabst's Milwaukee Beer. Wallace & Miller operated a clothing store, while C.A. Hanson provided "good square" meals at his B.C. Chop House restaurant. Meals could also be obtained at the Owl restaurant, operated by Gaudio Salatore. The Cascade Boot & Shoe Store was owned by A.H. Bigney, while Joseph Schaich dispensed drugs and chemicals and sold wallpaper and stationery in his Cascade Drug Store. The Star Barber Shop was operated by Pribilsky & Thomas. Some other businesses included: H.H. Duff, blacksmith; John Dwyer, jeweller; S.W. Bear, sign painter, and D.D. Ferguson, contractor. Cascade also had a second hand furniture store, operated by Balwin & Chezun, and saddle horses could be rented at Tyghe & McKellar's Palace Livery Barn.

All of Cascade's businesses, however, were not legitimate enterprises. Although the town was still in its infancy, it could already "boast" of its own red light district. One man, Mike Downey, came up with a unique plan to deprive the soiled doves of some of their ill-gotten gains. Posing as a police officer, Downey visited "each of the houses with red lanterns" and asked for a contribution of $50, apparently, to permit them to continue their operations. Although details are lacking, the plan backfired, Downey was arrested, tried and sentenced to 12 months at hard labour.

Unlike the rough, wide open mining towns just south of the border, Cascade, and other Boundary towns, were reasonably law-abiding. Most of the incidents that did occur, happened during the early history of the various towns, before the appointment of policemen. Cascade was no exception.

The first incident was recorded in the November 26 issue of the *Record*. Upon reporting for work at the English Store one morning, manager Stanley Mayall was informed by his clerk that thieves had broken into the premises during the night and had stolen about "a dozen caddies of tobacco. . .worth about $130." The two burglars had left a clear set of tracks in the snow, but these were soon lost where they merged with other footprints. Mayall, suspecting that the thieves might try to sell the tobacco, immediately notified other Cascade residents to be on the alert. It was not long before this prudent move yielded results, Mayall being notified that a man named John Doon was, at that very moment, trying to sell tobacco at Francis & Milne's store.

Lacking a police constable, Mayall's bookkeeper, a man named Morgan, was hastily sworn in as a special constable. Doon was promptly arrested. "He was then taken to ex-constable Elkin's old quarters, but broke away, and did not give up until Mr. Morgan fired twice from a persuasive six-shooter. He was then ironed hand and foot."

In the meantime, Thomas Florence, Doon's accomplice, was unaware that his partner had been arrested and went to Francis & Milne's to look for him. He too was promptly arrested. Justice was not handcuffed with red tape in those days, and a trial was held that same evening before Paul Rochussen, JP. Doon and Florence were found guilty and sentenced to "six months at hard labor and a fine of $5 each, or 12 months if the fine was not forthcoming."

Two days later, Cascade was shocked by a more serious altercation. Around midnight on November 28, James Miller was arrested by Special Constable Darcy "charged with the theft of $1 from an Italian." Miller was locked up in the improvised jail, just behind the Commercial Hotel, where ex-constable Elkins formerly had his headquarters.

It was common practice for towns who did not have a police constable to hire a night watchman. Cascade had hired a giant Irishman named Pat Kennedy, and as he made his rounds at 5 a.m., he saw two men sneaking around the jail. The men were in the alley, and as Kennedy approached along the side of the hotel, one of them jumped out from his place of concealment and struck at him. In dodging the blow, Kennedy stumbled and fell down, and while in this position one of the assailants fired at him. "The bullet entered Kennedy's body on the side of the left breast, coming out under the arm, and doing no serious damage."

At this point Kennedy fired and struck one of the men, who later identified himself as Tim Sullivan. "The other man started to run, with Kennedy after him, and firing. He evidently struck him, as, early that morning, a man applied at the bunk house of the Lynch & Earl mill for some bandages, saying he had hurt his leg. He soon made himself scarce, and is probably safe on the other side, in Uncle Sam's domain."

The fusillade of shots soon brought a crowd to the scene and Sullivan was taken to the Cascade Hospital. An examination revealed that the bullet had passed through the kidneys, coming out on the other side. Dr. Foster did not think Sullivan would survive, and he was soon proved correct.

On Wednesday, Sullivan asked for the services of a priest, and Father William Palmer, of Trail, who was in the city, spent most of the day with the wounded man. During that time the dying man confessed that Sullivan was not his real name. He had given a false name because "he did not want his family and friends back east to hear of his trouble and probable untimely death."

The shooting affray caused a great deal of talk all over the city, and it was the general opinion that, if Cascade had had a suitable jail "where prisoners could be securely kept, the affair would not have happened."

Kennedy, meanwhile, was placed under a $650 bond and ordered to appear before justices Ross and Rochussen for the shooting of "Sullivan." Provincial Constable Dinsmore, of Grand Forks, investigated the incident and found that Kennedy had indeed fired in self defence, so he was exonerated of all blame.

These two incidents drove home the fact that, as a thriving, growing city, Cascade needed proper jail facilities. The death of Sullivan made it a pressing concern, and on December 10, the *Record* announced that a new jail would be built. Not only that, but Att.-Gen. Joe Martin gave assur-

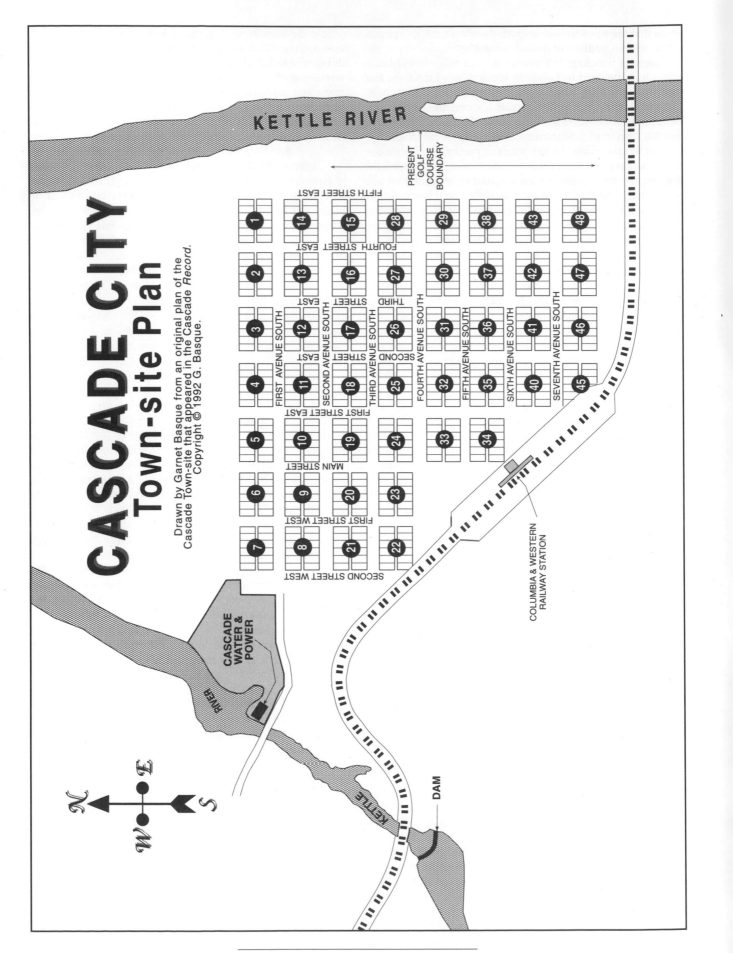

CASCADE CITY
Town-site Plan

Drawn by Garnet Basque from an original plan of the
Cascade Town-site that appeared in the Cascade *Record.*
Copyright © 1992 G. Basque.

KETTLE RIVER

PRESENT GOLF COURSE BOUNDARY

FIFTH STREET EAST

FOURTH STREET EAST

THIRD STREET EAST

SECOND STREET EAST

FIRST STREET EAST

MAIN STREET

FIRST STREET WEST

SECOND STREET WEST

FIRST AVENUE SOUTH
SECOND AVENUE SOUTH
THIRD AVENUE SOUTH
FOURTH AVENUE SOUTH
FIFTH AVENUE SOUTH
SIXTH AVENUE SOUTH
SEVENTH AVENUE SOUTH

COLUMBIA & WESTERN RAILWAY STATION

CASCADE WATER & POWER

RIVER

KETTLE

DAM

N
E
S
W

ances that the town would also receive "a permanent police officer and an additional Justice of the Peace. . . ."

George Stocker, the town-site agent, informed the paper that the deed to Lot 16 in Block 8, located on the flat below Black's Hotel, had been donated to the government for a jail. A week later a contract for construction of the building was awarded to N. Robinson for $445. On December 21, Const. D.J. Darraugh, formerly of Burton City, arrived to take charge of the police department. Three days later the *Record* informed its readers that Robinson had ordered the lumber for the jail and that construction would begin "next Monday morning. He (Robinson) also says that by Saturday night the jail will be complete and ready for guests. It will be 20x30 feet, one story, and contain three cells, a court room and apartments for our provincial police officer."

On January 14, 1899, the *Record* provided further details on the now completed jail: "The cells are made of 2x6 timbers, laid flat and spiked to one another, the six sides of each cell being fitted in this way. The windows to the building have iron bars, there of course being no windows in the cells. The contract price is $445, but extras will run up to over $100 more. The building is well suited for the purpose for which it was built."

Meanwhile, the Dominion Mining & Development Agency was formulating plans to install a "water and light plant" in Cascade. On November, the *Record* announced that the company intended to "install a 60 horse power engine, to pump the water to a large tank, to be erected on the hill west of

The Hotel Cascade, gaily decorated in celebration of the Queen's birthday.

town. Then a four inch main will be laid on First and Second avenues and on Main street, which will be large enough to put in hydrants for fire protection, if deemed desirable. This plant will be located near the bridge, close to where preparations are being made for the construction of the large power house.

"If an electric light plant is installed, as seems likely, a motor will be put in sufficient to run 500 sixteen candle power lights, and the service will be extended all over the city. Mr. Simmons is a practical electrician and machinist of many years' experience, and consequently thorough(ly) at home in matters of this kind. With Wm. Anderson, the supervising engineer, he assisted in the construction and installation of the great Bonnington Falls plant, near Nelson."

Cascade thriving economy had not gone unnoticed in banking circles either. Although Cascade never did get its own bank, there was plenty of interest. In late November John Smith, manager of the Rossland branch of the Bank of Halifax, was in Cascade. He was returning from Grand Forks, where a branch was to be established. Several officials of the Bank of Montreal also examined Cascade potential an a site for a bank. In the end, they went to Greenwood.

As the year drew to a close, there seemed to be no end

of new businesses. L.K. Larson, formerly of Slocan City, started a cigar, tobacco, fruit and confectionery store. J.H. Kellog erected a 24x36, two-and-a-half story building on First Avenue. Kellog operated part of the lower floor as a cigar store, putting the balance up for rent. G.T. Curtis sold tea, canned goods, tobacco, pipes and stationery from his First Avenue store, while John Lyngholm sold boots, shoes, rubbers and clothing from a store on the corner of First Avenue and Main Street.

Cascade also had four new hotels. The Roma, situated on First Avenue and owned by C. Davin, opened for business in late November, about the same time that Tom Lake & Max Hickmann began construction on the Royal. The Grand Central, owned by Captain Ritchie, was situated on Second Avenue, opposite the B.C. Stables. It was a 26x40-foot, two-story building with a 14x16-foot addition. It opened around mid-December. Cascade's seventeenth hotel, owned by Sam McOrmond, was also under construction by late November. However, its name was not recorded.

On December 31, the *Record* announced that railway contractors Mann, Foley Bros. & Larson were about to move their headquarters from Brooklyn to Cascade. This was a serious blow for Brooklyn, already reeling from a dramatic economic downturn, but it added more fuel to Cascade's economy. According to the newspaper, several teams had already been sent "across the mountains to Brooklyn for this purpose. It is said further, that by the early part of next week a dozen four-horse teams will be employed in the work."

A week later, on January 7, 1899, the *Record* announced another tremendous boost to Cascade's economy. W.H. Aldridge, manager of the Trail smelter, had arrived in Cascade accompanied by L.E. Campbell, manager of the West Kootenay Light & Power Co., and by C.A. Stoess, an experienced rail and general engineering surveyor.

"Mr. Aldridge," noted the paper, "came by special appointment to confer with the owners of the Cascade townsite, relative to the erection of a large smelting plant near the city, which is to be utilized in the treatment of the Boundary, Christina Lake and Burnt Basin ores. All day Thursday was spent in looking over the immense power of the falls and in tramping over the site selected for the smelter, about one and a half miles south of the city, on a high bluff above the Kettle river.

"For some time negotiations have been quietly going on between Manager Stocker, of the Townsite Co., and the land department of the CPR, and with the exception of some minor details of little interest to the general public, the matter is now in definite shape. After his final conference with the townsite owners, Mr. Aldridge explained the plans to some extent in regard to this new enterprise, to a representative of the *Record*. Asked in regard to the capacity of the new smelting plant, Mr. Aldridge said:

"'We will probably make it a 1000-ton smelter, so as to

The Columbia & Western station at Cascade, showing one of the first passenger trains to arrive.

be able to handle all ores that are likely to be offered. We do not believe in erecting a 200 or even a 400 ton plant here, as we would find it more economical to haul the ores to Trail for treatment if no more daily tonnage than that could be obtained in this district.'

"The cost of building a smelter of 1000 tons daily capacity will exceed $500,000, and will give steady employment to upwards of 500 men when completed. The stack alone will require 800,000 bricks and the buildings in connection in proportion."

On February 4, the *Record* reported on Stoess' progress during the previous month. He had found the clay to be admirably suited for the manufacturer of the 2,000,000 bricks that would be required for the construction of the many buildings needed for smelter purposes. Ample lime, for fluxing purposes, could be had within two miles of the smelter site. By the first week of February, Stoess was "running lines and taking levels for the flume which will be used to furnish the water supply for the smelter." This flume was to be a mile long, at least two-and-a-half feet square, with an intake near the dam currently being constructed above the cascades.

Ironically, despite the initial early interests and efforts, little was heard of Cascade's smelter until mid-November, when the *Record* expressed its disappointment that the CPR smelter had not materialized. Instead, the CPR had apparently decided it would make better sense to have "other parties" construct smelters throughout the Boundary. The railway, in essence, had decided to concentrate on transporting ore, not refining it.

By this time, Cascade's heyday had long since passed. In fact, when the *Record* had decreased in size to eight pages back on January 14, 1899, it marked the end of Cascade's tremendous boom. Although Cascade would be robust for many months, and survive in lesser stature for years, it would never achieve its greatness again.

As with all depressions, it takes a while before the economic problems become evident. One of the first establishments to feel the pinch was the B.C. Tobacco Co., which went out of business in mid-February. Three weeks later

T.E. Mahaffy decided to close out his business and offered his entire stock of men's suits, "shirts, hats, gloves, socks, shoes, rubbers, blankets, underwear, pipes, tables, oil cloth, Flannelettes, ladies rubbers, embroideries, stockings, towels, etc, etc.," at cost.

Then, between Wednesday morning, March 30, and Thursday evening, March 31, three small fires occurred. Two of these were in a small barbershop adjoining the Roma Hotel, "and were so palpably the result of almost criminal negligence, that the fire wardens have already read the riot act to the proprietor. . . ." The other fire occurred in the house of D.L. Barclay, opposite the *Record's* newspaper office. The roof, which caught fire from sparks, was quickly put out. Fortunately, the three fires were quickly contained with minimal damage.

Meanwhile, two more establishments had gone out of business. However, instead of pointing the finger at Cascade's faltering economy, the newspaper wrote: "It is a curious fact that none of them were advertisers in the *Record*."

As the summer wore on, Cascade put these setbacks behind it and tried to move forward. By late May a new post office had been constructed by postmaster Cameron, and a new telephone office had been established. On May 24, the city held its first ever celebration for the Queen's birthday, drawing spectators and participants from many miles around.

"With the cornet band of 14 pieces from Bossburg came the base ball club and many others of the same town. From Grand Forks, it is said that nearly 50 teams were dispatched with visitors to the Gateway City celebrations. Prospectors, miners and railway men from the adjacent mountains made it a point to be here on that day. Gladstone, Christina Lake, Columbia and Greenwood also contributed their quota of pleasure seekers, and they were not disappointed.

"The entire business portion of the place was decorated with bunting and flags and presented a most attractive appearance. At the east and west ends of town were banners stretched across the street with the word 'welcome' thereon in large letters, while in the centre of town was another lettered with 'God Save the Queen.' In fact, with the evergreens and other decorations Cascade took on a most inviting holiday-like appearance."

The festivities included a baseball game between Bossburg and Grand Forks, which was won by the latter 16 to 11. A rock drilling contest, held in front of the Hotel Cascade, was won by C. Sadner and George Moore. These events were followed by horse races, bicycle races and track and field events. There was even a prize awarded for the best decorated building, which was won by C.H. Thomas of the Hotel Cascade. Special mention was also given to the Montana and Scandia hotels.

By mid-June, C&W track layers were west of Gladstone. Although 15 trestles had to be built between there and Cascade, and construction was progressing slowly, it was still hoped that the railway would reach Cascade by the end of July. The anticipation of the C&W's arrival gave Cascade a brief, but much needed, economic spurt.

"Cascade continues to grow slowly but in a substantial way," noted the *Record* on June 24, "and this summer will see quite a number of new buildings erected in the town. The school trustees have been advised by Alex. Robinson, superintendent of instruction, that the provincial lands and works department will proceed at once with the work on the new school building. It will be remembered that the government this year set aside $1,500 for school progress in Cascade. This should provide a commodious and comfortable building."

The B.C. Hotel, shown here, survived the fire which claimed six Cascade hotels in 1899.

Finally, on August 12, "at exactly 27 minutes past 10. . . the first locomotive to enter the Boundary Country, crossed the 1600-foot-long, 135-foot-high Kettle river bridge at Cascade, and is now busy laying the heavy 73-pound Carnegie steel rails in the Cascade yards. The engine is a powerful one, with eight drivers. It is numbered 403, and has H.N. Atkinson at the throttle and James H. Baxter as fireman, two excellent mechanics. Last night the engine was decorated with bunting, and presented a gay appearance today, as it pushed the track-laying machinery before, which was putting down the heavy steel at the rate of one rail, 30 feet, every two minutes.

"The track was laid to the other end of the bridge last Monday, but has been delayed for want of the 30-foot bridge stringers which were en route from the coast. However, Supt. Stewart and Chief Engineer Tye set the wires at work, a special steamer was sent up Arrow lakes, and the result of their unremitting energy is seen in presence of the snorting iron horse in the Gateway City today.

"A car of hogs and sheep, for P. Burns & Co., was brought down to the bridge yesterday, but had to be taken back to the siding at Sutherland creek. This will be brought in this afternoon with seven other cars of merchandise.

Orders were sent out yesterday to rush all Boundary freight via Robson to Cascade.

"It is certain the CPR expects to do an immense business at this point, as three experienced employees have been sent here to care for it. As soon as possible a neat and commodious station will be erected, the carpenters being already on the way here."

By this time, work was well underway on Cascade's new Presbyterian Church. Constructed at a cost of about $850, it was 24x36 and had the capacity to accommodate over 100 of the faithful. Construction was also about to start on the new 27x33-foot schoolhouse. Although the completed school could accommodate 56 pupils, it would never hold half that amount. At one end of town construction of the new two-story, 40x50-foot railway depot was about to commence. Cascade could also boost of several new homes.

On September 18, the first passenger train ever to enter the Boundary Country, rolled into the Cascade depot. "The train consisted of a passenger coach, a combination baggage and smoking car and a locomotive, Conductor Ed Chesley being in charge. Every seat in the coach was occupied, there being about 75 passengers aboard."

The event marked another turning point in Cascade's fortunes. It was a happy occasion, of course, because Cascade now had railway connection to outside points. But, paradoxically, it would also prove to be a sad occasion. History had shown that by the time the C&W had actually reached a town, that particular town was already dead or dying. This had already happened in Brooklyn and Gladstone, and other smaller settlements or roadhouses, like the Mountain House, Summit House, Half Way House and Peterson's Hotel, between Brooklyn and Cascade, had all shut down.

Residents of Cascade were optimistic the same fate would not befall their town; and they had ample reason to be encouraged. Four factors had contributed to Cascade's prosperity in varying degrees: it was a mining centre, transportation hub, railway headquarters and a potential supplier of hydro-electric power. Unfortunately, however, one by one each of these economic building blocks were whittled away.

With the establishment of the C&W into Cascade and beyond, freight transportation through Bossburg quickly disappeared. While the railway now transported the bulk of goods and supplies, it did not contribute to the town's economy as had the freight wagons of old. Also, by the time the first passengers reached Cascade, the bulk of railway contractors and workers were many miles away, boosting the economy of new boom towns, particularly Niagara. Thus Cascade turned from being a railway centre to little more that a railway depot along the line. When the Burnt

Basin proved to be little more that a surface wonder, Cascade's mining fraternity left for greener pastures, and another economic base was lost. Only the potential of Cascade's hydro-electric power continued to hold promise for the future. But this alone could not create enough employment to maintain a town as large as Cascade had been.

However, residents of Cascade, if they were even aware of what the future implications might be, had little time to worry about them, for, only 11 days after the arrival of the first passenger train, Cascade received a terrible baptism by fire.

"It was 12:30 this morning when the dreaded cry of fire resounded through our streets and the fire alarm triangle began to be rung," reported the *Record* on September 30. "Fire was first discovered by Mrs. Mahoney, who had a room in the Britannia hotel. As she looked out of her window the one-story shacks between the Britannia and Club hotel was all ablaze, from what source is not known. Quicker than lightning the flames leaped up and were soon licking up both hotels and spreading westward, fanned by a northwest wind.

"In quick succession, the Grand Central hotel, Railroad Headquarters hotel, Scandia hotel, Francis & Milne and the Hotel Montana were eaten up by the fiery demon and reduced to ashes. Six hotels and one cigar store were destroyed, in an hour's time, and nothing remains today but a heap of smouldering embers, marking what was once the busiest part of the Gateway City.

"When the fire first broke out it was evident that the block, if not the entire city, was doomed. Everyone of the buildings had sleeping occupants, some of whom escaped with but scanty attire. When it was realized that everything in the path of the fire demon must go, a frantic effort was made to save goods, furniture, personal effects, etc., but little, however, was rescued from the flames.

"Then a futile effort was made to save the last building on the block, the Montana, by blowing up the Scandia with dynamite. A box of 50 pounds was touched off with a 50-foot fuse. The building rose with a deafening roar and then collapsed, and the flames rushed on as though nothing had happened, engulfing the Montana and the log building in the rear.

"Alex Arvoll, who had been employed by C.J. Eckstrom, was one of the hardest workers, of the several hundred willing ones endeavoring to rescue property. He was imprisoned on the sidewalk in front of the Scandia by falling walls, and before he could possible be rescued, the sea of flame swept over him, carrying him to eternity in a most horrible manner.

"Several times efforts were made to drag him out, but human endurance could not possibly stand that intense heat. He could be heard piteously calling for help, yet it was not possible to get him out in time.

"When the dynamite was placed in the Scandia, loud warnings were given in every direction to give the building a wide berth. Arvoll saw a drunken man run back into the doomed building and he rushed after him to get him out. The man was saved, but at the cost of his brave rescuer's life. It was a heroic action, and his name will live long in the memory of those who witnessed it.

"Every man in town organized himself into a fire lad-

die, and splendid work was done in many instances. With no water supply and no fire fighting appliances, it was a foregone conclusion as to the result, when the flames were fairly started. No human ingenuity could have saved the fated block. Mark Tracy with his water wagon did excellent service, continually refilling it at the river as fast as the bucket brigade emptied it.

"This water was used to save the buildings on the south side of First Ave, and though at times it seemed doubtful, the effort was finally successful. Angus Cameron's postoffice building was one of these, and the heat was so intense that it blistered the water carriers, but they held on and it was saved. The postmaster was away on Huckleberry mountain, but his brother Jim and sister Kate were there. The same experience was had with the Kelliher building adjoining, and also with the feed barn and old custom house.

"The Cascade Drug Co. and Wm. Wolverton's pioneer store were also given attention with water and wet blankets and the fire prevented from spreading eastward on the street.

The losses totalled between $20,000 and $25,000, of which only $4,450 was covered by insurance. The heaviest loser was S.F. Quinlivan, whose Club Hotel, stock, furniture and fixtures was valued at $3,800. Oscar Stenstrom lost $3,400 when his Scandia Hotel went up in flames. C.H. May's Hotel Montana was worth $2,500. The fire also consumed $300 in cash. None of the above had insurance to cover their losses. Nelson, Olson & Bergman lost $3,500 in the Britannia Hotel, $1,000 of which was covered by insurance. The grand Central Hotel, owned by Flood & McDonald, was valued at $4,500, $1,500 of which was covered by insurance. E.C. Eckstrom lost $2,000 in stock, fixtures and personal effects when the Railroad Headquarters Hotel was destroyed. Eckstrom was one of the most fortunate of the fire's victims, for, not only did he have $1,000 in insurance, but he was able to save both his piano and billiard table. His partner, B.F. VanCleve, was also fortunate in that his loss, after insurance, was only $850. Francis & Milne carried no insurance to cover their building and stock, which was valued at $1,000. There were also a number of other smaller losers.

This disaster could not come at a more inopportune time. A few, like C.H. May, who leased the International Hotel, renamed it the Montana, and opened up for business a week later, continued to have faith in Cascade. But they were the exceptions. Most realized that Cascade's glory days had passed and her future was beyond recovery.

With six of Cascade's hotels destroyed in the fire, those that were still operating did a landslide business, the *Record* stating that: "Never in the history of a town have the hotels been better patronized than now, every room being occupied nearly every night." However, the paper was forced to admit that "on the whole," business was quieter, although it asserted that "mining development" and "permanent business" was improving.

That, however, was apparently not an opinion shared by many, for, in its December 2 issue, the *Record* printed this item in defence of Cascade's faltering economy: "Some people have erroneously got the idea into their heads that Cascade is going backwards. This is a mistake, to prove which is not difficult. During the past few months Cascade has built a nice little church and a pretty, commodious school house. A splendid large residence has been erected on the plateau near the river in the northwest part of town. The work on the foundation for an electric plant of great magnitude is going forward, Work is already progressing on the big dam. Mr. S. Mayall and Mr. T.F. Canden have both built fine residences, the town site people have erected five cottages, additions have been made to several buildings already standing, including the English Store and Montana hotel. In fact, no other town of no more pretentions than our's can show a much more steady and substantial growth."

Despite the newspapers bluster, however, the signs were clearly visible for those who cared to look. In early December, Const. D.J. Darraugh was transferred to Phoenix, and a week later, when the Boundary Licence District Commissioners met in Cascade, only three Cascade hotels had their liquor licenses renewed: Roma, Cascade and Black's. Cascade received another blow in early January, 1900, when contractors Mann, Foley Bros. & Larson decided to move their headquarters from Cascade to Trail.

Despite the gloomy situation, the March 10, 1900 issue of the *Record* tried to reassure its readers that the outlook for Cascade was improving. "There is a decided improvement in the general outlook in Cascade. Renewed confidence in the stability of the community is apparent on every hand. The winter season, with its depressive conditions, which have been present in a marked degree for the past three or four months, owing to open weather and impassable roads, is rapidly passing, and the awakening influences of springtime are inspiring new hopes, new ambitions and renewed effort. The past two weeks the town has been filling up with the coming of strangers and the return of former citizens. Several new businesses have been opened up, and there are others in prospect. Altogether the

indications for the future are quite reassuring."

Granted, there were some minor improvements later that month. Bill & Duncan, who had formerly owned and operated a stage line between Cascade and Bossburg, but had sold out to G.H. Williams in 1899, started another line. On the hotel side, Black's, which had been closed, was leased by Andrew Ravine and reopened. But even these brief turnarounds were deceiving. Ravine, for example, retired from the hotel business one month later.

Even Wilcox, publisher of the *Record* eventually had had enough. On April 7 he sold the newspaper to his editor, H.S. Turner. Turner, who had been with the paper for five months, probably should have known better. One has to wonder if he was deceiving himself or trying to deceive others when, on June 16, he wrote: "While other over-boomed towns of the Boundary are floundering in the gloom of despondency which comes with reaction in such cases, Cascade is just beginning to shine by reason of its true merits."

On September 22 the *Record* shrank to four pages from eight. The following month, T.E. Mahaffy started selling off his stock of clothing at "greatly reduced prices." What remained was shipped to Moyie where Mahaffy opened up a new store. In early November, Sam Handy sold his interest in the water delivery business to C.H. Thomas, and he too moved to Moyie. On November 10, John Simpson, principal of the Cascade school, resigned his position. In late November, John Lyngholm decided to pack up his stock of clothing and footwear and take a "vacation until next spring." But the vacation became permanent when, in February, 1901, Lyngholm shipped his goods to the Crow's Nest loop.

On November 10, as the *Record* marked the beginning of its third year of publication, an optimistic Turner editorialized: "Apparently the *Record* is here to stay. Editors may flourish and decay, may come and go, but the local journal greets its readers regularly once a week, in boom times and in times of depression, and in the perhaps remote future when it is printed on a $30,000 press, and its types are set

The dam at Cascade.

(Above) The powerhouse of the Cascade Water & Power Co. Note the old wooden trestle which has since been replaced by a modern bridge. (Left) Interior of the power-house.

with a $4,000 typesetting machine, its present efforts and persistency will be reverted to with pride by the historian. So it steps off in the beginning of the third year of its career with as much determination and hope as inspired it the day it slid from the dry dock into the sea of journalism."

Turner continued to be optimistic, and on December 22 he wrote: "There are not quite as many people in town as formerly, but the buildings are all here yet, and by June next there'll not be an unoccupied one in town. The growth that will be witnessed here in the spring will not be 'bloat,' but bone and sinew.

"We who stay here this winter and keep things moving steadily along, and thus maintain our faith in the final outcome, will enjoy the pleasure of greeting the return in a few months of many familiar faces, whose wearers will admit they, too, would have done better to have remained here."

Despite this optimistic forecast, however, there was little to report in Cascade for the first four months of 1901. Then, on May 11, the following two lines appeared on the editorial page: "The Cascade *Record* is for sale." In its June 27 edition, the small "for sale" notice had disappeared, and in a brief editorial, Turner explained why.

"This issue of the Cascade *Record* is the final one.

"The writer has fought the battle of life in the treadmill of journalism for nearly 38 years, covering a range of territory extending from the Atlantic to the Pacific coast, and now we take to the woods, having amassed a sufficient competency to enable us to lead a quiet comfortable life amid genuine rustic surroundings, provided we meet with ordinary success in hunting, fishing and trapping.

"To be truthful, though, as we have always been with the pen, we will say that for the past year or more we have been preparing to go into the farming and livestock business, and we have now got where our entire time and attention is required to this new enterprise, and having, during our 38 years' effort at journalism, set reform movements in motion that will eventually evangelize the world, we think we can be spared from the journalistic field."

An optimist to the end, Turner continued: "At no time since our sojourn in this field has the outlook for Cascade assumed a brighter hue. From this (time) on Cascade will thrive, and while we have prospered in the past, we could do much better in the future, but we have made other plans which we do not care now to abandon. Cascade will not be long without a local paper. Some one will see and seize the opportunity here offered. To our local friends we wish to express our gratefulness for their steadfast and liberal support, which has enabled us to keep ahead of the hounds.

"The few who have paid subscriptions in advance will be rebated what is their due, which will be accompanied by a prize picture of the editor."

With the *Record* now gone, we must rely on other Boundary newspapers for news of Cascade, although, admittedly, there was little to report. Only the Cascade hydro-electric power situation continued to make the occasional headlines.

In December, 1899, the Grand Forks *Miner* had reported that the development of hydro-electric power at Cascade was "proceeding with a large force of men. . . . It will take a year more to complete the work and have the plant ready to deliver electric power. In some respects it is an enterprise of greater magnitude than that carried out at Bonnington Falls by the West Kootenay Light and Power Company and which is now delivering electric power at Rossland, Trail and other points in that part of the country.

"The work at Cascade involves the construction of a flume 2,700 feet long, most of it through solid rock. This is over 2,000 feet longer than the flume at Bonnington and the fall is 150 feet, which is 116 feet more than the fall at Bonnington. An equal service can be done at Cascade by one-fourth the water as at Bonnington."

On April 14, 1900, the *Record* announced that the hydro-electric project had been purchased by the London & British Columbia Gold Fields Co. However, nothing further was forthcoming until May, 1901, when the *Record* informed its readers that the long delay in completing the Cascade power company's project was at an end. "Orders for all the necessary machinery have been placed with the Westinghouse Electric & Manufacturing Co. of Pittsburg, Pennsylvania, and tenders for furnishing poles to extend the wires from Cascade to the mining camps in the neighborhood, are asked for. . . . It is expected the machinery will be installed, and the entire plant completed and in running order by Christmas."

On August 24, the *Pioneer* published a detailed article about the Cascade hydro-electric power project. For the development of the power, a dam, consisting of timber cribwork filled with 10,000 cubic yards of rock, had been constructed at the head of the gorge. The dam. 40-feet thick at the base and 24-feet wide at the top, was 400 feet long. It measured 50 feet from the top of the dam to the deepest part of the channel, tapering off to a height of 25 feet on the sides.

"The site is on solid rock-bed throughout, and the foundation timbers are solidly bolted to the rock. The permanent water level is to be 10 feet below the top of the dam, and provision has been made to control the water level during periods of high water by a series of sluice ways, 12 in number, which can be opened up to a depth of 12 feet below the normal level. This will give an area of about 2,000 square feet of waterway through which to pass the flood water. The sluice ways are closed by means of stop logs, 12 inches square, dropped one on top of the other in a grove provided for their reception.

"A steel rail track will be placed on the top of the dam on which a travelling winch can be run over the sluiceways for the purpose of drawing up the stop logs as the water rises during floods. This winch will be operated by hand or electric motor."

To illustrated the strength of the dam, the *Pioneer* related an incident that had occurred during high water of the previous June, when a large log boom broke loose. The logs, "a few hundred yards above the dam, gave way and about one million feet of logs were thrown against the dam in a solid mass, and at a time when the water was at extreme flood, without inflicting the slightest damage on the structure. The unexpected test of the dam fully demonstrated its stability."

The water was conveyed from the dam to the powerhouse, "first by an open rock cut 225 feet long, from this point a tunnel, 12x14 feet, is driven for a distance of 410 feet through solid rock, thence by another open channel for a distance of 500 feet. At this point a concrete bulkhead will be placed and the water conveyed in a circular flume of 12 feet to the power house. Over 35,000 yards of rock have been excavated for the open cuts alone. The area of the open cuts and tunnel are so large that no appreciable loss of head will occur, and the water will enter the flume with a head equal to the level of the water in the dam."

The powerhouse itself was erected on a natural bay at the foot of the falls, where about 7,000 cubic yards of rock had to be excavated for the purpose. The building, a substantial 45x200-foot fireproof structure of brick and stone, can still be seen today as you cross over the modern bridge leading into the Cascade town-site. The inside contained the latest and most up-to-date Westinghouse electrical machinery.

To transmit electrical power the 22 miles to Phoenix, a 132-foot-wide right-of-way had been cleared. Then, from November, 1901, to February, 1902, a small force of men were engaged in getting the power lines in place. Although there had been some delay because of the non arrival of insulators from Germany, on February 22 the *Pioneer* was able to report:

"These have now arrived and cars containing them, as well as the heavy copper wire, have been delivered to Hartford Junction, Columbia, Gilpin's and Cascade. Putting up the wire is to be started next week.

"The work of erecting the poles and crossarms was completed about Christmas time, when the force was reduced and the balance of men set at work putting in the bolts and clearing the right of way in better shape.

"In addition to this an engineer has been busy nearly all winter in going over every foot of the line, for the purpose of measuring and counting every stump on the right of way. It appears that when the right of way, about 22 miles long, was cut over two years ago, the Cascade Water, Power and Light Co. managers thought the charter held by the company gave them the right to cut and dispose of the timber on mineral claims which they crossed. This, however, appears to have been an error on their part, and a costly one, too. Every tree that was cut down will have to be paid for, which is the cause of counting the stumps by an employee of the company.

"Of course, owners of claims are not disposed to sell the timber after it has been cut for any more than they think they can get, and as a result they are getting all that they can get. Randolph Stuart, of Greenwood, is attending to the settling of the stumpage matter, and it is said that he has arranged to pay for stumps at prices ranging all the way from 20 cents each up as high as $1 each. One claim owner, at least, across the corner of whose ground the line goes, wanted and got his full dollar for every tree cut down. However, nearly or quite all of these stumpage claims have now been adjusted.

"Thus far the company. . .has spent nearly $250,000 in the work, and by the time it is completed it will represent an expenditure of about $400,000. The cost of power all through the Boundary will be largely reduced from the expense of steam production, and will enable the working of low grade mines at greater profit than heretofore. The city of Grand Forks is already negotiating for the power to light that municipality, and it will be used in the cities of Greenwood and Phoenix as soon as it can be had, for the same purpose. The line is expected to be completed and in operation by June."

Despite that optimistic prediction, it was about December 1 before everything was in readiness and the current was turned on for the first time. This initial power enabled the Granby Company to fire up all its furnaces. Previously, two had been idle because of lack of power.

But the joyous celebrations that came with the switching on of the Cascade power plant was to be short-lived, as bad luck continued to plague the venture. Only a week later, on December 10, Thomas Bagley was fatally electrocuted. The same evening, valves in the big pipe that supplied water to the powerhouse, broke. According to the Boundary Creek *Times*, this created "an enormous quantity of water which struck the power house carrying away a portion of the wall and doing other damage. Fortunately, none of the costly machinery was damaged. The accident will force the closing down of the plant for nearly two months."

This was a major setback, not only for the power company, but also for the Granby Smelter, a number of Boundary mines and the city of Phoenix. For another year they would have to make due with inadequate power supplied by the Greenwood Electric Co. Finally, on January 25, 1903, the electric current from Cascade was used to light the city of Phoenix for the first time.

Cascade, meanwhile, continued to wallow in its own problems. Back on September 11, 1901, the town suffered another blow when a fire destroyed several businesses. The fire originated in Black's Hotel and quickly consumed the hotel, an adjoining jeweller's shop, and the Columbia Hotel, causing $5,000 in damage. Ironically, Black's Hotel, which had been closed for some time, had been purchased by Abe Hall of Phoenix and only re-opened on August 6.

By June, 1902, Cascade had only two licensed hotels; the Cascade, owned by pioneer resident C.H. Thomas, and the Commercial, owned by C.E. Johnson. Six months later, only the Cascade was still in business, a situation which continued until May, 1904, when the *Pioneer* reported that J.A. Bertois had purchased the old Commercial Hotel from George Stocker.

Bertois renamed his establishment the B.C. Hotel and applied for a business license, which was granted. However, when the liquor licensing board met the following year, the inspector recommended that only one license be issued in Cascade. In what the *Pioneer* described as a "strenuous fight with the license commissioners" for that single license, Thomas emerged triumphant. But, for Thomas, it proved to be a short-lived victory. Two weeks later Cascade was ravaged by another disastrous fire which destroyed most of the buildings that had survived the previous two fires.

According to the July 15 issue of the *Pioneer;* "The fire started in a barn near the Cascade hotel. It quickly communicated to the Cascade hotel, owned by Charles H. Thomas, and then to the livery stable of J.A. Bertois on the same side of the street. Then the flames went across the street and licked up the general store of William Wolverton and a number of small buildings to and including the old Commercial hotel, where it stopped for lack of fuel.

"There is no water supply in the town, and no possible way of fighting the fire once it got started. The loss is estimated at between $25,000 and $35,000 with no insurance. Mr. Thomas had the only licensed hotel in the place, and there is now but one standing, that of J.A. Bertois, who was refused a license a few weeks ago. But one store also, that of R.G. Ritchie, is left standing in Cascade.

"Nearly six years ago Cascade had a fire that wiped out five (sic) hotels and destroyed $25,000 in property. A little later another fire cleaned up a goodly share of the buildings left. Consequently, it was difficult to secure insurance at any price. In the boom days of CPR railway construction, 1898-99, Cascade had 17 licensed hotels and other businesses in proportion. William Wolverton and Charles H.

Thomas were the pioneer settlers there, and had been in Cascade about 10 years."

Cascade now found itself in a unique situation. Bertois had a hotel without a license, while Thomas had a license without a hotel. Although the loss was a terrible blow to Thomas, who had only $1,000 in insurance, he briefly contemplated rebuilding the hotel. But the situation was resolved when Bertois bought out Thomas' property, "including ranch, livestock and license, for a sum stated to be $3,000 cash." Thomas later moved to the McMynn Ranch, west of Midway, and erected another hotel. However, according to the *Pioneer*, the merger of the hotel interests in Cascade was apparently "no less acceptable to residents of that place than to the licensing commissioners, to whom the squabble had been anything but pleasant."

During 1906, the Cascade, Power & Light Co. again made headlines. This time they were battling to prevent the West Kootenay Power & light Co. from expanding into the Boundary Country. On February 3, 1906, the *Pioneer* explained why it favoured the expansion:

"Up to last winter the service from Cascade was plentiful and efficient on account of the small amount of power needed, but when the water in Kettle river went down a year ago, the power went down also, and the company was not able to supply all the demands made upon it, let alone take care of an increase in demand which was to be used in a few months, and which has now already arrived in this section. These are facts beyond contradiction, and every resident of the Boundary is aware of them. The output of the Boundary a year ago was curtailed to the extent of thousands of dollars because the Cascade concern could not supply the power, due to extreme low water — and that extreme might come again any season. As it stands today the amount of power will be so greatly increased, due to the improvements being made at the several Boundary smelters and mines, that there is not enough power to supply this demand with the present Cascade running at its maximum.

"When the West Kootenay Power & Light Co. agreed to furnish the needed power, it was given contracts, and has constructed its long distance high tension lines into the Boundary for this purpose.

"If the Cascade concern is or was willing to make an effort to supply the demand, why was it not done when an application to it was made?"

On November 17, at the annual shareholder's meeting of the Cascade Power Company, chairman E. Begg tabled his report, which included the following: "The West Kootenay Power and Light Company, having failed to obtain legislative powers, is for the present debarred from doing business in our area. The company had, however, spent large sums in building pole lines throughout our district and in erecting a fresh plant at their central station, and has also made provisional contracts to supply our customers — contracts which, of course, at present they cannot proceed with. We must, therefore, anticipate a keen fight in the legislature next year."

Unfortunately, it proved to be a short-lived victory, for on May 11, 1907, the *Pioneer* announced that West Kootenay Light and Power had purchased the Cascade works for between $250,000 and $500,000. This acquisition proved to be the final blow to what little remained of Cascade's economy. By August, the hydro-electric plant at Cascade had been shut down, power for the Boundary now coming direct from Bonnington Falls.

Prior to this, in March, George Stocker, manager and largest shareholder of the Cascade Townsite Co., had sold his residence and returned to Spokane. A month after the closure of the Cascade power plant, the *Pioneer* reported that the town-site was to be turned into fruit farms. But, despite it current lowly status from once lofty heights, Cascade was not officially dead. Bertois continued to operate his B.C. Hotel there until at least 1909. In October of that year the *Pioneer* reported that he was "adding a story to his hotel, providing accommodation for 17 more guests, and possibly for eight more rooms to be finished if needed. The growing summer hotel trade for Christina Lake necessitates increase of accommodation and Mr. Bertois is building with that business in view."

Today, much of what was once the Cascade town-site has been converted into a gold course. The powerhouse yet stands, forlorn and abandoned, and a couple of original homes yet remain. But of Cascade busy main business section, which had boasted 17 hotels, there are only a few rock foundations to indicate what once had been. It is sad that a town which once held such promise for the future has now been reduced to this. ❁

Niagara

THE ghost towns of the Boundary Country can be said to fall into two main categories; those which developed because of mining, and those which developed because of the construction of the Columbia & Western Railway (C&W). At various points along the C&W right-of-way, wherever contractors decided to establish major construction camps or headquarters, towns sprang up like mushrooms. Most of these towns enjoyed spectacular, rapid growth and phenomenal, although brief, prosperity. But, when the construction crews moved on to their next location, the towns wilted and died almost as quickly as they had been born. The same fate was to befall Niagara.

Prior to the arrival of C&W construction crews, a man named Jones had preempted a small ranch at the junction of Fisherman Creek and the North Fork of the Kettle River (now Granby River), about eight miles north of Grand Forks. Jones, apparently, was unable to afford proper doors and windows for his ranch, so he covered the openings with gunny sacks. Because of this, he became known far and wide as "Gunny Sack Jones."

On April 15, 1895, the Midway *Advance* printed this small article about Jones and his ranch. "Gunnysack Jones, an old prospector, is clearing and cropping a large portion of his ranch on Fisherman creek, some six miles above Grand Forks. He has already commenced a barn 20x90 feet. This ranch is by some considered as a prospective townsite. At all events, when the 320 acres belonging to Mr. Jones is all cleared, as a ranch it is sure to hold its own. Fisherman creek runs right through its meadow."

If the ranch was, as the *Advance* claimed, considered as a possible town-site as early as 1895, it must have been because of nearby mining interests. In any event, plans to develop a town were not consummated, and the ranch's town-site possibilities were all but forgotten about until the construction of the C&W once again stimulated interest in the area.

In the fall of 1898, probably during the month of September, George E. Seymour, a businessman from Greenwood, concluded a deal with Jones to purchase a part of his ranch. Seymour was the head of a group of Spokane capitalists that wanted to develop the property into a town-site, realizing its value with the C&W passing right along side it. How much Jones was paid for his property is not recorded, but by September 26, Sydney Johnson, P.L.S., had been obtained to survey about 40 acres of the ranch into town lots.

Two newspapers, the Grand Forks *Miner* and the Boundary Creek *Times*, both heralded the birth of Niagara in their October 8 editions. Although the town-site plans were not filed until December 29, and a crown grant was not issued until February, 1899, the *Miner* noted that "the advance sale of lots has been phenomenal," George Seymour, the town-site agent, having sold 53 lots since September 26.

"The town is beautifully situated at the foot of the mountain, on a level piece of ground in the bend of the North Fork river, where Fisherman creek with its never failing supply of cool spring water running through it, which with a comparatively small expense can be dammed a few hundred feet above the town, and piped to any portion of it — affording one of the most essential acquisitions necessary for the successful upbuilding of a town — an everlasting supply of pure spring water."

The *Times* also praised the new town: "Niagara, according to the proprietors of the townsite, is no temporary boom railroad town. It sprang into existence quickly but it came to stay. They point to the fact that the town will get a start because close at hand is several miles of exceedingly heavy rock and trestling. This will mean the employment of a large number of men whose headquarters will be Niagara. But they also point to important factors that go to make up the permanency of the town. Along the North Fork and adjacent to Niagara are some of the best farms in the Kettle River valley; across in another direction are the Volcanic, Pathfinder, Seattle and other important North Fork claims. Niagara is a good townsite. It is well situated on the North Fork, is comparatively level and is reached by a good wagon road from Grand Forks which is nine miles distant. The line of railway passes a few hundred feet above the town and land for a station and switch in the immediate vicinity has been acquired by the CPR."

By the time these two newspaper articles were printed,

as mentioned, over 50 lots had already been sold, most of them to Greenwood businessmen. The sound of hammer and saw was heard all over as carpenters rushed buildings to completion. As one of the town-sites owners, Seymour had such faith in the new town that he sold his Windsor Hotel in Greenwood and started to erect one in Niagara. Joe McDowell, also of Greenwood, was building a livery barn and blacksmith shop. While his new 24x40-foot building was being erected, D.W. Hicks conducted his restaurant from a tent. Rendell & Co. were erecting a branch of their Greenwood store. A second hotel, 25x50 and three stories high, was being built by Shaw & Lawder, while William Brown was establishing a 24x40-foot general store. A Mr. McCoon, of Grand Forks, was building a feed and provision store and J.G. White was building a real estate office on Columbia Street. Three residences were also under construction, and scattered amid the construction scene were numerous tents.

Mann, Foley Bros. & Larson gave the new town instant credibility when they began negotiating for sites to erect a large warehouse and hospital. On October 15, the *Times* reported that carpenters were "kept busy erecting business houses and residences for the large number of people who are rushing in. Some are doing business in tents until more substantial premises can be erected. The town has a busy appearance and from early morn till late at night, the sound of saw and hammer can be heard." E. Stack was the busiest contractor. Of the 19 buildings currently under construction, he had a contract for six and had 12 men at work.

A number of new businessmen decided to establish themselves at Niagara the following week. W.M. Law & Co., which operated a store in Greenwood, were about to open a general store. Gus Vossholm, of Rossland, and J.E. Ahlmstrom, of Northport, Washington, had purchased a block of six lots on Main Street and had let a contract for three buildings, one of which was to be a 30x65-foot, two-story, 20-room hotel constructed of logs. Oliver, Stabile & Arena were also erecting a "large and commodious hotel."

In addition to Hicks' restaurant, which was open and doing "a big business," Stack & McDowell had opened a livery stable. However, the latter company already had "insufficient accommodation for their numerous patrons" and were waiting for a load of lumber with which to build an addition.

By this time a daily stage was running between Grand Forks and Niagara, and as the rush for lots continued, the Niagara Townsite Company hired 10 men to clear and grade the streets while another eight were employed at improving the wagon road between Niagara and Grand Forks. The company had also let a contract to Alec Smith for the construction of a heavy bridge across Fisherman Creek and Columbia Street, which was to be completed by October 30.

By October 22, the railroad construction camp of Pat Welsh, "large enough to accommodate over 1,000 people," was taking shape just outside the town's limits. Within the town itself, meat king Pat Burns had purchased three lots on Columbia Street and was preparing to enter competition with a butcher shop operated by W. Gray. A week later Niagara's first two hotels opened for business.

Although, at its peak, Niagara could boast of 12 hotels,

very little information has survived concerning them. However it appears that the Niagara, owned by Shaw & Lawder, and the Fisherman, owned by Wilberg & Benson, both opened on October 29. Construction of the 15-room Niagara Hotel had begun in the first week of October. Immediately upon completion, work was commenced on a 20-foot, two-story addition. The Fisherman Hotel must have originally been rather small, for after a new three-story, 20x24-foot addition was added in December, it had been enlarged to 22 bedrooms.

Niagara's third hotel to open, the Windsor, owned by George Seymour, was the first to be started. In mid-October, Oliver, Stabile & Arena began construction of a two-story hotel which was called the White Star. By the time it opened a month later, Pete Arena had sold his interest to his partners and had started construction of a new three-story hotel, the name of which is not recorded. The Stockholm Hotel, owned by Kempt & Lockhart, formerly hotel-keepers at Brooklyn, was constructed at a cost of $3,000. It had 20 bedrooms and a 25x60-foot barroom with a billiard parlour. The two-story, 33x55-foot Scandia House, was owned by Oscar Stenstrom of Cascade. In mid-November, John Wisner, formerly of Gladstone, purchased a lot and building on Main Street from a man named Fraser for $950. The building was then moved to the back of the lot and a 25-foot addition was built to the front. The completed hotel, called the Wisner House, opened for business on December 16. The Columbia Hotel was owned by a man named King. The name of two other Niagara hotels are known: Cosmopolitan and Tunnel, but their owners are not recorded. Thus the names of 11 of the 12 hotels are known.

Of the last three, one was a two-story, 20-room structure owned by Gus Vossholm & J.E. Ahlmstrom. Another belonged to a Mr. Woolf, who arrived from Toronto in mid-November and erected a hotel on Columbia Avenue. The third, located on Main Street, was started on December 27 by a man named Reeve.

Meanwhile, by mid-November, 1898, about 40 buildings had already been completed. Four of these were hotels, but the rest contained a variety of businesses. Edward White, of Cascade, had erected a 30x45-foot "lunch counter and fancy confectionery store" on Main Street. Another Cascade businessman, A.G. Williamson, had also purchased a lot on Main Street and was erecting a 20x30-foot "gent's furnishing store" to accommodate the large clothing order already in transit from Montreal. Two blacksmith shops were competing for business on Columbia Street, one owned by a Mr. Armstrong, the other by a Mr. Simpson.

In its continuing coverage of Niagara, the *Miner* noted during the same week that a desperately needed sawmill would be in operation within the week. It also informed its readers that a Greenwood businessman named Robins had purchased 20 horses from the Okanagan and started a daily stage line between Greenwood and Niagara. On the lighter side, the *Miner* wrote: "An Italian camp on Main street caught fire last night and was reduced to ashes. The loss of vermin in the blankets must have been appalling."

Unfortunately, during its brief existence, Niagara did not have its own newspaper, although two parties did express an interest. The first was a man named Fleming, of Wardner, Idaho, who arrived in town on November 29 and announced plans to start publishing the Niagara *Weekly Times* as soon as his printing plant arrived. This never happened, however, and in mid-December R. Nesbit, editor and publisher of the short-lived Cascade *Maple Leaf* was in town "sizing up the situation with a view to moving his plant here."

On November 26, the *Times* reported that Mann, Foley Bros. & Larson were about to move their railroad headquarters from Brooklyn to Niagara. This news, coupled with the fact that railroad contractor Pat Welsh was expecting to double his workforce to 800-900 men within two weeks, created considerable excitement in the new town. In the end, however, Mann, Foley Bros. & Larson went to Cascade. Nevertheless, by the end of November, three stages were running between Niagara and Grand Forks, and the owners were "doing a rushing business."

On December 3, the *Times* announced that Niagara was to have its own waterworks system. "Mr. S.F. Crocker has secured the water right and has ordered 5,000 feet of piping. A dam is being constructed on Fisherman Creek, 1,500 feet above Niagara, and the water will then be carried down in mains through Mr. Ward's preemption, thence through Greenwood Street. The Windsor, Cosmopolitan, Columbia, Tunnel and Wisner hotels have already made arrangements for water to be laid to their houses.

"A large tank 20 feet long is being constructed and will be placed on Main St., so that numerous freight teams driving through will be able to secure water for their horses free of charge."

Business activity continued at a hectic pace throughout the month of December. A. Yorke & Co., a firm of Spokane butchers, were offering mutton, beef, pork and oysters from their Main Street store. Two weeks later they received a large consignment from Manitoba containing 200 cases of eggs, 50 tubs of butter and four crates of plump turkeys in preparation for Christmas celebrations. During the same time, R.J. Reitch, of Trail, was building a large general store and waiting for a consignment of goods from Vancouver. A week later, a Mr. Ernst, of the California Wine Co., of Nelson, purchased six lots on Columbia Street and two on Main Street and revealed plans to build a wholesale wine and cigar store. On Jones Street, meanwhile, contractors McNee & Stuart were erecting a 20x30-foot building for William Bros., while a Mr. Armstrong was building a public hall with a seating capacity for 300. On the corner of Greenwood and Main streets, Hughes & Crawford were erecting a substantial store from which they intended to sell hardware and dry goods.

As 1898 drew to a close, Niagara had 11 hotels, nine general stores, three butchers, two blacksmiths and a variety of other businesses. Although Niagara could never boast of having a real bank, two private institutions were established in December. The first, a branch of Beer & Dunlop of Grand Forks, was a "brokerage and safety deposit office" which included a 3,000-pound safe imported from Chicago. The second establishment was operated by Frank Oliver and Gracchino Stabile, who were also partners in the White Star Hotel. This second institution, however, was anything but reputable.

The first indications that something was amiss occurred on December 12 when Stabile was nearly killed by "an infuriated drunken Italian." The man, armed with a Winchester rifle, was about to shoot Stabile "when two men seized him from behind and wrestled the gun from him. It had seven cartridges in the magazine and one in the breech." If the two men had not intervened, Stabile would certainly have been murdered. Because Niagara did not have a policeman, the man was able to escape. With him went the motive for the attempted murder.

This narrow escape must have been too close for comfort for Stabile and Oliver, for on December 31, the Cascade *Record* reported: "Frank Oliver and Gracchino Stabile, who have been posing as Italian bankers on the railway construction, are now anxiously wanted by a number of irate fellow countrymen around Niagara and elsewhere, who assert that money entrusted to them for transmission to the old country, has never reached its destination.

"Al. Rizzuto of Niagara, came to Cascade on Wednesday, to try and trace Stabile and Oliver, who he said had skipped out a day or two before, one going to Nelson and the other to Spokane, but so far has not been able to get them. He, with A. Sprovieri, who now run the White Star Hotel at Niagara, were formerly in partnership with Oliver and Stabile, but recently bought the bankers share of the business. He asserts that there is a large number of Italians at Niagara who would make it decidedly warm for the pseudo bankers if they could be got at.

"Oliver had a contract at the switchback last summer, and Stabile, who is a fluent linguist and had had the confidence of his countrymen, formed a partnership with him in Brooklyn. Later they came to Niagara and gave it out that they would establish branches all over the country.

"Mr. Rizzuto returned this morning to Niagara, to get further information from the dupes of the so-called bankers."

A week later the *Record* was able to add some further information. The con men had apparently absconded with about $4,000 which had been entrusted to them by their fellow countrymen for forwarding to Italy. When it was learned that none of the money had reached its destination, some of the men became uneasy, and Stabile and Oliver decided it was a good time to leave town. The *Record* also revealed that Oliver was only an alias for a man named Raphel Vungaro, who was apparently wanted in Nova Scotia for having committed murder. Unfortunately, there is no record of either man being captured or punished for their deeds.

On December 10, a more serious altercation occurred near Foss & McDonnell's camp, six miles beyond Niagara, when a quarrel between John Lawler and Harry Green resulted in the latter being stabbed several times with a pocket knife. Constable Dinsmore of the B.C. Provincial Police arrived in Niagara the following day to investigate the situation, and Lawler was subsequently arrested. Fortunately for Green, his wounds were not serious.

It was probably as a result of the attempted murder of Stabile and the stabbing of Green that the government decided to station a policeman at Niagara. The man chosen was D.G. Cox, who had previously been stationed at Golden. Cox had initially been instructed to report to Brooklyn, but before he reached there that town was virtually dead, so he was ordered to report to Niagara instead.

By this time, however, Niagara's boom days were also a thing of the past. On February 18, 1899, the *Record* noted that a crown grant had been issued for the Niagara townsite and George Seymour was finally able to issue deeds to the property owners. However, by the end of that month, Seymour sold out his interest in the property. The name of the new owner was not revealed. However, since the newspaper reported that he wanted to rename the town "Jonesboro," after his own name, it seems likely that Gunnysack Jones may have been the purchaser. In any event, some time later Seymour also disposed of his hotel, for by June it was being run by Gus Vossholm.

When W.S. Torney visited Niagara at the end of March, he told the *Record* that the "little town is just alive." An indication of how tough times were becoming might be suggested by the fact that the Niagara area was faced with several acts of lawlessness. One serious incident occurred at the end of March when a blacksmith named Bresser was robbed of $140. Bresser, who was employed in McLellan's Camp near Niagara, slept in a tent. One night he was awakened suddenly by the cold muzzle of a revolver pressed against his head. While one man kept him covered in this threatening fashion, Bresser could barely make out two shadowy forms rifling his clothes, but it was too dark to identify them. However, while the robbery was in progress the moon came out and provided sufficient light for Bresser to get a good look at his assailants. The next robbery he went to Grand Forks and swore out warrants against three men, Foust, Brault and Everett.

Brault, the proprietor of the Tunnel Hotel, was arrested immediately, but the other two temporarily eluded the law. Thoedore Foust crossed the border to Republic, Washington. There he was arrested and escorted to the international border at Carson, where Constable Dinsmore was waiting to take the fugitive into custody. A week later Everett was captured at Midway.

Unfortunately, Brault, the first to be arrested, had been released on bail, and when the date of his trial arrived, he was nowhere to be found. Theodore Foust, probably the worst of the three criminals, decided to turn Queen's evidence on his two companions, and was released. Thus Everett was the only one to serve time in prison for the robbery. It was not long, however, before Foust was again in trouble with American authorities, this time for robbing an Indian at Molson, Washington, of $20.

Meanwhile, Niagara's days were numbered. By the end of June only five hotels, Columbia, Scandia, Windsor, Wisner and Niagara were still operating. By the time that CPR track-layers reached Niagara in mid-September, the town was so quiet that Const. D.G. Cox had been transferred to Cranbrook some two weeks earlier.

For some reason, Niagara did not rate another mention in any of the local papers until June, 1906, when the Phoenix *Pioneer* noted that a liquor license had been granted to E. Vassholm. Applications for two other liquor licenses, by Octave Blanchet and Chris Matla, were temporarily deferred. However, Matla's application was later accepted.

The original town of Niagara died as suddenly in 1899 as it had been born a few months earlier. From then until 1906 it did not exist, although a few residents and one or two businesses might have refused to give up the ghost completely. Then, in the summer of 1906, during the construction of the Kettle Valley Railway (KVR), the old townsite enjoyed a brief resurgence. However, except for the brief notice pertaining to the issuing of liquor licenses, all information concerning Niagara centred around one despicable incident that occurred at the Canada Hotel on November 18, 1906.

On November 24, under the large front page heading "ATROCIOUS CRIME AT NIAGARA," the Grand Forks *Gazette* related how the Canada Hotel had been destroyed by dynamite and fire. One person was dead and nine others were injured, and a $1,000 reward had been posted for the culprit.

The Canada Hotel was owned by a French-Canadian named Peter Roi (French for King, the name used in most accounts). Since it is described as a two-story log structure, it was probably one of the original Niagara hotels constructed in 1898. Assisting in the running of the establishment was Mrs. King and an 18-year-old daughter named Louise. Prior to the incident, King had been boarding a number of Italians who were working on the grade of the KVR. However, it appears that Mrs. King had, in her husband's opinion, become a little too friendly with some of these workers, so on Sunday morning Peter told six of them they had one day to find alternative lodging.

One of the men, Frank Cedio (or Agilio, as his name appeared on the payroll of the KVR), resented being told to leave, and during the day he began to drink heavily. About 5:30 that evening, Cedio went to Chris Matla's saloon where he continued his drinking. Cedio's room mate, Sam Rovella, accompanied Cedio to the saloon and later testified on Cedio's actions there, stating that at one point he "put his watch on the bar, smashed it with his hand and raised a disturbance, pulling out a knife, cutting his hat to pieces, and pulling his coat off and swearing. Also took his vest and shirt off slashing them with his knife, and called 'come on boys'."

Rovella testified that Cedio then followed him and another man named Caglisto towards the Canada Hotel, saying "some one will pay for this tonight," but he left them and went off towards the timekeeper's office. Rovella went on to state that he was eating supper at the Canada Hotel a short time later when he heard a loud noise upstairs. Rovella said he accompanied King, who was carrying a lantern, upstairs to investigate. When they entered Cedio's room, Cedio smashed the lamp with his rifle, and King bolted back downstairs. A short time later Cedio went downstairs armed with a knife, smashed two chairs, then left the building.

Meanwhile, Mrs. King and her daughter, afraid of Cedio, went to the home of Movarelli, the railway foreman. Around 7 o'clock, Cedio also arrived at Movarelli's, and the Kings then returned to their hotel and locked the doors. Cedio apparently tried to persuade Mrs. Movarelli to leave her husband and go away with him, hinting that something would happen to Mr. King shortly, and Mr. Movarelli would leave her for Mrs. King. When Mrs. Movarelli turned him down, Cedio left. About an hour later, Cedio and Rovella tried to get back into the Canada Hotel, but were not permitted entry by Mr. King.

It was probably at about this time that the men went to

the powder magazine of R.W. Tierney & Co., the railway contractors. Rovella, who of course denied any part of the subsequent explosion, had the keys to the powder magazine. Meanwhile, denied access to the hotel by the main entrance, Cedio had apparently reentered his room by the back stairs, as King heard footsteps going up and down. On one occasion King actually encountered Cedio upstairs, and although the latter was empty-handed, King was suspicious and afraid and quickly rejoined the crowd downstairs. It was during this period that the stolen dynamite was apparently being carried into Cedio's room. Later investigation showed that at least three boxes, and possible as many as five boxes, had been removed from the powder magazine.

Meanwhile, in the hotel's barroom, which was directly under the room occupied by Cedio and Rovella, there were 10 or 11 men drinking. Suddenly someone noticed flames through the cracks in the floorboards overhead and gave the alarm. The warning of fire drew everyone's attention upward just as the first explosion shattered the hotel. The force of the blast was so great that logs were scattered for hundreds of feet, and what remained of the hotel burst into flames.

As most of the men in the bar had been looking upwards at the time of the explosion, most were injured in the face. The worst of these was A. Donati, who suffered a fractured skull, five broken ribs and a punctured lung. His son suffered lacerations and burns to his face and chest. They, and two other men, had to receive hospital care.

Mr. King, who was on the second floor, was thrown out of a window by the detonation. In addition to lacerations and burns, he lost his hearing. Mrs. King and daughter Louise were together on the second floor at the time of the explosion. Miraculously, Mrs. King escaped with minor injuries, but Louise was not as fortunate. Reported the *Record*: "The daughter Louise was blown to bits, hardly enough of the remains being gathered to hold a coroner's inquest over."

Rovella and another man were promptly arrested, but of Cedio, there was not a trace. However, the provincial government was determined to apprehend the fiend who committed the atrocity, and they offered a reward of $1,000.

On December 1, the *Gazette* reported that the coroner's jury had decided that the death of Louise King had been caused "by dynamite or other explosive, deliberately and maliciously used by Frank Pain Blanc, also known as Frank Cedio, who was assisted by an accomplice, Sam Rovella."

Meanwhile, Cedio had escaped across the border and for over a year he would be successful in eluding the police. Finally, on February 8, 1908, the *Gazette* announced that Cedio had been captured. After escaping from Niagara in a load of hay, Cedio and another Italian stole a CPR speeder at Grand Forks and made their way to Marcus, taking the train from there to Spokane. Cedio then travelled from state to state until he settled in Salt Lake City. There he remained unmolested for nearly a year.

Chief Devitt of Nelson had learned some time earlier that Cedio had been spotted in Spokane, Washington, and he went there to investigate. Although Cedio had already left, Devitt was able to trail him to Salt Lake City, where the fugitive was taken completely by surprise by a Salt Lake City policeman. Cedio fought extradition for some five weeks, but in the end he was turned over to Canadian authorities.

On May 27, 1908, after a brief one-day trial, Cedio was found guilty of the murder of Louise King at the supreme court in Greenwood, and was sentenced to hang on July 31. Cedio's face paled when the verdict was read, but he showed no other emotion. The jury needed only an hour to reach their decision.

On August 8, the *Gazette* reported on Cedio's execution at Kamloops. However, Cedio's death left many questions unanswered. Prior to the execution, Cedio had given a statement to Father Pecoul concerning the murder which implicated two other Italians, Movarelli and Caglisto. Movarelli had actually been arrested and held for six months following the explosion, but was eventually released for lack of evidence. His whereabouts were now unknown, but had Cedio been captured earlier, his fate might have been different.

Cedio claimed that Movarelli had a "vulgar interest" in Mrs. King, who had left her husband and taken a private room in the hotel. Caglisto, the other Italian implicated, had been, according to Cedio, courting Mrs. King. Both men had a motive for killing Mr. King. Cedio claimed he knew that the dynamite was being taken into the hotel and tried to warn Mr. and Mrs. King. Unfortunately, according to Cedio, he could not speak any English, and as he was drunk and still had a knife when he tried to warn them, they misinterpreted his actions as threats. Cedio added that he was innocent of the crime, and the others had made him swear an oath over crossed daggers never to speak of the incident. He also claimed they gave him $20 and told him to take a train to Salt Lake City, and that the first time he heard about the explosion was while in that city.

Cedio's statement had the effect of postponing his execution for an hour while Victoria and Ottawa were informed of the latest developments. However, at 9:15 a.m., the execution was carried out. Was Cedio's statement one final chance to save his life, or was it the truth from a man who simply wanted to clear his soul before meeting his maker? Unfortunately, we will never know. ❦

B I B L I O G R A P H Y

PRIMARY SOURCES
Anaconda *News.*
B.C. Mining Record
B.C. Minister of Mines Reports
Boundary Creek Times.
Brooklyn *News.*
Cariboo *Sentinel.*
Cascade *Record.*
Grand Forks *Gazette.*
Grand Forks *Miner.*

Greenwood *Miner.*
Midway *Advance.*
Nelson *Miner.*
New Denver *Ledge.*
Okanagan Falls *Mining Review*
Phoenix *Pioneer.*
Rossland *Miner.*
Trail Creek *News.*
Victoria *Colonist.*
Other newspapers as quoted.

SECONDARY SOURCES
Boundary Historical Society Reports.
Glanville, Alice. *Schools of the Boundary 1891-1991.* Sonotek, Merrit, B.C., 1991.
Iverson, Robert. *Camp McKinney, Then & Now.* 1984.
Paterson, T.W. *Encly. of Ghost Towns & Mining Camps of British Columbia (Vol 2),* Sunfire, 1981.
Other books as quoted.

I·N·D·E·X